WOMEN, IDENTITY AND PRIVATE
LIFE IN BRITAIN, 1900–50

WOMEN'S STUDIES AT YORK/MACMILLAN SERIES

General Editors: Haleh Afshar and Mary Maynard

Published titles

Haleh Afshar (*editor*)
WOMEN IN THE MIDDLE EAST: Perceptions, Realities and Struggles for Liberation

Haleh Afshar and Carolyne Dennis (*editors*)
WOMEN AND ADJUSTMENT POLICIES IN THE THIRD WORLD

Judy Giles
WOMEN, IDENTITY AND PRIVATE LIFE IN BRITAIN, 1900–50

Joanna de Groot and Mary Maynard (*editors*)
WOMEN'S STUDIES IN THE 1990s: Doing Things Differently?

Haideh Moghissi
POPULISM AND FEMINISM IN IRAN: Women's Struggle in a Male-Defined Revolutionary Movement

Anna Reading
POLISH WOMEN, SOLIDARITY AND FEMINISM

Rebecca Stott
THE FABRICATION OF THE LATE-VICTORIAN *FEMME FATALE*

Women, Identity and Private Life in Britain, 1900–50

Judy Giles

Senior Lecturer in English and Women's Studies
University College of Ripon and York St John

MACMILLAN

First published 1995 by
MACMILLAN PRESS LTD
Houndmills, Basingstoke, Hampshire RG21 2XS
and London
Companies and representatives
throughout the world

ISBN 0–333–62242–1 hardcover
ISBN 0–333–64083–7 paperback

A catalogue record for this book is available
from the British Library.

10   9   8   7   6   5   4   3   2   1
04   03   02   01   00   99   98   97   96   95

Printed in Great Britain by
Antony Rowe Ltd
Chippenham, Wiltshire

For Nettie, Dorothy and Catherine

class system 133

W.C 47
49
50
53
G2 - 3
o Into toMC 93 2
M.C. 95.
108
136
137 (Men in Service)
138
139
171-2.

Femunity

$2L

Add women & litact
to conclusion.

Through examining the develop
of womans lives during the 30,
it is clear that its not a justified claim
that the 1930's was an
insignificant period of time

Contents

Acknowledgements

I would like to thank the Norwegian Research Council for granting me a research fellowship in Autumn 1993, which allowed me to complete this project, and the University College of Ripon and York St John, which enabled me to take up this opportunity. Thanks are also due to colleagues and friends at Telemark Regional College, Norway, and Agder Regional College, Norway, for their hospitality and welcome, in particular Tørun Gulliksen, Ragnhild Eikli and Annabelle Despard.

Over the years of involvement with this research I have received encouragement, criticism and suggestions from numerous friends, students, colleagues and scholars. I am grateful for this community of support, which seems to me to truly embody a spirit of cooperation rather than competition and which, on a personal level, has sustained me through the inevitable troughs that accompanied the writing of this book.

Finally, I acknowledge my debt to the women who allowed me to enter their lives and record their pasts and who willingly and generously shared with me their thoughts and feelings. I hope the experience was not simply one way.

JUDY GILES

Introduction

In 1912 Virginia Woolf attended a meeting of the Women's Co-operative Guild at which women delegates debated and formulated their most pressing needs and the political strategies best suited for achieving these. The letter Woolf wrote to Margaret Llewellyn Davies based on her experience of this meeting became the introductory letter to *Life As We Have Known It*, a collection of narratives by working-class women, detailing their experiences of working-class life and the part played by the Co-operative Guild in offering both education and support (Llewellyn Davies, 1931/1977). Throughout Woolf's introductory letter she grapples with her own ambivalence to a social structure, based on differences of class, which she believes to be ultimately divisive, however sympathetic she might be personally to the women's cause as articulated by the Guild delegates and by the stories that make up *Life As We Have Known It*. The gap between middle- and working-class women was, for Woolf, so great that, however much one wished to make common cause,

> [o]ne could not be Mrs Giles of Durham because one's body had never stood at the wash-tub, one's hands had never wrung and scrubbed and chopped up whatever the meat may be that makes a miner's supper. The picture therefore was always letting in irrelevancies. One sat in an armchair or read a book. One saw landscapes and seascapes (Llewellyn Davies, 1931/1977, p. xxiii).

This book is about the divisions Woolf identified and their manifestation in the social practices, cultural forms and individual subjectivities that made up women's lives in the early years of the twentieth century. Woolf's acute awareness of class and her self-conscious ironising of what she calls her 'comfortable capitalistic head' renders visible the specific sites where class divisions between women were most fully articulated at this specific moment in history (ibid., p. xxi). Domesticity, the home, housework and 'private' life shaped the day-to-day existence of most women and, despite expanding employment opportunities, continued to be the arena in which women of all classes sought to define and understand themselves, whether as wife, mother, housewife, servant or mistress. As Woolf recognises with her usual perspicacity 'the

1

imagination is largely the child of the flesh'; subjectivity is neither a transcendent essence nor is it formed in a culturally neutral, ahistorical and social vaccuum but is the product of specific cultural articulations and the material experiences of day-to-day existence.

Virginia Woolf and Mrs Giles of Durham may share the same sex but neither can experience 'being a woman' in the way the other does: both experience their bodies and the materiality of their day-to-day lives differently. Woolf sits and reads, Mrs Giles stands and scrubs; Woolf 'desires Mozart and Einstein' whilst Mrs Giles needs 'baths and ovens' (ibid., p. xxviii). For both women their experience, their imagination and their identity is differently shaped and understood, and the meanings attributed to their ontological status as women varies according to class, age and historical moment. Moreover the physical tasks expected of their bodies function as signifiers of difference and division – one sits, the other stands – and, for Woolf, these significations are located in the very arena conventionally ascribed to women – the home and 'private' life. 'Home' for Mrs Giles, according to Woolf's representation, means washing, scrubbing and preparing meals for a hungry breadwinner; 'home' for Virginia Woolf could mean the privacy and leisure in which to read and in which to imagine 'landscapes and seascapes'.

This book, then, is also about the meanings and experience of 'home' and 'privacy' for certain women who grew up before 1950 in England and it is about the ways in which women's understanding of themselves in relation to the home and what has conventionally been referred to as the private sphere, shaped the versions of femininity available for self-definition according to class, age and historical moment. How to understand and explain the centrality of domesticity to women's experience has consistently exercised feminist theory, whether in the present or the past. Home has been posited alternatively as a location where specifically feminine virtues of 'maternalism' and connectedness counter the impersonal and power-ridden (masculine) worlds of work and the state, or has been understood as a site of oppression, gender struggle and/or the privatised reproduction of the labour power required to fuel capitalism (Rich, 1977; Elshtain, 1981; Barrett and McIntosh, 1983; Ferguson, 1984; Ruddick, 1984). As Jane Flax has observed,

> The complex fantasies and conflicting wishes and experiences women associate with family/home often remain unexpressed and unacknowledged. Lacking such self-analysis, feminists find it difficult to

recognize some of the sources of our differences or to accept that we do not necessarily share the same past or share needs in the present (Flax, 1987, p. 639).

It is my contention that the home may be understood as both constricting and fulfilling; domesticity is an arena in which women experience and live out our deepest fantasies; the nature of these fantasies and the understanding of 'home' in producing and articulating our profoundest wishes has varied over time and across cultures. As Virginia Woolf recognised, the needs that home and domesticity speak to are themselves produced through imaginations shaped within social structures and the material embodiement of lives lived within specific social and historical parameters. 'Home' is both a historical and a social construct, as well as a profoundly resonant metaphor for psychic needs. Women do not, as Flax points out, 'share the same needs' nor do we today share the same relation to the home and to domesticity as did our mothers and grandmothers. Moreover, any historical reconstruction of women's relationship to the home requires a recognition that it was precisely in the domestic sphere, so often valorised in feminist analyses as a site of female bonding, that the deep divisions that have for so long structured social relations between women in Britain were forged and sustained via the system of domestic service (Cott, 1977, pp. 67–74; Smith-Rosenberg, 1975).

This book asks questions about the desires that 'home' articulated for certain women at a particular moment in history and addresses the ways in which these desires might be created differently according to social class and historical context. For example, did working-class mothers understand domesticity in different ways from their daughters who entered domestic service; or from those middle-class women who found a professional role in advising and supporting mothers and housewives through their work for a newly emergent welfarism; or again from the middle-class employers of domestic servants; and did the daughters and granddaughters of these women find, in domesticity, joys and resentments very different from those of previous generations?

However it is not simply differences understood as relativity that I am interested in but the ways in which those differences interrelated and functioned in terms of power and conflict across a range of social relations, including women's relations with men, women's relations with women, mothers' relations with daughters and daughters' relations with fathers. In order to explore these issues I draw upon the oral testimony of twenty-one working-class women, on autobiographical accounts by both middle- and working-class women, on letters, on fiction and on the written pronouncements of professional observers, both male and female.[1] I have quite deliberately used a range of sources, including both those conventionally understood as 'literature' and those more usually associated with the social sciences and historical scholarship. The intention is to suggest that in placing alongside each other sources usually kept apart and subjected to different methodological analyses, it becomes possible to read *across* as well as *into* the written and spoken expressions of historical experience. For example to read Stephen Taylor's medical pronouncements on 'suburban neurosis' alongside Daphne Du Maurier's *Rebecca* reveals not only the anxieties and fears of middle-class men and women centred around the home but also the ways in which such anxieties found articulation in differently conceived figures of the 'lower' class woman. The oral narratives of working-class women read in conjunction with middle-class writings offer insights into the ways and forms in which such women might and did contest at some points the subjectivities offered by dominant cultural forms to produce self-dignifying ways of seeing themselves.

The period between 1900 and the end of the Second World War provides an ideal focus for exploring the questions raised above. The figure of the 'ordinary housewife' dominated media, social policy and even, albeit to a lesser extent, feminist debates about women's position in 'modern' society. Post First World War reconstruction policies focused on the family as the political means of achieving stability in the wake of war. Implicit in this was the idea that a return to the normality of established gender roles would secure and reinforce wider social and economic reconstruction (Beddoe, 1989; Brookes, 1988, p. 10). Policy makers assumed that all married women would remain financially dependent on their husbands, despite increased unemployment as the postwar slump gripped, and even the minimal welfare provision of the immediate postwar years assumed the existence of a male breadwinner earning a wage adequate to maintain himself and dependents. National Health Insurance did not cover dependents and married women's entitlement to benefit rested on joining the insurance scheme as insured workers, a limited option as many of the occupations employing women, for example domestic service, were not part of the health insurance scheme. Educational policy was predicated on the assumption that women would only engage in waged work prior to marriage and thus formal schooling need only prepare women for 'filler' occupations between school and marriage. Such ideas were officially sanctioned by the introduction of marriage bars in the Civil Service and in the teaching profession in the 1920s, and, even where there were no formalised marriage bars, generally accepted policies about retirement on marriage meant most married women expected to become full-time housewives with occasional and seasonal supplements to the family income via part-time and casual work (Giles, 1989, pp. 82–4, 91; Lewis, 1984, pp. 199–200; Stevenson, 1984, pp. 218–20; Gittins, 1982, pp. 33–68). As the educationalist Sir Charles Cheers Wakefield commented in his book, *On Leaving School*,

> a small wage, some leisure and more freedom, is all that the young, intelligent, and above all attractive girl needs until she marries some five or six years later ... many girls are so obviously and happily destined for the married state, that their parents need not very seriously consider an alternative location as a permanent one (cited in Brittain, 1928, p. 196).

The editorial of the first edition of *Good Housekeeping* in 1922 offered its readers a celebration of 'modern' femininity:

> Any keen observer of the times cannot have failed to notice that we are on the threshold of a great feminine awakening. Apathy and levity are alike giving place to a wholesome and intelligent interest in the affairs of life, and above all, in the home. We believe that the time is ripe for a great new magazine which shall worthily meet the needs of the housekeeping woman of today (*Good Housekeeping*, 1922).

Good Housekeeping addressed 'modern' women, women who in 1918 had obtained the right to vote, who had access to higher education, whom war had freed from the constraints of Victorian chaperonage and who were participating in an apparently ever-widening variety of professions and occupations. Such women, *Good Housekeeping* assumed, would wish to play a full part in the reconstruction of postwar England not as 'career' women but as 'housekeeping' women.

The increase in women's magazines devoted to home and family after 1918 testified to both the popularity and the desirability of the figure of the housewife for a media wishing to attract the custom of advertisers and manufacturers, who were themselves seeking new home markets for a growing range of consumer durables and processed foods (White, 1970, pp. 103–17; Melman, 1988, Pt 3; Fowler, 1991, pp. 51–71). Prior to the First World War women's magazines had fallen into two categories: those produced for women managing servant-run estab-lishments and those, such as *Peg's Paper*, targeted at working-class women and consisting mostly of sensational and romantic fiction. *Home Chat* and *Woman's Weekly*, both launched before the First World War, were the forerunners of the new service and information magazines that proliferated between the wars: magazines, such as *Woman* and *Woman's Own*, aimed at middle- and lower-middle-class women with small, servantless homes to run and at the more affluent amongst the working class who were enabled to rent or purchase a whole house rather than 'rooms' (White, 1970, pp. 96–8, 311–13).

These magazines, focusing as they did on the tasks and duties of the 'housekeeping' woman, played a significant role in disseminating im-ages of women that linked them tightly to the home and their role therein as domestic managers (housewives). In doing so these maga-zines attempted to construct the housewife as an homogenous figure, occupying the middle ground between the very wealthy and the very poor; neither the mistress of servants nor the over-burdened mother of six. As housewives, *Good Housekeeping* suggests, women were being offered a 'new' role in the 'new' world of postwar reconstruction: an important role commensurate with their new political status but one that built on and thereby maintained intact the doctrine of separate spheres. As Alison Ravetz has suggested, by 1950 the term 'ordinary housewife' had come to denote

> the middle-class wife [who] had finally and irrevocably lost her ser-vants and the working-class wife [who] had gained, or was in the process of gaining, a whole house to look after (Ravetz, 1989, p. 189).

The idea that women of all classes could best deploy their abilities in the home as homemakers and mothers or as domestic servants received legitimation from elementary school curricula that insisted girls learn needlework, cooking, laundering and homemaking and secured large blocks of timetabled hours in which to teach 'housewifery' (Giles, 1989, pp. 140–7). The Consultative Committee on the Education of the Ado-lescent reported in 1926 that '[w]e consider that courses in housecraft should be planned so as to render girls fit on leaving school to undertake intelligently the various household duties which devolve on most women' (HMSO, 1926, p. 224), and the problem facing those who were developing secondary school curricula was to 'find out how the natural instincts of the girl may be used to best advantage in assisting her all-round development while at school and in fitting her for home-life as well as for a professional or business career' (HMSO, 1923, p. 72).

Neither were the fundamental assumptions about separate spheres that underpinned such policy seriously challenged by feminist discourse (Harrison, 1987; Alberti, 1989, Dyhouse, 1989; Pugh, 1992). After 1918, as suffrage issues no longer dominated feminist campaigns, feminism turned to a wide variety of concerns. Prominent amongst these was the plight of women as wives and mothers, particularly poorer women whose inability to sustain their families was part of a wider social agenda dominated by the need to rear a healthy citizenry. Eleanor Rathbone, in her fight for state allowances for mothers, never seriously questioned the prevailing assumption that the final responsibility for domestic life and childrearing rested with women who were 'the natural custodians of childhood. That at least is part of the traditional role assigned to us by men and one that we have never repudiated' (cited in Lewis, 1984, p. 105). Even those like Winifred Holtby and Vera Brittain, whose concern focused on achieving equality with men ('a fair field and no favour') in employment opportunities and conditions, tended to view paid employment and a career as incompatible with marriage, motherhood and housekeeping. For Brittain the solution was a developed system of domestic service, and whilst Holtby argued for streamlining housewifery – '[w]omen really determined to spend no more time that was absolutely necessary upon domestic labour could have revolutionised housekeeping within a decade' – she too favoured the use of 'professional employees' to enable 'women better equipped to be engineers, lawyers or agricultural workers' not to 'waste their time on domestic activities' (Brittain, 1928, p. 31; Holtby, 1934, pp. 146–50).

Neither Rathbone's 'new feminism' nor the equal rights feminism of Brittain and Holtby challenged the assumptions upon which the sexual division of labour, both within the home and as an organising feature of wider society, were founded. Women were either wives and mothers *or* 'career' women, and men were always 'career' men. The early twentieth century offers an ideal moment at which to examine women's relation to the home: it represents an historical period when women's various roles in society were in the process of being redefined culturally, socially and politically. In the wake of the First World War, a changing economic structure and political ideas about citizenship and a 'modern' society offered women a wide range of positions from which to contest subordination and secondary status.

Nonetheless the ways in which women were enabled to make sense of their lives remained closely tied to the home and discourses of femininity continued to organise themselves around concepts of privacy, motherhood, homemaking and 'service'. Moreover, as Davidoff and Hall have noted, 'the language of class-formation [was] gendered': opposing terms of the period such as 'servant'/'mistress', 'lady'/'woman', 'respectable'/'rough' represent women as dichotomously positioned in the very heartland of female experience – the home and private life (Davidoff and Hall, 1987, p. 450). Although such language was specific to the period before the Second World War, nevertheless the significations embedded in dualisms such as 'lady'/'woman' remain traceable in contemporary attitudes, both feminist and non-feminist. To dismantle the oppositional positioning inscribed in such thinking, and thus to be in a position to contest the social practices legitimated by such articulations, requires an understanding of how such divisions are formed and maintained and the role of language in this formation. We need to understand the ways in which our mothers and grandmothers saw themselves in relation to the home as well as the ways in which dominant cultural formations invited them to see themselves. We need to understand the desires and aspirations that historically specific expressions of the domestic embodied, and that may differ amongst women as well as between women and men.

HISTORY, POWER AND DIFFERENCE

The absence of women from conventional historical accounts, discussion of this absence (and discussion of the real archival difficulties that lie in the way of presenting their lives in a historical context) are, at the same time, a massive assertion of what lies hidden (Steedman, 1992, p. 164).

Feminist history over the last fifteen years or so has been concerned with the recuperation and 'assertion of what lies hidden'. In recovering 'hidden' lives, feminist historians have drawn attention to areas of the past that remain uncharted, beyond history, visible only perhaps in the memories of those who survive. Women's history, like histories of other invisible groups, has implicitly drawn attention to those aspects, events and lives that are forever lost, in the sense that we have no archival sources, no documents from which to reconstruct a factual version of the past. In constructing a history of women's domestic experiences we rely to a considerable extent on the stories told us by women, on autobiographical accounts, on fictional recreations and, if we are lucky, on diaries and letters written at the time. This raises questions about the extent to which 'that which is gone, that which is irretrievably lost, which is past time, can be brought back, and conjured before the eyes "as it really was"' (Steedman, 1992, p. 163). Whilst the impossibility of knowing exactly how 'it really was' or how women 'really' interpreted their relations to and within the home at the time rather than in their retrospective memories need not be cause for despair, neither should it be a license to write those stories or myths which best suit our current political purposes. Accepting that historical reconstruction has a story-telling and mythic function does not mean, as Linda Gordon has argued, dispensing with 'verifiable, fact-based truth'. It would be wrong, she argues, 'to conclude, as some have, that because there may be no objective truth possible, there are not objective lies . . . there are degrees of accuracy; there are better and worse pieces of history' (Gordon, 1986, p. 22).

Any attempt to write a history of women that focuses on their experiences and understanding of the domestic sphere is particularly caught within this tension. Because the sources are limited, frequently biographical and autobiographical writings or oral testimonies, verifiable, fact-based truth is harder to come by and the temptation to create mythical figures from the fragments of lives offered is seductive. In the 1970s and early 1980s numerous autobiographies were published in which women recalled poverty-stricken and deprived childhoods in the years before the Second World War (Scannell, 1974; Forrester, 1981; Dayus, 1982; Foley, 1974; Hewins, 1986; Willmott, 1979). Reading such accounts there is a very real temptation to write a history of working-class women that, in focusing unquestioningly on their struggle against poverty, drudgery and ill-health, posits a generation of working-class women whose fight against insuperable odds fills us with admiration. In our desire (rightly) to document not only the damage and oppressions suffered by women in the past but also their achievements, we construct strong heroines whom we represent as resisting the victimisation and humiliation, contingent upon the structures of domination. In doing so, however, we face the danger of creating quasi-myths that function to prevent any confrontation with the relations of women across a range of social boundaries, of which gender is but one, and which might equally include race, class, age, education, sexuality. We also fail to confront the very real pain and injury that, without detracting from the myriad victories of women's lives, subordination, oppression and poverty give rise to.

In reconstructing histories of women's 'private' lives in which subjectivity and consciousness are foregrounded it becomes imperative to read and hear the stories women tell us, but we need to do so in ways that locate those stories and the events of those lives firmly in the historical and social contexts that produced them. It is not intended to explore methodolgies for reading and hearing women's stories and oral narratives here as these issues will be considered more fully in a later section: the point being made is, following Gordon, that whilst we need to be aware that any historical reconstruction requires negotiation between the demand for myths and the demand for fact and truth, we should resist the impulse to seek resolution and synthesis in carefully balanced accounts (Gordon, 1986, pp. 20–3). The tension between fiction and 'objectivity' in reconstituting history can be a productive one for feminism precisely because, in its refusal of any universalising teleology or its rejection of the generalising tendencies of metanarratives, it allows for the possibility of multiplicity and difference. In the tension between our search for appropriate myths for different situations and our equally dedicated desire to be true to the facts, we may be enabled to see more clearly the ways in which simply being female does not mean we share the same past or the same aspirations. Equally, such a tension makes it possible to deploy appropriate methodological and analytic tools for different purposes. To write of women's private lives may require different sensitivities, different sources and a different understanding of the fiction/'objectivity' tension than a reconstitution of, for example, the political activity of women in the Labour Party. Neither approach invalidates the other nor is this intended as simply an assertion of multiplicity understood as variety and relativity in a liberal pluralist mode.

The concept of sexual difference that developed from feminist theories of gender is one of the organising principles of women's history. Most historical writing that deploys gender as an analytical tool also relies on polarised models of sexual differentiation to explain both work-place practices and domestic experience, and indeed these very locations are fixed within the dichotomous thinking of sexual difference

– work place = male; domestic = female. As a consequence the questions we have asked have assumed this polarisation: thus, for example, historical studies may seek to discover how far women brought the values of domesticity to the workplace or how far domestic values opened up routes of influence for women (Kessler-Harris, 1983; Smith-Rosenberg, 1986). In concentrating on gender as sets of dichotomised and even opposed attributes we run the risk of limiting women's potential to only one set of values, those of the feminine, and and we may thus find ourselves affirming quasi-essentialist forms of difference and separation in which the structuring relations of dominance and submission are softened or neglected (Bock, 1989, pp. 15–17; Kessler-Harris, 1989, p. 37). Following Gisela Bock I would argue that whilst we need to retain the force of gender as an analytic concept, we need to do so in ways that recognise gender as 'one constituent factor of all other relations', and we need to do so in ways that are 'understood in terms of relationship – with other women and with men' and not simply in terms that affirm 'difference and apartness' (Bock, 1989, p. 21; Rosaldo, cited in Bock, 1989, p. 16). Gisela Bock has called for a 'gender-encompassing approach' in our study of women, which would mean a recognition that

> gender relations are equally as important as all other human relations, and that gender relations contribute to and affect all other human relations. Conversely, all other human relations contribute to and affect gender relations (Bock, 1989, p. 21).

Hence, insofar as this is possible given the sources, I have attempted to interpret the experiences and understandings of women within the network of social relations that constituted their daily lives – these include women's relations with men, with other women and with children, who themselves are gendered persons, as well as relationships based on age, geographical location and employment (Thorne, 1987, pp. 85–109).

More recently the use of the term 'difference' has come to signal differences *amongst* women as well as differences *from* men. Black women in particular, angered by white feminists' assumptions of an homogenous female voice, asserted a 'different' feminist perspective. Whilst such approaches have provided important insights, nevertheless, in the same ways that the male response to feminism has often been simply tolerance of difference, so too have white feminist perspectives frequently failed to do more than accept black women or working-class women's analyses in anything other than a tokenistic and liberal way. The easy seductions of a libertarian acceptance of multiplicity and difference place at risk the critical edge of feminist history, which must continue to insist on the relations of power and hierarchy that concepts of difference inscribe. As Gisela Bock and Alice Kessler-Harris have observed, gender identity is not the only form, nor even the most significant form, of self-definition (Kessler-Harris, 1989, p. 37). Race, class, age, family role and work-place role are all potential identifications that may or may not structure consciousness at different times and in different ways.

All of these identifications exist in relation to one another and the boundaries between may overlap. Nonetheless the relations in which such identifications are constituted are relations of power, and as such relations of dominance and submission: it is the constantly intersecting dynamics of such relations that structure experience and imagination rather than any single essentialist polarisation such as sex or class. Moreover, to lack formally legitimated power is not necessarily to be power-less although it may mean being less powerful. The circuits of power function via the potential positionings available in any situation: a women may be debarred from wielding power in certain situations but not in others. The home, as I shall argue, has been an arena where women have experienced both power and powerlessness: social relations legitimated some women's subordination to others via the system of domestic service; sexual relations between women and men offered opportunities for dominance and submission, violence and manipulation; relations between mothers and daughters could move around experiences of conflict as well as solidarity; professional women have spoken for 'ordinary housewives'; and in all these instances wealth, education, age have intersected with gender to create the possibilities for oppression and resistance, for authority and deference, for domination and resistance.

If gender is a social relation interacting with a variety of other social relations then women's history must, in some sense, be social history. However 'social history' as defined since the 1960s has been predominantly the study of social class and histories of class formation in which gender, along with other social relations such as family and ethnicity, has been perceived as 'something non-social' (Bock, 1989, p. 18). This has at times led to a situation in which claims are made for the importance of class over gender and in which class, like gender, has been represented as polarised and homogenous social groupings operating along lines of solidarity and common interest. Moreover, many social histories in this vein failed to recognise the ways in which class cannot be and has not been conceptualised in the same way for women as for men. Women's social class is constituted in their relations with men as fathers and husbands; for men class is understood in terms of the workplace and their relation to capital. Moreover it is not only gendered differences that may divide members within a class: education, age, relative wealth, religion and, as will become apparent, suburbanisation are all factors that may promote conflict or common interests and may function to constitute complex networks of social relations that remain resistant to the two-class conflictual model of Marxist theory.

As Bock observes, 'both class and gender are context-specific and context-dependent categories'. They are also lived relations. For example, according to certain categories of social history, my father's occupation (solicitor) and my upbringing precluded me from categorisation as working class during my marriage to a semi-skilled manual worker and I have never identified myself as such. Nonetheless I experienced myself in relation to people who did perceive themselves as working class and amongst whom I lived for many years. Moreover, and I think, most significantly, I lived within the economic and psychological conditions of working-class existence as experienced by manual factory workers and their wives, in which money and time carry very different meanings from my present experience as a highly educated and well paid woman. Trying to make sense of the contradictions inscribed in my own experience is, of course, one of the compulsions behind the writing of this book. However this is not simply a desire to find ways to explain the social relations in which I can narrate my own life but rather a wider concern to explore cultural and political articulations that could explain *all* those social relations which do not readily fit the central interpretative forms available. Thus, although throughout this book the term 'working class' is used as a shorthand by which to identify certain groups whose lived experience was shaped by specific relations to money, time and health, I remain aware of the ways in which such a definition is always striated by other factors such as gender, age, education and environment, and hence the impossibility, and indeed dangers, of assuming any kind of homogenous class group based around common interests.

Michel Foucault argues in *The Use of Pleasure* and *The Care of the Self* that social agents cannot simply remain the 'docile' bodies implied by his earlier analyses of the institutional regulation of crime and madness, but need to 'struggle against the forms of subjection' imposed by 'the kind of individuality which has been imposed on us for several decades' (Foucault, 1978, 1985, 1986, 1982, p. 216). This argument asserts individuals as active subjects who are able to act autonomously and freely to fashion both experience and understanding, 'not as a liberation of a true or essential inner nature, but rather as an obligation, on the part of the individual, to face the endless task of reinventing him or herself' (McNay, 1992, p. 89). Foucault is not here returning to humanist and essentialist conceptions of a transcendently unique self, for he continues to stress that the ways in which individuals shape their existence ('practices of the self') are always determined by social and cultural contexts. Yet, whilst the individual may only engage in practices defined by the socio/cultural context such practices are never reducible to that context. The construction and representation of the self as posited in *The Use of Pleasure* and *The Care of the Self* is posited as 'a necessary non-correspondence, but mutually determining relation, between the individual and society' in which the individual is accorded a degree of autonomy but is not returned to an essentialist conception of the subject (McNay, 1992, p. 62). Foucault suggests that

> the subject constitutes himself [sic] in an active fashion, by the practices of self, these practices are nevertheless not something that the individual invents by himself. They are patterns that he finds in his culture and which are proposed, suggested and imposed on him by his culture, his society and his social group (Foucault, 1988, p. 11).

Similar ideas about the ways in which individuals constitute themselves and are themselves constituted within the social, historical and cultural context they inhabit have been proposed by other social theorists, in particular Giddens, who argues that the relationship between social structures and individual agency needs to be conceptualised as a dynamic rather than a static one: 'existing structures are reproduced by human agents who modify and change these structures to differing degrees as they are shaped by them' (Giddens, 1979, pp. 70–2). The idea that social actors can effect change at various political levels from the macro-politics of state institutions to the micro-political level of personal relations opens spaces for individuals to 'understand and intervene in the processes through which meaning is produced, disseminated and transformed in relation to the changing configurations of modern power and domination' (McNay, 1992, p. 115). This approach is of particular value for feminist historians, concerned as historians with the unique and particular and as feminists with the politics of radical change. It allows the stories and voices of women from the past an autonomy that, whilst not located in essentialist conceptions of an 'authentic' femininity, can intervene in the processes and meanings that reconstruct and shape their lives.

PUBLIC/PRIVATE

The concept of separate spheres in which a 'public' arena of activity and debate is set in contrast to a 'private' world of opposing values has dominated women's history for the last fifteen years.[2] The 'private' sphere, which, in feminist theory, has encompassed activities and ideologies associated with the privatised world of (the mainly middle class) household, has also stood for intimate personal life and sexuality and has come to mean in certain contexts the idea of an 'inner life' in which resides authentic selfhood. 'Private' has a further sense in terms of socio-economic relations: it refers to private property in a capitalist economy and as such can refer to interests that are frequently antithetical to those of women. For example, the concept of 'private' property in the nineteenth century was extended to legitimate the legal construction of dependent family members as the 'private property' of the (male) head of the household. The rhetoric of domestic privacy and the rhetoric of economic privacy both serve to prevent the public discussion and contestation of certain issues that predominantly concern the well-being of subordinate groups. For example, wife battering, marital rape and incest were for a long time labelled 'private' family matters; it was believed that to open up such issues for public debate would be to infringe certain individual freedoms enshrined in the concept of 'private life'. Equally, economic privatisation functions to cast issues of affluence and access to wealth and property 'as impersonal market imperatives or as "private" ownership prerogatives', which removes these issues to 'specialised discursive arenas and thereby [shields] them from general public debate and contestation' (Fraser, 1991, p. 73). In both cases the concept of a 'private' sphere is used to construct social and cultural classifications which then legitimate continued subordination.

Feminist theory has reconceptualised the idea of the 'private' sphere in ways that serve to valorize women's activities and values. Kessler-Harris has observed that

> Historians, who first perceived separate spheres as an ideology adopted by women to justify their exclusion from public life and to rationalize the effects of an economy that increasingly removed production from the household, have, more recently, found in the idea the capacity of women to create networks of female power and access routes to political influence. . . . Thus the notion of separate spheres, which once suggested the limits of family life, is now offered by many historians as the most important source of female power (Kessler-Harris, 1989, p. 32).

There are dangers in travelling too far along this route, as Kessler-Harris recognises, not least because the dichotomous thinking behind any conceptualisation of separate or different spheres simply recreates new versions of the public/private opposition (Flax, 1987, p. 639; Kessler-Harris, 1989, p. 35). Revaluing the domestic sphere as a site of women's power, whilst revealing women's strengths as well as oppressions, is, of course, a revaluation that takes place within a public arena that is itself neither gender-neutral nor culturally transparent,

> public spheres themselves are not spaces of zero degree culture, equally hospitable to any possible form of cultural expression. Rather they consist in culturally specific institutions – including, for example, various journals and various social geographies of urban space (Fraser, 1990, p. 69).

Put another way, feminist discourses of the 'private' do not simply supersede previous conceptualisations, rather they exist in relation to the prevailing and dominant discourses, one of which is the idea of economic privatisation. The overlapping and contradictory interconnections of the discourses of privatisation were rendered visible, as will be discussed more fully in Chapters 2 and 4, in the ideal of home 'ownership' and property rights, and in the system of domestic service, both of which were subject to the rhetoric of both economic and domestic 'privacy'. Attempts to recreate the 'private' sphere as a space where praiseworthy 'female' values predominate and oppose the aggressive and competitive worlds of men, fail to confront the ways in which 'private' life, not just between men and women, but between women and women, between adults and children, sanctions different forms of aggression, anger and conflict, some of which are organised around and legitimated by economic privatisation.

Moreover, too rigid an adherence to theories of separate spheres prevents any exploration of the ways in which the public/private split was understood and experienced by working-class people. Most of the work by feminist historians based on the ideology of separate spheres has focused on the middle-class nineteenth-century family in Britain and North America, and in the words of Carroll Smith-Rosenberg's pioneering work has recuperated a 'female world of love and ritual' (Smith-Rosenberg, 1975). Historians of the working-class family and women's role therein have emphasised less the bonds between women than the ways in which working-class women tended to see their own and the family's interests as inseparable. Thus female networks, where they exist, focus on the needs of the whole family within a specific system of economic organisation rather than on concepts of supportive and empowering sisterhood (Roberts, 1986; Ross, 1985, 1986; Jamieson, 1986; Chinn, 1988; Sarsby, 1988).

Furthermore the distinction between public and private has been, historically, considerably more blurred for working-class than middle-class women. Working-class women until the early years of this century had few opportunities to experience the privatised household of separate spheres theory: family life was less separate from the workplace, particularly where women undertook paid work in their own homes – taking in washing, childminding, hat-making, sewing, and running small businesses such as a corner shop or boarding house. The home cultures of mid and late Victorian urban working-class areas were lived publicly in the streets and courts where children played and women gossiped. Working-class women, unlike their middle-class counterparts, were not chaperoned in public areas and moved freely around the streets of their localities, where they were considerably more exposed to the violent and/or sexual dangers and attractions of urban street culture (Walkowitz, 1992, pp. 15–39). As I shall argue, in such circumstances 'private' life could take on different meanings and practices, meanings in which the domestic values of the middle-class home (modesty, nurture and piety) might take different forms.

Equally, whilst the urban geographies of public space might define and regulate working-class women in certain ways, for example the term 'streetwalker' was not only gendered and classed but also signified an urban as opposed to a rural world, the public arenas of discourse and debate in which such definitions were constructed have never been fully accessible to working-class women *as women*, although they were to become so increasingly for middle-class women during the period under consideration. Even where working-class women have entered public discourse, as for example via their stories in *Life As We Have Known It* or *Working Class Wives*, their right to speak and debate on their own behalf has been mediated by middle-class social reformers (male and female) or the male-oriented and family demands of trade union politics. Moreover, in the late nineteenth and early twentieth century the figure of the working-class woman frequently entered public discourse as an object of pity, fear or pathology, as her sexuality and her 'private' life were surveilled and probed by an increasing number of educationalists, social reformers, health visitors and housing officials.

When the focus is removed from middle-class domestic life and middle-class understandings of the term 'private' we are forced to confront not only the variety of meanings connotated by the concepts public and private but equally the impossibility, even if such a project were desirable, of fixing such meanings in permanently oppositional terms. The danger of remaining committed to a rhetoric of domestic privacy, be it feminist or non-feminist, is both to reproduce the exclusion of certain issues and groups from discussion and to fail to confront the constantly shifting relationship between the meanings assigned to each term. The concept of privacy depends for its meaning on its relation to the concept of the public: changing the meaning of one means changing the meaning of the other; private means 'not public', to understand the meaning of the one to specific groups we need also to understand the meaning of the other.

Alice Wilkinson, born in York in 1913, became a farm servant and later a general maid in a York hotel. Alice believed that the lessons she learned from her mother were precisely those that were mirrored in her experience at work:

> If there was a litle mark at all at the side she [mother] would make me do that over and over and over again . . . it had to be done right. She used to say to me 'if you can't do a job right, don't do it at all'. Or 'it's not worth doing' but she would teach me and I hated anybody standing over me and telling me to do anything when I was at work because it was drummed into me that much you know when I was young, but I realise now that she was in the right.

Such an account refuses feminine maternalism as entry to a separate sphere of private and affective relations but posits mothering on a continuum with public and workplace relations and the structures of authority that underpin these.

Finally, the problems indicated above in thinking in terms of separate spheres has led to considerable ambivalence and difficulty for feminist theory when it has confronted women's relationship to domesticity. The historical legacy inherited by feminists in the 1960s and 1970s produced the issues that would dominate a reemerging feminism. The decline and demise of domestic service and the dominant versions of femininity in the 1950s (sexual object or housewife) made it hardly surprising that second-wave feminism would place domesticity at the centre of its polemic. 'The housewife syndrome' was attacked as the source of women's oppression and feminist thought stressed the impor-tance of 'killing the Angel in the House' and liberating women from what was perceived as a limiting 'incarceration' in the home (Friedan, 1965; Gavron, 1966; Oakley, 1974).

At its best this assumption that domesticity is *always* monotonous and *always* stifling for all women has led to a lack of sufficient will-ingness to confront what it is about housework and homemaking that gives pleasure to many women. At its worst, feminism's insistence on seeing domesticity as either degrading and constraining *or* the source of 'true' female virtue serves to reproduce precisely those structures which supported the system of domestic service and further divides women across the barriers of class, education and affluence. For many women in the past as today both their livelihood and their sense of worth are closely tied to their domestic skills: white, middle-class femi-nism's refusal to confront this question, except in its own terms, runs the risk of excluding and alienating vast numbers of women. The women whose oral testimony informs this book washed nets, cleaned windows, scrubbed paths and doorsteps; they married, bore and reared children, sometimes they worked part time in other women's homes as servants, all of them left school at 14 with no qualifications for anything but low paid, low status jobs. Their aspirations focused on the home and the comfort it might provide; they were variously motivated by dignity, love, pride and the satisfactions of an ordered environment. They must also and equally have experienced exhaustion, anger, envy and resentment. They were neither saints nor victims but 'ordinary' women whose place in history is assured as our mothers and grandmothers. To avoid dis-cussing *their* relationship to the home or to conceive it in inappropriately dichotomous terms, is to avoid confronting the ways in which both pleasure and aggression might be internalised and expressed by women, not only in the culturally and socially sanctioned public arenas of politics, protest and writing, but in the 'private' heartland of the home (Giles, 1993, p. 240).

CULTURE, DISCOURSE AND STORY

In order to think about women's relationship to the home and the domestic I have necessarily drawn upon a range of sources that cut across the conventional distinctions between historical documents and literary fictions. These include women's accounts of the past as narrated via oral interviews in the present, diaries, letters, autobiographies and fictional accounts, as well as accounts of women's lives by social reformers and other professionals. Foucault has shown us the importance of detailing 'the interconnections between knowledge claims' and the ways in which competing discourses create power as an effect rather than a transcendent property owned by virtue of wealth, status or gender (Flax, 1987, p. 633). Authority and suppression, the strategies that create power effects, are deployed in a range of practices and discourses that vary across the positionings of class, gender and generation. Working-class mothers could, for example, draw on those discourses of 'good housewifery' and respectability to assert supremacy and authority over both children and 'bad' housewives; speaking for the needs of working-class women from a discourse that emphasised female homogeniety provided authority and professionalism for some (middle-class) women; and the denial of sexual desire or 'sentiment' sanctioned by the anti-heroic, anti-romantic discourses of post First World War England functioned to suppress those discomforting aspects of the psyche which might jeopardise material security. Hence to make sense of the various accounts and sources drawn upon it has been necessary to understand them as participating in these wider discourses, of which they are fragments. Equally, it is important to be aware of the ways in which social actors deploy the cultural narratives and iconographies that are constituted in discourse in order to make sense of their own experience and in order to place themselves in relation to others, relations that are context-specific and thus may be more or less powerful at different moments but remain experienced within oppressive social and economic circumstances.

The anti-heroic and anti-romantic mood of post First World War England was to produce new versions of femininity in a world where the carnage of trench warfare and the war work of women rendered untenable those gender distinctions based on Victorian theories of sexual differentiation. Masculine heroism and feminine fragility were rewritten in the years after the war in terms that, at least on the surface, attempted to minimise sexual difference. Heroism became optimism and endurance ('smilin' thru') and could be refigured as the cheerful, indomitable heroines, played by Gracie Fields in *Sing As We Go* (1934) and *Sally In Our Alley* (1931) whilst 'the little man', content with his garden, home and domestic ideals and epitomised in the nation's image of prime minister, Stanley Baldwin, offered a 'feminised' form of private life to men psychologically exhausted by the demands of imperialist masculinity. And it was, of course, precisely the 'cheerful housewife' in the stories of Jan Struther's Mrs Miniver who was to become one of the central iconographic figures of Second World War propaganda and heroic celebration. As Alison Light has pointed out, it is only necessary to think of Celia Johnson playing the middle-class housewife in David Lean's 1945 film, *Brief Encounter*, based on Noel Coward's play, *Still Life*, to recognise the attributes of common sense, restraint and endurance that characterised representations of English identity both before and during the Second World War, here presented as a domestic and feminised version of the masculine 'stiff upper lip' of Victorian narratives (Light, 1991, pp. 208–10).

Thus, whilst the discourses of medicine, science and psychology posited a 'modern' woman freed from the constraints of Victorian 'repression', her apparently newly acquired robustness and common-sense were to be at the service of marriage, housewifery and motherhood. Mothers were advised that physical exercise, plain food, sleeping on a hard mattress alongside an open window, cold baths and discouraging 'sentimental and morbid devotions to an individual' would ensure the stable and healthy development of their adolescent daughters and provide a firm preparation for their ultimate fulfilment as wives and mothers (Webb, 1932, p. 13). Physical health and 'moral hygiene' would ensure a sensible attitude to sexuality and avoid the excesses of passion, intensity or yearning desire. This disavowal of sentiment and intensity, which found its expression in the pronouncements of medical practitioners, psychologists and women's magazines, such as *Home Chat* and *Woman's Weekly*, that offered a service to the 'housekeeping woman of today', coexisted with the much-criticised narratives of 'glamour' and 'pulp' fiction, whose targeted readership was working-class women and girls (Melman, 1988, Pt 3). *The Oracle, Red Star Weekly, Silver Star* and *Lucky Star* offered stories with titles such as 'Scandal Ruined Her Life', 'Branded by Satan' and 'Three Years of Stolen Love' in which, despite the visibility of passion and glamour, intensity of emotion and sexual desire were represented as roads to ruin and misery or the attributes of a demonised 'other' woman (Jephcott, 1943, pp. 98–111; Melman, 1988, Pt 3; Fowler, 1991, pp. 51–71). The following extract from a story called 'Love's Sinner' makes clear the punishment contingent upon excessive emotional behaviours:

> [Ruby] would never get her man. Clenching her fists, tears of fury in her eyes, Ruby ran upstairs, and back in her bedroom stripped off the peach satin nightdress, trampling it beneath her feet. She could have torn it to shreds, as willingly as she would have torn Hagar had she been at her mercy just then. Jumping into bed she curled up like an animal, snatching viciously at her pillow . . . I'll kill her if she doesn't get out of the way, she thought (cited in Jephcott, 1943, p. 106).

Educationalists and youth workers were anxious about the influence of such fiction on the ideals and dreams of working-class girls, seeing it as offering them spurious fantasies of romance and adventure outside the parameters of their class and gender. Pearl Jephcott for example writes:

> [Girls] want desperately to know what 'love' is, and the publishers, knowing their young clients, cater for this demand. What they provide, however, are stories of sex and sentimentality, not love. 'The kisses, the love stuff' are thrown at the readers. Every page is sickly with them. Only very *immature* people or girls whose tastes have begun to be *perverted* could endure the constant repetition of this kind of description: 'Glyn Curtis was the only man who could make her heart throb with longing – the longing to be taken into his arms, to feel his lips upon hers. Not lightly, caressingly as he had kissed her before but – ! (Jephcott, 1943, p. 110, my emphasis).

The point I want to make is that in the 1920s and 1930s the dominant and acceptable response to the longings suppressed by the discourse of healthy, 'common-sense' was to denigrate such yearnings as 'silly', 'perverted' and 'immature', irrelevant and inappropriate to the 'real' experiences of a woman's life, which consisted of prudential marriage and the provision of a comfortable, hygienic environment in which to sustain a male breadwinner and healthy children (Giles, 1994).

Discourses of femininity that stressed cheerful common-sense, brisk competence and 'ordinariness' were easily imbricated with the discourses of home and family that focused on concepts of 'national efficiency' and the role of mothers in raising a physically fit and emotionally stable citizenry. For 'womanly' common-sense and competence would rear healthy babies, maintain 'homes fit for heroes' and produce the secure home life necessary for national stability. Moreover the discourses of welfarism and reform that created the social policies of the years after 1918 argued, as indicated above, for the importance of the family and its maintenance as an economic and social unit. The discourse of welfarism, linked as it was to debates around ideas of 'national efficiency', whether in the form of infant welfare or maternal need, addressed, at least partially, the needs of working-class women and as such indicated a change in dominant perceptions of 'the poor'. The numerous social surveys of the 1920s and 1930s, often inspired by the spectre of mass unemployment, which was itself so much at odds with 'national efficiency', suggested a growing investment in alleviating the worst excesses of industrial capitalism and a concern to tackle the structural causes of poverty and ill health. At the very least, this signalled a social and political recognition of the poor as members of society with certain rights, although, in contradiction, this ran alongside neo-Malthusian and eugenicist discourses that questioned the rights of the poor to reproduce and hence to exist at all. Nonetheless such conceptualisations were reinforced by the discourse of citizenship in which a belief in the rights and responsibilities of those deemed 'citizens' extended to adequate housing, education and political participation and overlapped with the construction of the housewife as consumer in an economy increasingly dominated by the manufacture of consumer durables such as electrical products, processed foods and mass-produced clothing (Glucksmann, 1990, pp. 226–56). Thus the dominant discourses of housewifery were produced from an intersecting nexus of medical, political, economic and psychological discourses in which women were positioned as wives, as mothers, as consumers, as citizens, and, for working-class women, as 'the poor'.

Women of all classes were able, up to a point, to adapt and expropriate these discourses for their own purposes. As we shall see, middle-class women inserted themselves into the discourses of welfarism and reform by stressing their empathy as women with the wives and mothers of 'the poor'. Working-class women, particularly those who were able to benefit from the opportunities for affluence and improved housing available in the period, found a cultural ideal and a social space in the figure and practices of the housewife and adopted the discourse of housewifery in order to develop their own forms of respectability and self-definition. Whether in doing so new and different relations between women and women, between men and women, and between mothers and daughters were created is the subject of the chapters that follow.

Finally, I want to examine how we might read primary sources as texts and as history. Recent work on language, text and subjectivity makes it impossible to treat oral narratives or autobiographies as simply reflections of an unproblematic external reality. Even those sources closer to the traditional historian's heart – the official report or survey – have only the power to authorise or refuse certain readings and do not contain within themselves, sealed away as it were, events as 'they really happened'. Sometimes in these pages I relate facts: when people were born or married, where they lived, the size of their families; information that can be verified and provides a chronological framework, which is the basis of all historical scholarship and writing. At other times I speculate on attitudes, beliefs and motivations from the written and spoken material I have to hand. This task can be conceptualised as the second layer of history writing, hermeneutics and narrative, in which cause and effect, character and significance are mapped onto the chronological chain.

However I have also attempted to construct what Carolyn Steedman has called 'psychological history' by treating the various narratives to the methods of textual analysis and by considering the accounts women have given of the past as synchronic stories in which recurrent motifs and symbolic expression produce further layers of meaning and subjectivity (Steedman, 1992, pp. 125, 41–50). My intention here is to draw attention to the ways in which both written and spoken sources represent rather than simply reflect their subjects' worlds. Furthermore, as Lynn Hunt reminds us,

> as historians learn to analyze their subjects' representations of their worlds, they inevitably begin to reflect on the nature of their own efforts to represent history; the practice of history is, after all, a process of text creating and of 'seeing', that is, giving form to subjects (Hunt, 1989, p. 20).

Hence I am aware that my own 'voice' is part of the 'process of text creating and "seeing"', and thus my own positioning within and towards the material I deploy is neither transparent nor neutral and does need to be accounted for.[3] Storytelling is one of the ways in which we make sense of our experiences and our past, whether we do so through the literary forms of autobiography or through the oral history life story. Unlike historical narrative, the story of a life depends for its meaning on the presence, either literally or through the narrative personna, of the story's teller. The presence of the teller in the present legitimates the 'truth' and the significance of the story – 'and that's why I'm here today'.

Historical narrative on the other hand, despite the necessary technical closure of the narrative at a certain point, always remains unfinished. The historian's craft is to seek out continually more details of the particular research topic in hand. All historians know that it is impossible to state a final conclusion. We can only ever possess fragments of the past from which we continually attempt to create a whole; new evidence may come to light and new interpretations can be formed by using different sources or deploying established sources in new ways, as well as from controversy and debate. On the other hand the life story, whether written or oral, finishes in the present of the teller and as such can be approached as 'a meaning system complete unto itself' but, I would add, one that can only be apprehended by locating it both in the moment of its telling and in the moments it recalls (Chanfrault-Duchet, 1991, p. 77). Stories are ways in which we not only make sense of the world from the vantage point of the present but also claim for ourselves a self-hood and subjectivity in which we are positioned as both subject and object of our own narration.

Hence in order to understand the stories related to me by women it is necessary to examine the form as well as the content of those narratives, for in the choice of linguistic and cultural forms may lie deeper articulations of relationship and affect. I am not suggesting that the following accounts of women's lives are in any sense definitive or 'objective' versions of the ways in which certain women understood and made sense of their experiences. The versions produced below are readings of the stories women told to me and as such they are readings that draw upon my concerns and preoccupations as a feminist historian in the late twentieth century. Katherine Borland has demonstrated how an incident in her grandmother's life was read differently by herself and by her grandmother. Borland produced a feminist interpretation of the event, her grandmother refused this version. As Borland points out, neither reading was invalid but they were produced from different standpoints and for different purposes; in allowing both readings to coexist in her text Borland refuses the tendency of dominant (phallocentric) cultures to suppress those readings which threaten claims to authority and knowledge (Borland, 1991). Yet, as Borland notes, we are still left with questions about her role as author and researcher, the 'expert' through whom her grandmother's story is mediated, and our roles as readers of this story:

> How then might we present our work in a way that grants the speaking woman interpretive respect without relinquishing our responsibility to provide our own interpretation of her experience (Borland, 1991, p. 64).

I shall return to this issue, but for now I believe (or I want to believe) that the historical imagination (both of the researched and the researcher) is as valid in exploring the past as historical causality. There are no primary sources by which I can verify the 'truth' of the many things I was told, nor can I provide quantitative or empirical data to reinforce some of my interpretations. I can, however, identify common patterns and tropes in the narratives and I can use these judiciously to ask questions about how myth and chronology, fact and story, memory and history are used to reinvent subjectivities that both expose and hide selfhood, and that tell us not only about the individuals who created these definitions but also about the historical circumstances from which they were produced and in which they intervened.

To turn then to some specific features in the accounts: the use of repeated refrains, key phrases and pronouns frequently expressed the relationship between teller, history and her social world. For example, in all the interviews I recorded and in many autobiographies by working-class women of this period there is a recurrent use of the phrase 'in those days you had to'. This suggested to me a distancing of the self by the speaker from the rules of her social world and a distancing from that past in which such impositions occurred; a distancing that, as I shall argue in Chapter 3, was reinforced and sanctioned by the social imperatives of respectability. Equally, in telling her story each woman chose a mode in which to represent herself: she might represent herself as fighter or victim, as stoic or rebel, as excluded or as belonging. In order to do so women selected from the repertoire of cultural myths and iconography available and *acceptable* to them. For example, no working-class woman in the stories I heard or in the autobiographies I have read presents herself as a romantic heroine, despite the fact that many working-class women read and enjoyed romantic fiction. Equally and connected, none of the women interviewed (not surprisingly) represented themselves as 'rough', all of them self-identified as 'respectable', although some would have not been thus defined by their peers. 'Being swept off your feet', falling in love, sexual yearnings were, as we have seen, represented culturally as 'immature' behaviours, often closely linked to 'roughness' and 'otherness' and as such unacceptable to women who, as we shall see, aspired to maturity and belonging in a 'modern' world that appeared to offer the material conditions for securing this.

Such representations are also, of course, produced from the social and historical contexts in which the teller is located. When I set out to record interviews I was concerned to create a situation as close as possible to a private conversation. Nonetheless social markers such as my professional position and the switching on of the tape recorder signalled something very different to the interviewees, who, I came to realise, understood the situation not as a private dialogue, but as a public performance with myself as 'first audience' (Stuart, 1993, p. 81). Conversant with media conventions in which interviewers with microphones ask people to say 'a few words', the women interviewed were understandably concerned about performance: 'will I have enough to tell you?', 'it won't be very interesting', 'you'd do better to ask my husband', 'you'll have to tell me what you want me to say' were common responses to initial requests for interviews. And, arriving to interview women, I was initially surprised to be met by respondents who had quite obviously dressed for the occasion as well as cleaning and tidying the room and providing tea in the best china. These women, historically debarred from performance in public arenas, were more used to being spoken about and for, and over a long period have developed strategies for resisting and 'escaping' their observers (including myself).[4] The 'performance' many gave was intended to reinvent a self appropriate for public consumption and as such emphasised prudence, restraint and self-sufficiency and 'forgot' romance, desire or intimacy. The frequent use of the pronoun 'You' signalled this need to split the self, 'I', who might have desired from the public 'You' who related and existed in a certain social world (Giles, 1995). Women have always relied on oracy as a means of communicating our selves, our stories and our lives – we tell friends, children, and lovers anecdotes and stories about our history but these are often in the context of a personal relationship, an intimate conversation or, where written, in letters or diaries. The oral lifestory is produced in a social context that to the narrator signifies entry into a public arena of discourse and that can be alien to her usual mode of speaking and conversation. Hence any understanding of the women's stories requires recognition of them as public statements in which the articulation of unacceptable or 'deviant' emotions may remain both coded and obliquely embedded in the language.

Finally, I want to discuss the ways in which the following chapters are organised and the rationale for this structure. Chapter 1 explores what it meant to be both female and working class at a specific moment in history. For example, the experiences of poverty and the proximity of death provided images and understandings of the world that found articulation in ideas about 'making do' and 'getting by'. I also explore the relations between parents and children, particularly mothers and daughters, as one of the locations in which women could see themselves as both powerful and powerless within the structures of working-class life. I also ask to what extent relations between men and women within the family, as husbands and fathers, were touched in various ways by the outbreak and aftermath of the First World War and the reinvention of masculinity contingent upon this. I focus in this chapter upon the 'voices' of working-class women, drawing on oral testimony and autobiographical accounts, in particular their recollections of childhoods lived alongside poverty, war and death, and attempt to map these onto the wider historical circumstances within which these women experienced their lives.

Chapter 2 picks up on the aspirations and dreams of working-class women for a better future than their mothers. It explores the ways in which post First World War housing policies made such dreams possible via renting or buying a home in the expanding suburbs and the ways in which this dream was experienced differently for men and women via ideas about citizenship and property. Housing designers and housing officials used housing as a means of defining the 'respectable' family, and housing discourses often used the figure of the 'modern' housewife and the 'good tenant' to represent the ideal working-class family. At the same time the growth of suburbia occasioned considerable hostility, and my analysis of Dr Stephen Taylor's 1936 article in *The Lancet* on 'suburban neurosis' explores the gendered focus of this and the needs and interests served by his construction of the 'suburban neurotic'. We hear the 'voices' of some of the working-class men and women who became suburbanites in a correspondence that took place in the columns of the *Birmingham Mail* in 1931, and my juxtaposition of this with the official 'voices' of housing policy and medicine is intended to suggest the ways in which hegemonic discourses may provide spaces in which specific groups can articulate their own needs and interests. This is taken further by considering the ways in which some women, in telling their life stories, represented suburbanisation as a positive experience in which they recalled neither 'neuroticism' nor isolation. Nonetheless suburbia made possible forms of reinvented social divisiveness articulated in numerous contemporary accounts.

The desirability of 'keeping yourself to yourself' was frequently expressed by the women interviewed, and Chapter 3 attempts to analyse exactly what made up the cluster of attitudes and behaviours associated with 'keeping yourself to yourself'. It also explores the needs that could be met via reserve and distance. I argue that 'keeping yourself to yourself' was not simply a social practice but an emotional imperative, particularly at a time when the developing practices of social welfare increasingly observed working-class women in their roles as wives and mothers. Health visitors, social scientists, welfare and housing workers, as well as educationalists and writers were all observers and recorders of working-class family life. One of the aims of Chapter 3 is to investigate how far and in what ways working-class women internalised the versions of themselves offered by middle-class observers and how far they deployed ideas of 'keeping yourself to yourself' as a resistance and protection against the intrusions of observers. But I am also concerned to speculate on what needs were served by home visiting, social work and welfare reform for those middle-class women who were enabled to enter such professions. To suggest the interactions between working- and middle-class women around issues of 'good' housekeeping, motherhood and sexuality I draw upon writings by Marie Stopes, The Women's Hygiene Committee and Pearl Jephcott, and in order further to suggest how these related to the ways in which men represented themselves as social reformers, I have briefly considered George Orwell's *The Road to Wigan Pier*. However an exploration of 'keeping yourself to yourself' also requires a consideration of the concepts of a 'private' self and an 'inner' life, and this raises questions about the ways in which women from different classes might represent themselves sexually as well as socially.

The final chapter focuses on the relationship of women of different classes via the system of domestic service. The demise of residential domestic service, the 'feminisation' of the occupation, middle-class anxieties over 'the servant problem' and the advent of labour-saving devices and smaller homes represented the relations between mistresses and servants in different and changing ways. This chapter will address such relationships as articulated in the autobiographical accounts of service produced by Jean Rennie and Winifred Foley and in the fictional representations of mistress/servant relations offered in Jan Struther's *Mrs Miniver*, amongst others, as well as in the diaries and autobiographies of middle-class women. I am concerned here not simply to recount the conditions of domestic service but to explore the 'psychological history' produced from such relations. One of my concerns is to suggest how 'privacy' for middle-class women, reliant upon domestic service, might have had very different meanings from the conceptualisations of 'keeping yourself to yourself' explored in the previous chapter. I end the chapter by juxtaposing two stories of mistress/servant relations: one as told me by Doris Arthurs, a working-class woman from Birmingham, and the other, Daphne Du Maurier's *Rebecca* in which the sinister figure of the servant/housekeeper and her relationships with the mistresses of Manderley could suggest powerful meanings for middle-class readers in the 1930s organised around the centrality of domestic service in their lives.

Thus my intention is to build up layers of meaning in order to demonstrate some of the ways in which a variety of subjectivities, imbricated in generational, gender and class relations, were (and are) articulated and experienced. In doing so I shall suggest the ways in which none of these relations can be understood independently of those others upon which they impinge and depend. Thus domestic servants were often the fourteen year old daughters of working-class mothers; mothers who might dominate daughters in one area, might ally with them against 'outsiders' in another; mistresses and mothers might share authority over young working-class girls; working-class fathers could be experienced and understood in relation to mothers; and relations with husbands might be negotiated and made sense of in relation to parents and other authority figures. What I am suggesting is that power, manifested in dominance, authority and claims to knowledge was a constantly shifting effect, produced within particular sets of specific relations. Some men and some women, of course, were socially positioned in ways that made it possible to sustain power effects over more people, for longer periods and in more arenas than others.

1 'Making Do' and 'Getting By'

Doris Arthurs observed of her childhood in the rural North Midlands:

> it was really hard you know. I wouldn't like to think mine had to go through anything like that now. Mind you we was happy because we didn't know anything else. That was your life.

Doris, like all the women interviewed, articulates an acute awareness of the structures within which her life could be understood, 'that was your life', alongside a (contradictory) desire for life to be better and a fierce pride in having survived and endured. Throughout the interviews the women used phrases such as 'lucky if you just got by', 'it was a hard life but a good one' and 'better just to get on with things'. 'Getting on with things', however, suppressed the myriad disappointments and exclusions that constituted the complex existence of these women in a society structured around the divisions of class and gender. I want to suggest that rather than simply reading the life stories of working-class women as accounts of a gritty stoicism, or as celebrations of the strength of 'Mum', or alternatively, in some instances, as narratives of escape through education or affluence, such stories can also be understood as obliquely wrought expressions of the disappointment, resentment and envy that asymmetric class and gender systems must engender in the psyches of those who experience such injuries. As Jane Flax has pointed out, we cannot assume, as we so often tend to, that 'the oppressed are not in fundamental ways damaged by their social experience' (Flax, 1987, p. 642). Growing up in the early part of this century was to experience the social practices of poverty and femininity in ways that differed both from what went before and from what was to come after. Girls acquired a knowledge and understanding of what it meant to be female and what it meant to be working class both from the social practices they experienced and from the ways in which class and gender were culturally articulated from a range of positions. Doris knew it was 'hard' but she also understood her life as 'happy' – this chapter attends to the ways in which women such as Doris were enabled to see their lives as 'happy', the negotiations, suppressions and evasions that were necessary in order to make sense of the injustices inherent in their class and gender positions, and the forms in which these experiences could be expressed.

Moreover, as Alice Kessler-Harris has argued, people, as historical agents, did not simply imagine themselves as gendered or classed beings. A working-class woman would not necessarily define herself thus. Such social categories as 'woman', 'working class' certainly functioned in part to structure consciousness, but they were constantly intertwined with a range of other self-definitions of which class and gender are but two. Alice Kessler-Harris offers the image of 'intersecting circles which together' create a web of experience and understanding not rooted in a single variable but participating in and moving around sets of interacting self-identifications, amongst which might be age (adult/child), family relationship (daughter, sister, brother, father, uncle), economic role in family (dependent, provider), geographical location (urban, rural, suburban) as well as ethnicity, class and gender (Kessler-Harris, 1989, p. 37; Thorne, 1987, pp. 85–109). The women I interviewed made sense of their lives from their experiences of these relationships and the cultural repertoire of images available in which to express their understanding and definition of a sense of self. In order to try to offer a sense of 'intersecting circles' I shall focus on women's childhood experience and understanding of poverty, respectability and affluence, which necessarily involves exploring issues of class and gender but which were also made sense of from a variety of positions. Although I have subtitled the sections of this chapter 'Growing up female' and 'Growing up working class' this does not preclude other variables, as will become apparent, nor does it deny the myriad ways in which consciousness and internalisation of one category intersects with another. Before turning to the variety of ways in which girls made sense of their lives however, it is necessary to sketch the historical contexts in which understanding and experience were rooted.

The women interviewed were born between 1895 and 1922. The world they found themselves in was dominated by the First World War and, later, the Second World War. Yet it is not these cataclysmic events that are recalled in their retrospective accounts but the day-to-day experiences of poverty, survival and hard work, and their aspirations for a better life than that of their mothers. War is mentioned only insofar as it impinges on daily life and none of the women made any reference, for example, to the general strike of 1926. What the women offer in their accounts of the past is not a chronological sequence of verifiable

historical events but the 'psychological history' discussed in the Introduction (Steedman, 1992, p. 125). Their concern in telling their stories
in the present is to explain who they are rather than what they did,
although I would not want to suggest that they were themselves aware
of this distinction, nor would I wish to suggest that the historical and
political realities of war or industrial unrest were in any way insignificant. It is the way in which the events of the past were imaginatively
recreated in the construction of a story that explain a consciousness,
and the way in which the past is made sense of in the present that offers
a psychological narrative of selfhood, a narrative that is not necessarily
bounded by or imagined in terms of chronological categories – although it will, of course, occur within a linear time structure – but that
nonetheless offers an imaginative reality that we might equally wish to
call 'history'. The two world wars and the peace between form a metaphoric as well as a material landscape in which women found ways of
articulating lives dominated by poverty, affluence, survival and death,
as well as experiencing the daily circumstances of such realities. War
was articulated as part, albeit a more dramatic part, of a continuum in
which injury, disease, loss, survival and death form a framework for
living.

Nevertheless, of course, the aftermath of the First World War and the
growing possibility of the Second did have very real material implications for daily life. Graves and Hodge observed that the First World
War 'killed off one eligible man in every seven and seriously injured
another', and in 1927 it was estimated that there were two million
women in excess of men in the population of Britain (Graves and
Hodge, 1940, p. 45; Jeffreys, 1985, p. 173). Young women reaching
adulthood in the 1920s found themselves in a social world still committed to marriage as the sole locus of a woman's fulfilment at a time
when the actual supply of men to marry was seriously depleted. This
and the anti-heroic mood of post First World War Britain (and latterly
the fear of another world war) produced a social and moral climate that
disavowed romance, sentimentality and displays of excessive emotion
in favour of 'common-sense', prudence and reserve, particularly for
working-class women for whom an 'imprudent' choice of marriage
partner could seriously jeopardise their future lives. For all the women
interviewed, poverty, hard work and the expectation of marriage structured their lives and their imaginations as they grew to adulthood and
struggled to make sense of their place and purpose in society.

In the first half of the twentieth century a large proportion of the population continued to exist in conditions of more or less extreme poverty, and of the 21 women interviewed all but one experienced childhoods marked to a greater or lesser extent by material need. In 1911–13 an estimated 170 000 persons owned 65.5 per cent of Britain's wealth, whilst nearly 17 million of the property-owning population owned only 8.5 per cent (Pollard, 1983, p. 1). As Deirdre Beddoe points out for the 1930s, whilst *Good Housekeeping*, a magazine targeted at a middle-class readership, estimated that between 12s. 6d. and £1 was the minimum upon which one person could survive for a week, many working-class women struggled to feed a family of five on 14s 3d a week (Beddoe, 1989, p. 5). The social surveys of Charles Booth and Seebohm Rowntree revealed that approximately 25–30 per cent of the population of London and York experienced relative degrees of poverty at various times in their lives, and for at least 10 per cent of the population poverty was a permanent feature of their lives. Even those, comprising the bulk of the working class, who did not experience the extremes of poverty, lived

> not quite destitute but always in fear of destitution through illness, accident or old age, not unemployable but always in danger of unemployment, not without homes but often living in slums (Read, 1972, p. 41).

In 1901 it was estimated that 8.2 per cent of the population lived in conditions of overcrowding, where overcrowding was defined as more than two persons per room per tenement (Read, 1972, p. 27). Working-class homes were usually rooms and many large families lived in two rooms, sharing beds and sleeping, eating, cooking all in one general living space. Water had to be carried from a standpipe, often up steep flights of stairs, and there was little light and less fresh air as much urban working-class housing, except for that of the most affluent, was squashed between factories, warehouses, workshops and railways before the advent of cheap transport made it possible for working people to live at a distance from their employment. The harmful consequences of lack of ventilation and light were exacerbated in urban slums by primitive sanitary arrangements, piles of rubbish 'distributed promiscuously over the yard or court' and, on washing-days, 'pools of water . . . which gradually percolate through to the damp and unsavoury soil below' (Rowntree, 1902, pp. 153, 154).

Girls born at the beginning of the century were born into a world dominated by disease, ill-health and death in ways unimaginable to us today. Mortality rates were high even before we add the loss of lives contingent upon the First World War: in 1900 life expectancy for men was 46 years and for women 50. Widowhood was a very real possibility for many women. Rowntree estimated that between 1897 and 1901 almost half of those applying to join the army in Sheffield, Leeds and York were rejected on medical grounds, and TB alone claimed 51 000 lives in 1910 (Stevenson, 1984, p. 203). For women, complications in or after childbirth were second to tuberculosis as a cause of death but constant pregnancies and lack of antenatal care caused serious health problems for those who survived. Moreover infant and child mortality rates, although considerably reduced from their mid-nineteenth-century figure, were very high at 151 per thousand live births in 1901 in England and Wales (Read, 1972, p. 23). At the turn of the century in London approximately 15 per cent of infants died before their first birthday and many more died between one and five years of age. In Hackney in 1880 it was estimated that nearly half of the deaths for the borough as a whole were children under five (Ross, 1986, pp. 81–2).

Growing up before the First World War was very much a matter of survival: it could never be assumed that a child would reach adulthood and even then, if we discount death or injury from war, the risks from infectious diseases, pregnancy, and industrial accidents were high. Dolly Scannell recalled her mother's pride in having borne and reared ten children, all of whom reached adulthood (Scannell, 1974, pp. 24, 29). For many life was interspersed with sibling deaths, the deaths of relatives, neighbours and even parents. Even if actual death was escaped, ill-health and, after 1918, war injuries could be an integral part of family life, with the male breadwinner incapacitated or a mother struggling against her own ill-health. Disease and injury seriously threatened the survival of whole families at a time when insurance schemes were rudimentary and trade union benevolent societies, friendly societies and kinship networks provided often inadequate safety nets.

Even where illness or death were avoided, many families, both urban and rural, were headed by one or more parents who drank heavily, or by a brutal and violent father, or by a male breadwinner who simply upped and left. Working-class children before the First World War, even where their immediate families were non-drinkers, were likely to have had some experience of alcoholism, drunkenness and related problems. In 1914 there were 3388 convictions per week for drunkenness in England and Wales, licensing hours were long, extending from 5 or

6 am until 11 pm or midnight. In 1900 there were 102 000 licenced premises and an estimated £195 million was spent on alcholic drinks. The topography of working-class areas included numerous public houses, as well as off-licences, and it was an accepted activity for working men, if not their (respectable) wives, to spend their evenings and leisure time in the cosy amiability of the public house, where clubs and associations might be formed as well as drink consumed (Marwick, 1965, pp. 63–8; Read, 1972, p. 52). Male violence, either physical or verbal, even when not exacerbated by drink, could be legitimated as an extreme manifestation of male authority, endorsed by the husband's role as primary breadwinner in return for which he was owed work by his wife. The failure of wives to carry out their side of the marriage 'contract' by cooking and cleaning was frequently cited by men as full justification for beating their wives, a justification that many women appeared, at least on the surface, to accept (Ayers and Lambertz, 1986, pp. 194–219; Ross, 1986, pp. 84–5; Ross, 1982, pp. 575–605).

Finally, all but one of the women interviewed were born into large families. Large families were the norm for working-class marriages before the 1920s: the decline in family size before the First World War was mainly attributable to middle-class fertility patterns (Banks, 1954; Gittins, 1982; Habakkuk, 1971; Levine, 1987). By 1940 average family size for all classes had fallen to two children whereas in 1900 it was common for working-class mothers to have four or more children (Wrigley, 1969, p. 197; Halsey, 1972, pp. 55, 57). Once again this was part of the visual landscape in which girls grew to adulthood: a landscape, whether rural or urban, in which children of all ages figured prominently. In 1901 young people under 30 comprised 60 per cent of the population (Read, 1972, p. 23). Urban streets might be full of children playing, schools were overcrowded and families might range in age from a baby to an adult worker. Without prams, cots or playpens mothers would take their babies everywhere with them, constantly holding them or passing them to others to hold. As Ellen Ross has argued, in such conditions 'the real mother–child "dyad" existed only for a short time', before the birth of the next child and older children from six years upwards were expected to look after themselves, to help with household chores and above all to mind the smaller children (Ross, 1986, p. 84). In such circumstances to be the youngest child was indeed a privileged position.

Growing up in the first decades of this century therefore meant inhabiting a world where extreme degrees of wealth and poverty created, not only a world of vastly differing social practices, but a visual landscape offering a range of images from which men, women and children might know who they were and where they belonged. The crowded, insanitary warrens of urban back-to-back housing provided a stark visual contrast with the tree-lined roads and avenues of middle-class suburbia; the industrial landscape of cities such as Birmingham and Manchester with the countryside of Worcestershire, Herefordshire and Kent; the well-dressed 'lady' with the uniformed domestic servant; and the cloth-capped working man with the top-hatted 'gent'.

Moreover there were equally potent contrasts in the homes of the population: working-class and poor families rented rooms, shared toilets, washhouses, play areas and beds with each other and with other families. Homes contained very little furniture and even less ornamentation. In contrast the homes of the middle and upper classes were large, each family member had a bedroom and there would certainly be more than one living area. Such homes were well furnished and contained ornaments, pictures and books to a degree unheard of in poorer homes. More than anything else perhaps, as Robert Graves and Alan Hodge noted in their social history of the interwar years, was the appearance of people and most particularly the looks of women: '[t]he most remarkable outward change of the Twenties was in the looks of women in the towns. The prematurely aged wife was coming to be the exception rather than the rule' (Graves and Hodge, 1940/1991, p. 75).[1]

Poverty, as well as wealth, was visually marked by clothing, house interiors and topography, but equally by its embodiment in the figures of women, aged and diseased by hard work, numerous preganancies, bad diet and insanitary conditions. Illness and injury manifested itself in the numerous crippled or wounded young men and in the figures of older men, for whom respiratory and bronchial diseases revealed themselves in the constant and unpleasant use of the spittoon. Dolly Scannell 'knew' her mother loved her father because she 'even washed and disinfected his spittoon, daily' (Scannell, 1974, p. 22). My point is that the ways in which women made sense of themselves, placed themselves in relation to others, found ways of 'getting by', and secured for themselves a reasonable way of living were shaped by this historical landscape and by the cultural explanations and psychological strategies they were able to bring to the conditions in which they found themselves.

All the women interviewed aspired to a better life than their mothers and it was precisely against the background outlined above that they measured their success in achieving this: smaller families, a reasonable income, better health for themselves and their families, a comfortable home and a less arduous round of daily tasks were the forms in which they expressed their yearning for life to be better than it was. Virginia Woolf was absolutely correct when she observed in her letter to Margaret Llewellyn Davies that working-class women were more concerned with 'baths and ovens' than 'Mozart and Einstein' and that their aspirations tended to be materialistic rather than spiritual (Woolf, 1931/1977, pp. xxi, xxviii). Where Woolf's own sense of class led her astray was in representing this division as evidence for a failure of that 'rich inner life' in working-class women who, in her eyes, remained one-dimensional, uncomplicated and undeniably alien figures, inhabiting a solidly physical landscape and lacking the 'romance' she associates with her own kind,

> they [working women delegates of the Women's Co-operative Guild] were not in the least detached and easy and cosmopolitan. They were indigenous and rooted to one spot. Their very names were like stones of the field – common, grey, worn, obscure, docked of all splendours of association and romance (Woolf 1931/1977, p. xxiv).

Woolf is enabled to create such images of working-class women precisely because of the forms of visual differentiation available to her. The women delegates of the Co-operative Guild no doubt gave the appearance of 'greyness', of being 'worn' and ordinary: they looked and dressed very differently from Woolf and her circle. They no less than Woolf must have been acutely aware of the differences. For them, however, such differences visually encoded their exclusion from the material benefits that accrued to the affluent and visibly expressed the permanent and persistent insecurity of their daily lives. Woolf, like many middle-class observers, may have regretted what she perceived as the lack of spiritual life in working-class women, but what she, and many others since, failed or preferred not to recognise was that the conditions of working-class life generated envy and desire, not for her 'culture' and 'inner life', but for her clothes, her house, her comfort and her leisure, and that this inexpressible and frequently unexpressed yearning might camouflage itself as belligerence, resentment, deference and a defensively proud assertion that 'we was happy'.

The language in which the psyche has been evaluated has so often been the language of class formations – 'materialistic'/'cultivated'; 'complex'/'simple'; 'mature'/'immature' – it has also and equally been the language of gender differentiation. Hence the class and gender formations in which women, born at the beginning of the century, found themselves invited them to define themselves via specific cultural discourses organised around conceptualisations of the 'cultivated' and the 'civilised', the 'materialistic' and the 'acquisitive'. Jeremy Seabrook, writing in the 1970s, continues this dichotomous conceptualisation in his assertions that working-class experience was shaped according to either a 'culture of poverty' or a 'culture of consumerism', both of which according to Seabrook's argument, although the former less so, seriously impoverish the psyche (Seabrook, 1982, pp. 21–37). How far the women interviewed interpreted, adapted, contested and inserted themselves into these dominant discourses and the social practices thus constituted is the subject of the following two sections.

GROWING UP WORKING CLASS

How then did girls growing up in the early years of the twentieth century understand and experience themselves as 'working class'? Poverty, as I have indicated, was the first experience of many girls and the ways in which it was marked and perceived by others shaped a consciousness of difference and exclusion. Mavis Kitching was born in Birmingham in 1916; she could not recall her father's occupation nor could she remember him working, although she did remember the illness that prevented him from working for the last nine years of his life. Mavis spent her childhood in Birmingham's jewellery quarter, a congested inner area of the city centre, where small workshops, warehouses, shops and residential housing rubbed shoulders. Mavis's mother undertook part-time cleaning to supplement the family's meagre income, working on the railway cleaning the toilets and later as a cleaner at the local hospital. She was also a teacher at the Salvation Army Sunday School and both she and Mavis's father were strictly teetotal and anti-gambling. Mavis left school at 14, worked as a kitchen assistant at a city centre hotel and married George, a chef, in 1936. In 1948, as a result of slum clearance, Mavis and George were rehoused in a new council house on the south-west perimeter of the city. By this time they had two small children, George had served in the army during the Second World War and both sets of parents had died. Mavis relished her role as a housewife and continues to bake and sew for her extended family,

People laugh at me – some people say they don't like housework but I love it. I love doing it, knitting, sewing. It's my favourite thing, sewing and altering.

Mavis's account of her life centres around poverty, illness and her pleasure in homemaking. Time and again she returns in her narrative to a childhood experience of poverty not uncommon before the Second World War – she received shoes and clothing from a local charitable organisation: 'You were given Daily Mail clothes, a big D.M. on the side of your boots, and your dresses were like prison dresses'. Mavis recalled how she was made fun of for wearing these boots and dresses, 'when you have the D.M. clothes they used to chase after you you know and used to hurt you'. The D.M. on the side of the boots was a concrete mark of social identity. 'Poor' meant you were different, available for ridicule and an 'object of charity' to be pushed around, excluded and chased, even by your playmates – the message was imprinted as firmly on Mavis's consciousness as its literal imprimatur on the heavy boots:

> I always said I would work my fingers to the bone rather than them have to have Daily Mail clothes because I knew what it was and I used to cry and I used to vow my kids will never have D.M. clothes . . . the boots used to be up here and they used to be really heavy when you walked and a big D.M. on the side so you couldn't pawn.

'Poor' also meant running errands to earn a few pence for the cinema, fetching coke from the gas works to keep a fire going and being given a holiday by the Girl Guides: 'the guides paid for me, they all put together so that I could go with them, I liked it all the way through'. For Mavis the experience of poverty meant both exclusion and dependency, hostility towards her tormentors and gratitude to her benefactors, anger and deference. Above all else poverty meant an acute awareness of the power of money, the apparent impossibility of ever acquiring quite enough and a willingness to undertake almost any task to procure a few pleasures. As Mavis recalled,

> We'd take a big basket to the gas works to sort the cokes for the fire and all the people you knew used to give you money to go to the pictures with – one penny or tuppence. . . . I have known my father

wheel a cartload of furniture on an ordinary hand cart from Vauxhall to Kingstanding for a packet of cigarettes.

However, whilst poverty might appear unchanging and inevitable to Mavis's parents, there was the possibility of a better life for Mavis's generation, for whom a developing agenda of welfare and social reform plus a market economy increasingly focused on domestic consumption made dreams of adequate housing, a reasonable income and smaller families attainable via marrying wisely, avoiding debt and working hard. Mavis loved her new council house, representing as it did her dreams of a better future for herself and her children, and she loved her treadle sewing machine, which was one of her first 'possessions' as a married woman. Her joy in acquiring her first sewing machine symbolically articulates her dreams of a future in which Daily Mail clothes are replaced by possessions and clothes of one's own and at the same time functions as a material object by which such dreams are concretely fulfilled. As a child Mavis understood very well that she would receive nothing without 'earning' it, either through hard work or via the emotional and psychological costs of gratitude and endurance. Providing clothes for herself and family was a means of owning and defining herself both psychologically and socially: making her own clothes and maintaining her own home was understood by Mavis as one of the ways in which she had 'earned' her right to belong in a society that constantly sought to position her otherwise. Nonetheless she also recalled the terms upon which this 'better future' of welfarism and affluence was granted,

When you first came up here every few months they used to come, a visitor used to come. She would turn your bedclothes back and lift your bed up and look underneath to see if there was any fluff or anything. . . . And they fumigated it before you come in it, they fumigate all your furniture from down town before you come into here. . . . They always made sure you was clean.

Poverty and the forms in which it was socially marked and culturally inscribed pervaded Mavis's account of herself from the story of her Daily Mail clothing, to the charitable help of the Guide movement, to her memories of struggling on George's army pay during the Second World War, to her recognition of the ways in which dirt, disease and 'otherness' constituted the elements from which she was invited to create a subjectivity by those who were in a position to grant her and her children a better future.

Being poor meant 'getting by', and getting by quite literally meant physical survival. Mavis's grandfather, mother and father all died when she was 19, leaving her to care for six younger siblings. Before she was born her mother lost two babies in infancy, two brothers died 'in the Army' and her first boyfriend died in India. Mavis's sense of herself is rooted in her knowledge that she has 'got by', that she has survived when so many did not. Often this knowledge is articulated in the language of superstition and chance. She told me how in the background of her wedding photographs was a gravestone with the inscription, 'Weep not for me my children dear. I am not dead but sleeping here. Christ did not die for me alone but loved me best and took me home', and how she insisted the photographer go to considerable lengths to block it out as 'I wasn't having that in the house'. Nancy Fellows, whose childhood in early twentieth century York was dominated by the poverty of her mother's widowhood, believed that 'you have got to be either born into it or you have got to have a bit of luck . . . others were lucky, but we never really got off the ground'. 'Luck' in Nancy's belief system meant financial security, survival and reasonable health. Mavis's narrative organises itself around accounts of death, sickness and ill-health; her Scarlet Fever as a child, her father's illness, nursing her mother-in-law, the time she feared her eldest daughter might have meningitis, and the time she injured her ankle and was bedridden, with George caring for the children and housework, as well as the countless deaths that punctuate her narrative. Lizzie Smith's story follows a similar pattern with accounts of her brothers' deaths in the First World War, the nine 'miscarriages' she suffered, her uncle's death of an ulcer at 24 and her own constant ill-health: Lizzie felt she had had very little 'luck' in her life. It may be argued that in old age people's memories turn more readily to sickness and death, but I believe the pervasiveness of these topics in so many of the accounts I received testifies to a consciousness shaped around a knowledge of the uncertainty of existence and a belief that survival and 'getting by' was largely a matter of luck, firmly rooted in the material conditions of physical survival and poverty.

Carolyn Steedman has suggested that the psychology of working-class children born before the Second World War has to be under-pinned by the inexpressible knowledge that their physical existence is a matter of pure chance and, particularly to their mothers, a piece of 'bad luck' (Steedman, 1992, p. 36). Of Kathleen Woodward's account of herself in *Jipping Street*, Steedman says 'she knew as a child that she was a burden to her mother, that she need never have been born, that mothers could indeed kill their children'. Steedman has said of her own childhood in the 1950s that had she grown up before the advent of welfarism, 'bottles of orange juice and jars of Virol', she might have found herself unable to believe in her own right to survival, that 'orange juice and milk and dinners at school . . . told me in a covert way, that I had a right to exist, was worth something' (ibid., pp. 36, 124).

Mavis's, Nancy's and Lizzie's insistence on stories of 'luck', death and survival taken from the community and family that surrounded them bears witness to a consciousness in which just to have survived their grim childhoods, to have 'got by' in a world that gave no visible or material sign that the survival of three working-class children was desirable, was felt to be worthy of attention. The narratives of all three women insist on drawing attention to those who have not survived, sibling deaths mourned but simultaneously unmourned because it was one less mouth to feed, violent deaths that suggest the women's under-standing of the world as a violent and uncertain place.

Lily Brown, born in 1895, begins her story with the death of her brother, aged 7, who 'was knocked down with a bike and died, he got his head bumped on the kerb' and continues with the story of her husband-to-be, who received a life pension for the serious wounds he incurred in the First World War, as well as the story of her sister's boyfriend, who came home from the war 'better than mine' but died just before they were married, and a brother-in-law who 'had his head off in the war and left a baby three weeks old'. Lily's narrative is full of explicitly violent deaths, recounted with a sense of pride in having witnessed, endured and survived such losses in a world where simply existing could never be taken for granted and in which it might be enough to say one had survived. Working-class tales of violence in which appalling accidents are recounted without apparent feeling or even with relish, and working-class pleasure in watching violence on film or television are frequently perceived as evidence of pathology and 'deviance'. As Valerie Walkerdine has suggested, such narratives may function to articulate fantasies of power: they may also simultaneously express a recognition and reassurance that physical survival is indeed a fragile and precarious thing (Walkerdine, 1990, pp. 173–204).

So often reading or hearing accounts of childhoods like these I en-countered the apparently contradictory view, that whilst life was hard people were happy. Lizzie told me 'there were no pleasures in them days, you know', but a few minutes later said 'they was happy days, they were happy folks'. There is a sense in all these accounts that people *ought* to be happy simply because they had survived; 'that being alive ought simply to be enough' and that existence was 'a gift that must be ultimately paid for' (Steedman, 1992, p. 38). The repetition of the phrase 'but we was happy' functions almost superstitiously, rather like Mavis's refusal to have a photo of a gravestone in the house. It works to ward off retribution for any ingratitude expressed or felt towards the fact of mere existence. Perhaps the main lesson working-class children learned, before the services of the welfare state mitigated the worst aspects of industrial capitalism, was how unwelcome pregnancies were to their mothers. Ellen Ross has said of working-class pregnancy in pre-First World War London that,

> Over and over again, we hear of preganancy as a period of special hardship. It involved more work and often less food than usual and could be accompanied by great anxiety, as women prepared for the confinement and tried to equip themselves for the new baby. 'Often weak and low spirited', 'depressed throughout,' 'much mental depression', the General Lying-In doctors wrote of their patients' pregnancies (Ross, 1986, p. 78).

In such circumstances children must have understood that new babies were a burden and hence that their own existence might be less than welcome, that in a very material sense it would have been better if they had not been born. Inhabiting a world in which subsistence was never taken for granted, in which, however hard mothers and fathers worked, there was never quite enough to go round, forced upon a child a recognition of her dependency and her dispensability. The psychological consequences of such recognition might be a deeply internalised denial of their right to be born, a denial that could manifest itself in a deferential and self-deprecating endurance expressed as 'it was hard but we was happy'. Yet the fierce pride with which women like Lizzie and Mavis narrated their survival testifies to an equally felt, if suppressed, anger at the injustice of their situation. As we shall see, this pride and anger was to manifest itself in adulthood in aspirations for a 'better' life, in a fierce determination to 'keep oneself to oneself' and an identification as 'respectable'.

Lizzie Smith was born in 1901, the youngest but one of six children and the only daughter. Her father was a brass furnacer at the railway engineering works in York and her mother earned extra income by taking in washing and casual cleaning jobs. Lizzie recalled her childhood as one of hard work and poverty; she also recalls her mother's violence and hostility towards her:

> She knocked me flying, oh yes she used to lay into you, pulled me around the house by the hair of me head if I wasn't in by a certain time.

When Lizzie was persuaded by her older sisters-in-law to have her hair 'bobbed' she recalls that her mother 'brayed' her to the extent that her elder brother had to drag the mother off Lizzie. In the next section I shall explore further the complex relations articulated between mothers and daughters: for now it is enough to note that Lizzie recalled her childhood and adolescence as a time of emotional and physical violence. Mavis too recalls her father's violence,

> Oh you couldn't cheek anybody. He used to have an army belt with a big buckle on, and you tell any lies or swear or anything that you shouldn't and you would get that round your back.

Childhood in such circumstances cannot be fitted into an account of working-class life which represents strict and even violent parental discipline as 'love', and the 'culture of poverty' as simply preparing children to accept with stoical resignation their future lives as factory workers or working wives (Seabrook, 1982; Roberts, 1973). To deny the pain involved in such childhoods is to refuse to confront the ways in which poverty and hardship, the outward manifestations of an economic structure organised around industrial capitalism, are more likely to damage rather than strengthen people's lives. Mavis, Lily, Lizzie, Nancy and the countless men and women like them may prefer stoically to recall the past as 'hard but happy'. This does not mean that resentment, envy and anger towards those who would never experience the psychological as well as social injuries and exclusions of poverty, Daily Mail boots, fumigated furniture and a perilous existence did not (and does not) exist. To put it another way, 'people stand in relations that are independent of their wills and of which they are more or less conscious. These relations do stamp a social character on people, but should not be *reduced* to relationships between people (of a nicer or nastier kind)' (Johnson, 1979, p. 222). We might add that these relations,

which are those of labour to capital, also produce psychological as well
as social 'character'. People forced by virtue of their position in the
social formation to expend all their energies on acquiring the means of
subsistence may have done so 'willingly, or with murder or even socialism in their hearts' but however they responded, they were forced
to continue expending such energy in order that neither they nor their
children starved or sank 'into still deeper dependency'(ibid., p. 223). A
knowledge and understanding of these fundamental economic relations
shaped very precisely the ways in which children like Lizzie, Lily,
Nancy and Mavis were able to define themselves in relation to the
world in which they (only just) existed.

Lizzie, Lily, Nancy and Mavis, like the other women interviewed,
told grim stories of childhoods marked by poverty, ill-health, death and
violence and they articulated a consciousness that, despite all the evidence to the contrary, they ought to be glad to have simply survived
and that, having done so, they should be happy. It is that lack of
gratitude for existence which all the women interviewed deplored in the
present. As Nancy said,

> I mean it is a terrible day and age that we live in and I am glad I am
> on this end of life ... they seem to get things on a plate so much to
> what we did and yet it is not appreciated. I don't think it is.

Resentment and envy, as well as hope, found articulation in their aspirations and dreams of a 'better future' for their children and in their
attitudes to the contemporary world. When women in interviews spoke
of their aspirations for their children it was always in terms of material
success. Lizzie described her daughter's home as follows:

> they have a garden at the front you know, a big, massive garden
> because you could get four cars down the drive, a beautiful house it
> is. A beautiful home. . . . in each place she has gone to she has had
> all lovely new carpets, lovely beautiful new carpets at every place. . . .
> She has got the kitchen done now and she has had the bedroom done
> and she is having the dining room done next, all emulsioned and that
> like, and then she is going to do the lounge before her birthday.

The 'better future' women dreamed of for their children was one in
which they never had to wear Daily Mail boots, or watch their furniture
fumigated, or know their mothers' agony at yet another pregnancy, or

hope for a hand-out, or scrap around amongst coke heaps for the means of warmth. It was a future in which success could be symbolically articulated via possession of a comfortable, well-furnished home, holidays and a degree of affluence; the icons of a capitalist society which it was believed expressed the right to belong to and share in the 'good things' of life, not as 'the poor' or 'the working class' but as fully integrated individuals. Mavis, like many of the women, maintained that all her hard work, all her sacrifices were to ensure an easier life for her children. Yet at the same time, like Nancy, she constantly complained that people today 'have it too easy'. Mavis and Nancy believed what they were told, that being a 'good' housewife and mother, working hard, providing clothes, food and comfort, working to provide a respectable home and background for their families would ensure a 'good start' for their children. History has proved them both right and wrong. Their children do not have to suffer the vicissitudes of poverty and disease that dogged their lives, but this is due to historical and economic forces rather than their housewifely efforts – in the end, not only was there no reward for endurance and hard work, but the world remained indifferent to these efforts. The self-deprecating gratitude for existence and survival engendered by the historical and economic conditions of childhoods such as Lily's, Nancy's, Mavis's and Lizzie's was no longer appropriate in the postwar world, where all children were perceived as valued investments, rather than burdens; a perception manifested in the post Second World War social agenda of welfare, education and health.

The belief, articulated by all the women, that people have things too easily today is an expression of resentment and anger for the economic and psychological security denied to their generation and a determination to extract a sense of self worth and reward from the sacrifices made on behalf of the next generation. Yet this in its turn produces new cycles of guilt, gratitude and obligation. Lizzie proudly recalled her daughter saying to her 'Mam I can never repay you for what you have done for me'. Such expressions of gratitude were Lizzie's reward for the hardships she has endured, but equally her desire for her daughter's thanks might express a balancing up of the record, a way of extracting from her child the guilt and obligation that was in childhood forced upon her. In this context it is worth exploring briefly whether expressed responses to this sense of obligation for survival were differentiated according to sex. This will lead into the final section, which considers in more detail the mother/daughter relationship. Here I shall concentrate briefly on the ways in which working-class boys responded to the burdens of working-class childhood via two autobiographical accounts.

Ellen Ross has suggested that for working-class boys 'helping mother' might be a long term dream, first envisioned in childhood and finally realised in the handing over of the first wage packet, and that in doing so, we may speculate, there would be the considerable psychic satisfaction of supplanting, or at least supplementing, the contributions of the father (Ross, 1986, pp. 87–8). Mr Dennis, born in 1910, with his mother's help got his first job in 1924 as an apprentice cabinet maker. He recalled how he had planned to 'make my mother a piece of furniture long before I was twenty-one', and how 'I made my mother a sideboard before I was sixteen years', and how 'I used to build trellises, sheds, etc., for neighbours and any payments I would get I gave to Mum; she treated me back well in return' (T. R. Dennis, cited in Burnett, 1976, pp. 348, 353). William Luby, born in 1883, explained that as a young boy he 'hadn't been used to much all my life, much like a dog or any animal. . . . I hadn't learned my rights as a human, you see' (Luby, cited in ibid., p. 96). Learning that he had a right to human existence was closely linked to paid work and the economic benefits William was able to bring to his family, 'my mother she'd got four of us, four she couldn't keep, so I had to start the best way I could' (ibid.)

For both men, the cultural discourses of working-class masculinity allowed them the possibility of defining themselves, as breadwinners, in terms that negated or alleviated any sense of their lives as dependent or burdensome. Bringing home the first wage packet signified adult status, manhood and freedom, at least on a conscious level, from the guilt of being an extra mouth to feed. Working class boys understood that manhood entailed economic responsibilities towards their families, and whilst these responsibilities might frequently be difficult to fulfil due to unemployment or sickness, nevertheless they provided a means by which they could, albeit at times precariously, assert their autonomy as a full member of society. The phrase 'a man's wage' not only signified the rise in income concomitant upon reaching the age of 18 but also the achievement of independent and adult manhood.

The importance of 'learning your rights as a human' existed as a cultural and social imperative of masculinity, even if the circumstances of working-class life frequently rendered this unrealisable. The rhetoric of citizenship (and of trade union politics) organised itself around ideas of human rights but had, since the eighteenth century Enlightenment, addressed itself to 'mankind', as for example in Tom Paine's *The Rights of Man*. Until 1928 women were excluded from full political citizen-ship, the most cogent form in nineteenth and twentieth century Western democracies for articulating human rights. Hence, whilst boys of all classes could choose to understand adulthood as achieving political and civil rights, becoming a breadwinner and entering the world of paid work, all arenas offering the potential (if not always the actuality) for autonomy and self-definition, entry into mature adulthood for girls was less sharply defined from childhood status. Adult 'womanliness' re-quired many of the attributes of 'the child' – dependent, deferential and positioned in the privatised arena of the domestic household. Moreover, ideological constructions not only likened women to children but 'closely and unreflectively tied [women] with children; womanhood has been equated with motherhood in a mixing of identities that simply does not occur for men and fatherhood' (Thorne, 1987, p. 96). For working-class girls the attainment of adult selfhood, defined in the terms of Western liberal humanism, was considerably more complex and could produce a fragmented psyche, split between the demands of femininity, the assumptions of adulthood and its 'rights', and the knowledge of their own dispensability

GROWING UP FEMALE

Working-class femininity was perceived by middle-class observers in the first decades of this century as 'a problem', whether it be in the form of adolescent girlhood, female servants or feckless, ignorant mothers. Working-class masculinity was, of course, also defined as deviant and problematic – men who failed to provide for their families because of 'idleness', drink or gambling, working-class boys and dis-satisfied workers all constituted problems – these were, however, usu-ally understood as problems of law and order whereas the 'problem' of working-class females organised itself around the 'personal' arenas of the home, family and sexuality. Working-class women were inscribed both in social practices and in cultural discourses within a limited range of roles: as overburdened victims of poverty, as sexual predators or as more susceptible to moral danger. Hence working-class girls acquired a knowledge of what constituted feminine behaviour from those rela-tions they experienced and understood as 'private' life, and in particular in their relationship to their mothers and fathers. At the same time they were invited to construct subjectivities from the cultural repertoire of images available in the discourses of middle-class observers; surveillers consistently anxious to define and fix working-class femininity as 'Other'. It was from such sources that girls might discover that not only were they a burden to their poverty-stricken mothers but a 'problem' for their teachers and advisors. Pearl Jephcott, educationalist and youth worker, succinctly articulated the 'problem':

> The working girl has a background that is very different from that of the much smaller number of girls who, at the same age, are still at school. Mr Seebohm Rowntree estimates that in York about half of the children of working-class parents spend the first five years of their life in poverty, and that about a third live below the poverty line for ten years or more. It is not surprising therefore, that when, at adolescence, the child is relatively free to adopt her own line she frequently chooses a 'take what you can get' attitude (Jephcott, 1942, p. 37)

The circumstances of working-class life produced, according to Jephcott, adults with a 'take what you can get' attitude and this was feared as considerably more problematic for a femininity defined as self-denying, nurturing and centred on motherhood than for a masculinity organised around the roles of provider and wage-earner. It was precisely around these attributes and particularly motherhood that an ideal of working-class femininity was constructed, an ideal that, as we shall see in Chapter 3, functioned to deny working-class female sexuality and to regulate its apparent potential for disorder, a concern frequently articulated in fears of 'cockiness' amongst the groups of working-class girls who increasingly frequented the cinemas, dance halls and public houses of large cities. If being working class meant defining an identity from the signifiers of poverty and disease and the social practices that attended these, then being female meant negotiating a selfhood from a range of social relations and a set of discourses in which working-class femininity was represented as a 'problem' to be probed, surveyed and regulated.

Working-class girls experienced themselves in relation to working-class men as fathers, to their mothers, to middle-class women and to middle-class men. All these relationships were experienced as relations of power and authority, dominance and submission, in which young working-class women found themselves relatively powerless, always dependent and often in conflict, sometimes in overt ways but frequently articulated covertly and obliquely. I want in particular to explore their understandings and experiences of mother/daughter relations and their apparently rather less conflict-ridden relationships with working-class men. Relations between middle-class men and women and working-class girls will be explored in Chapter 4 in the context of domestic service, so these will not be examined in detail here. The point I want to make is that the relationships working-class girls were able to forge with working-class men were a product of and interdependent upon their relationships with and experience of older working-class women, and in particular their mothers. I want first to consider the ways in which masculinity was represented and experienced by working class girls and then to identify the dynamic relation this might hold with regard to the, frequently resented but as frequently accepted, authority of the mother.

Women growing up at this time could not have remained unaware of the numerous men whom the First World War had incapacitated and permanently wounded, men hailed as heroes in the Reconstruction slogans, 'Homes Fit for Heroes' but appearing anything but heroic in their everyday lives. For the women interviewed, all of whom came to adulthood in the years immediately after the First World War, their understanding of what constituted masculinity was necessarily drawn from a repertoire of often contradictory narratives and images. On the one hand, in their early childhood they would have seen men, glamorous in soldiers' uniforms, heard tales of heroism and adventure and watched as fathers, brothers, uncles and cousins left for the front. Later they would have been witness to the return of some of these men; damaged, wounded figures whose painful struggle to come to terms with their war experiences was anything but heroic in the fictional sense of the term. Dolly Scannell's recollection of her father testifies, less to how he really was, than to her desire to remember him and rewrite him as the cheerful Cockney hero of First World War mythology:

> Father had been the bravest of soldiers, cheerfully suffering all manner of deprivations in the muddy Flanders trenches, but if he ever remarked on the days of the War (and he had his fiftieth birthday at Ypres), it was with humour (Scannell, 1974, p. 11).

Dolly was born in 1911 and her autobiography records her father's return from Flanders with breathtaking understatement: 'Father was very cross when he arrived home from the war; he thought Mother was turning into an extravagant woman, for she was to pay 2s. 6d. per week for this new furniture' (ibid., p. 70) The cheerful Cockney hero's return is here represented as little more than a minor domestic upheaval. Throughout Dolly Scannell's account there is a sense that having absented himself for a lengthy period her father had allowed, and his absence legitimated, the transfer of domestic power to her mother. In Dolly's story no-one takes very much notice of Father, despite his bluster and attempts to organise the household. But the war not only returned men to homes where their paternal power no longer held sway; it returned male figures whose wounded bodies belied aesthetic ideals of masculine beauty. One of Mary Hewins' earliest memories was of her mother tending her father's war wounds:

> I'd seen his wound once, when she was bathing him. He came home covered in coal dust, and chalk, and she bathed him by the fire. When she was bathing him, or me, or anybody, our Mother always kept the others out, but one day I rushed in and I *saw*. Horrible. He was covered in scars, and one side of him, low down, where there should a-been flesh, there was – nothing. You could see the bone! I'd guessed it would be horrible, like the butcher's shop. I'd seen his washing in the bucket, all blood and stuff, every day his clothes were put in to soak, but till you've really *seen*. . . . How could our Mother bear to touch him? And every day, well it seemed like every day to me, he was drunk (Hewins, 1986, p. 5).

Mary could not have been alone in her experience. Many girls must have grown up catching glimpses of repulsive wounds and misshapen limbs, of stained bandages and scarred flesh; many must, like Mavis and Dolly, have watched and heard the unpleasant symptoms of respiratory disease; many must have experienced the daily manifestations of depression, 'shell shock' and anxiety; and many must have grown up with fathers, older brothers and relatives home on leave or permanently demobbed, drinking to anaethetise the pain of war. Nancy Fellows, who was born in 1916, recalled, 'I was frightened of it [drunkenness]. I had seen that much of it'. Nancy was not alone, a number of the women interviewed recalled their fear of drunkenness and of physical contact with men: 'I was very, very frightened. Oh it was a long time before I kissed Jack. I wonder he didn't throw me on one side!' Although this fear can be readily explained in terms of girls' lack of knowledge about their own bodies and about sex, it has also, I think, to be understood in its specific historical context in which the actual physical embodiement of masculinity might be repugnant as a result of war or disease.

Romantic fiction and films continued to represent versions of masculinity in which strong, handsome men ruled their worlds with a benign and firm authority; men who, nevertheless, could display a tender, affectionate concern when in love with the 'right' woman. Such fantasies of masculinity were never simply produced as escapism for young women: they articulated social and psychic realities in which 'the actual operations of fantasy' were experienced in the lived relations of the family (Walkerdine, 1990, p. 204). Respectable masculinity meant 'looking after' and providing for a dependent wife and children; the struggle to be 'manly' was centred around being a 'big' man, a protector, and required for its realisation a 'little' woman who could be looked after and protected. Domestic versions of masculinity and femininity produced in romantic fiction and films of the period operate through an infantilisation of women and a 'toughening up' of men, which in turn represented and offered certain positions within domestic relations that could be attractive to both men and women. Men, wounded by war, exhausted by the struggle to provide, may well have fantasised about being the family protector, the one who fights the family's battles: equally such men may have yearned for the feminine infantilised position of dependence and passivity, and longed to be taken care of by a 'big man'. Women too fantasised about a strong protector who would love and care and provide a centre of safety in their precarious existence. Such fantasies articulate profound desires for nurture, dependence and care, and are less to do with any essentialist conception of feminine and masculine roles than with the potential for adopting different positions as social actors in living out these desires. As I shall argue, the mother in many working-class families might adopt the role of 'big man', although, of course, such roles were never fixed and various family members at various times might be provider or protector, dependent or protected.

Gladys Hutchings remembered the poverty of her childhood and her version of the ideal husband who could offer 'something that bit better'. He would be,

a decent lad who didn't take advantage of you, who was easy on the drink and that sort of thing. He would be of a good stable character . . . not a fly by night.

However the everyday reality of masculinity for many girls, as experienced in their relations with their fathers, was frequently an ineffectual and impotent withdrawal or the physical violence of frustrated anger. Lizzie commented on her father:

> Poor old Robert. He was like an old sheep was me Dad. He never interfered, she was the gaffer. He didn't like me Mam hitting me, and he never hit us. He never interfered.

In contrast Gertie Harris recalled her father's cruelty: he regularly used a belt with a buckle and she recalls her brother's back bleeding from a beating. Gertie also tells how when the family visited their more affluent relatives, Gertie's father forbade the children to take any food that was offered them because,

> He didn't want showing up, making them think he didn't feed you, you see. It was his background, not letting people think he didn't feed us like he should have fed us you see. This was the whole thing. He wouldn't want them to know he didn't. . . . And if you galloped your food and ate what was there then they would think he wasn't doing right by you and so you had to say no, and it was an awful, awful thing to say when your belly was nearly dropping. Your stomach was dropping through your skin for something to eat and you couldn't have it. It was really bad was that.

Gertie's father's cruelty and violence was such that when he signed up for the forces in 1914 Gertie and her brothers hoped he would never come back. In the event he returned a quieter and, if no less strict, a less physically violent man. Gertie's youngest sister, Ivy, was the only child born to him after the war and according to Gertie 'she was ruined' by both parents (ostensibly because of her predisposition to ill-health) and rarely suffered the cruelties meted out to the others. Mavis's father justified physically punishing his children in terms of 'discipline' and teaching correct behaviours. Mavis remembers that he would beat her if she was ten minutes late coming home from school, demanding to know where she had been and what she had been doing. This seems far less to do with 'discipline' and rather more to do with unconsious fears about and hostility to Mavis's vulnerability as a young female on the streets. Both fathers are represented in their daughters' accounts as 'fighters': Mr Harris, whose struggle to be 'manly' centred around his role as provider, and Mr Kitching, who is positioned as protector to his child-women whose 'feminine' vulnerability and innocence were threatened by their public presence on the streets.

Yet for both Gertie and Mavis their fathers' attempts at authority and control, whilst frightening and cruel, were narrated as a relatively legitimate and expected form of power, given the conditions under which they exercised it. Perhaps unsurprisingly, the women interviewed grew up eschewing romance and passion not only, as I have argued elsewhere, because the specific historical moment they inhabited endorsed an anti-romantic and anti-heroic consciousness, and not only also because the economic and social circumstances of the early twentieth century produced a cultural space in which it made sense for working-class women to define themselves as prudent, realistic and reserved, but also to protect themselves from the dangers of infantilisation inscribed in the social, psychic and cultural formations of masculinity and femininity (Giles, 1995). 'Being swept off your feet' by the seductions of romantic masculinity appeared, I suspect, not only faintly ludicrous but dangerous to contemplate for female subjectivities formed from poverty, ill-health, exclusion and the historicised masculinities of their time (Giles, 1992, 1995). In describing themselves as prudent and canny, young working-class women identified with and drew upon the social practices of older working-class women, particularly their own mothers; and the traditionally inscribed versions of motherhood available to them.

Many of the stories of working-class mothers at this time represent them as tough, matriarchal figures, strict, sometimes cruel, sometimes loving, but always enduring and always fighting (Hoggart, 1958; Roberts, 1973; Scannell, 1974; Foley, 1974; Hewins, 1986; Ross, 1986). Margery Spring Rice's *Working Class Wives*, despite its delineation of the impossible conditions and ill health in which many mothers reared their children, continues to celebrate mother as the

> abiding maternal personality [which] plays a large part in the stubborn persistence of the family tradition. Although with the increasing opportunities and complexities of social organisation, the activities and interests of the other members of the family tend to multiply, the magic of the hearth remains unchallenged. Undoubtedly it is rooted deep in all human nature, but the mother is the human anchor which holds it fast (Spring Rice, 1939/1981, p. 14).

The women interviewed, even where affection and pleasure characterised their relations with their mothers, remembered their mothers as
powerful, authoritative figures. Not one interviewee told me of a mother
who gave up or stopped struggling for her family: even where the
mother was recalled as 'restless' or 'difficult' as in Mary Porter's story,
she was still represented as an all-powerful and respected figure. Mary
Porter was born near Newcastle-on-Tyne in 1920. Her father died when
she was three and Mary and her two brothers spent the next six years
living with an aunt in Whitley Bay. When Mary was nine her mother
remarried and the family moved to Jarrow. There were frequent local
moves over the next five years and when Mary was 14 her mother,
now separated from her second husband, moved the whole family to
Birmingham. Mary's story presents her mother as a 'problem' and their
relationship as difficult – 'she was a very excitable woman. Flared up
and was very spoilt. . . . She was a good time person' – and Mary
resented what she perceived as her mother's partiality towards her two
brothers:

> Anything they did was right and everything I did was wrong. She
> didn't mind what they did. She used to clobber me one with anything
> handy but I only ever remember my brothers getting punished once.

Nonetheless Mary praised her mother's housekeeping skills – 'she was
a very good cook' – and her egalitarianism – 'there was one thing about
her she was never snobbish. She'd say "they may be poor but they're
clean and never look down on them because they are as good as you"'.
Later, when her mother was elderly and frail Mary looked after her.
Mary both respected and resented her mother: she resented her 'excit-
ability', which she saw as responsible for driving her stepfather away
and causing the frequent moves of her childhood, but she respected her
mother's understanding of class and her mother's acceptance of certain
tenets of femininity, linked to domesticity and homemaking. This
ambivalence towards mothers was present in a number of accounts;
resentment at the often inflexible authority wielded by mothers, respect
for the 'lessons' thus learned.

Mothers were the first and closest encounter working-class girls
had with authority. In many families the mother was positioned as 'the
fighter', the figure who fought officialdom, who provided meals, who
meted out discipline and who taught a moral law, iron-like in its rigid-
ity and immutability. This is not to suggest that in any simple way

mothers did not love their children or were not concerned for their welfare, but rather that caring for children was expressed and experienced as a struggle to survive that involved 'fighting', discipline and belligerence. As Walkerdine points out '[f]ighting is a key term in a discourse of powerlessness, of a constant struggle not to sink, to get rights, not to be pushed out' (Walkerdine, 1990, p. 187). This 'fighting spirit' could manifest itself in a determination to seek a reasonable life for one's children but, equally and also, it might take the form of sadistic and even physically violent encounters. Lizzie Smith's mother, who 'brayed' her round the room for coming in late or having her hair 'bobbed', later used Lizzie's illegitimate pregnancy in ways that structured the relationship between mother and daughter as one of power and powerlessness. Pregnant by a man whose mother, according to Lizzie, would not let him marry her, Lizzie was dependent upon her mother for survival. In the early years of the twentieth century there were three options open to a young woman pregnant outside marriage: marriage to the man involved; entering a home for unmarried mothers and giving the child up to adoption (in some cases girls were committed to mental asylums and declared 'morally defective'); or bearing and rearing the child with the help of family and relatives (Hewins, 1985, p. xiv). Lizzie was 'lucky', her mother agreed to look after the baby so that Lizzie could continue to work, but in Lizzie's words,

After he was born [Mum] took control of him. She never allowed me to bath him and you see when I had my wages I had to hand them over to her, I was never allowed no pocket money. After he was born you see, she was terrible.

When Lizzie broke her elbow her mother paid for an operation but refused to look after the baby when Lizzie attended the hospital for physiotherapy. There is a very real sense here in which Lizzie's economic powerlessness allowed her mother to exercise a moral power over her daughter, a power that operated within the intersecting circles of class and gender, but which formed within the mother/daughter dyad its own internal psychic structure of domination and submission. The mother's exclusion from economic or political power in the public arena could be compensated for by her moral authority in the domestic sphere: an authority that might take the form of withholding approval and adult privileges. In this way the daughter remains infantilised, dependent and punished and the mother is protected from confronting her 'real' lack of power as a woman and a mother, once she steps outside the closed circle of family and domesticity.

Nancy Chodorow's work on psychoanalytic theory and psychic structures argues for greater significance for the pre-Oedipal period in the psychological development of girls, when bonds with the mother-figure are particularly strong (Chodorow, 1978). Chodorow suggests that this first and early identification with femininity via the mother is important for both masculine and feminine gender identity formation but that it is particularly significant for female children as it is pre-Oedipal mothering that produces the adult impulse to become a mother and leads girls to be more concerned with relationships with others:

> from the retention of pre-oedipal attachments to their mother, growing girls come to experience themselves as continuous with others; their experience of self contains more flexible or permeable ego boundaries. Boys come to define themselves as more separate and distinct, with a greater sense of rigid ego-boundaries and differentiation. The basic feminine sense of self is connected with the world; the basic masculine sense of self is separate (Chodorow, 1978, p. 169).

Whilst Chodorow's account of the development of the feminine psyche provides a very useful model for considering mother/daughter relationships, when set alongside the experiences of Lizzie or Mary its ahistoricity and failure to locate psychic development within material structures raises problems. Is it possible to say that Lizzie learned to think 'maternally' because of her sense as a self-in-relationship, psychologically developed via her relationship with her mother? Any sense of 'connectedness' that Lizzie developed must equally have been forged in an acute recognition of the structures of power, of the potential for domination and submission, implicit in her sense of herself in relationship to others, particularly her mother. Equally Chodorow's theory that the capacity for mothering is developed in girls precisely as a result of their relationship to their mothers as daughters, a relationship in which, Chodorow argues, there is less psychic motivation than there is for boys, to achieve or assert separation, compels the question: what kind of capacity for mothering could be learned by girls whose experience as daughters was frequently one of powerlessness and whose sense of self in relation to the social and material world was often one of 'being an extra mouth to feed'?

It would not be surprising in the circumstances discussed here if girls grew up with an understanding and knowledge of 'mothering' as a potentially powerful and dominant relation within the family, and for that reason desirable. Hence it became possible to imagine and construct motherhood as a relationship in which authority and dominance, particularly in relation to daughters, could ensure material subsistence but could equally assuage the longing to assert that dignity and autonomy denied in childhoods lived under such mothering. 'Mothering' in such a scheme acquires an historical and class specificity that is denied it in many psychoanalytic accounts. Lizzie's sense of herself as a daughter and her sense of her mother, as a woman with whom she was encouraged to identify via cultural and psychological discourses, was an historical construct, produced from Lizzie's experience and understanding of poverty and the specific familial power relations thus engendered. Moreover if 'mothering' is taken to encompass a range of attributes, commonly associated with femininity – responsiveness to others, concern for the feelings of others – then how do we 'read' the models of femininity offered by working-class mothers at this specific moment? The mothers who feature in the stories of the women interviewed do not by any means always manifest a positive form of 'connection' or 'continuity with others'. Identifying with their daughters' needs meant for many mothers demonstrating the inevitable disappointment and futility of aspiration inherent in lives dominated by continuous pregnancy and poverty. Day-dreaming was sharply curtailed, domestic labour was expected from an early age and further schooling might be discouraged. Phyllis Willmott, sensing her mother's fatigue and depression, promises

Poor Mum, you have such a hard time because of us. But when I'm grown I'll buy you everything you want, even a fur coat for the winter

to which her mother replied,

When you're grown up you'll be doing the same as I am now – worrying where the next penny is coming from to feed **your** kids and how to keep their feet dry, never mind fur coats (Willmott, 1979, p. 75).

In a number of accounts fathers are remembered as allies against the injustices meted out by mothers. Lizzie recalled that her father would remonstrate, somewhat ineffectually, with her mother on the beatings Lizzie received, and Margery Crowe told me how her father protected her from her mother's anger and about their close relationship: 'I could pull his leg and I mean, my father and I was very close. We had laughs, we was always laughing'. As discussed above, fathers were not necessarily the powerful figures of patriarchal myth; many, like Margery and Lizzie's fathers, acted in ways that suggest 'feminine' responsiveness and, at time, passivity. Margery thought her father 'marvellous' because he brought her and her mother a cup of tea in bed every morning. For many working-class girls growing up at the start of this century their experience and understanding of masculine and feminine behaviours were not necessarily fixed to male and female figures: mothers might demonstrate a belligerent 'fighting spirit' whilst fathers might offer companionship and protection. Equally, of course, parents might act out different roles at different times and for different purposes. Nonetheless roles remained within the parameters of a socio/sexual system that legitimated and valued male power over female power, whatever form it took. Margery's father offered Margery affection and protection, but in doing so he was represented as being able to draw upon his privilege and power as the male head of the household. In Margery's story he deters Margery's mother from beating Margery by threatening the mother with a beating.

The point I want to make is that girls' knowledge of what it meant to be a woman was not only historically circumscribed and class specific but never complete and never coherent. Understanding what constituted femininity was a struggle for meaning in an arena where masculine and feminine relations were shifting and fluid and where the possibilities for power and powerlessness inscribed in such relations moved around a set of familial relations. For example, whilst the ways in which mothers might represent themselves offered a 'fighting' version of femininity, this was as equally contradicted by cultural discourses and social practices that inscribed femininity as childlike. Many of the women interviewed recalled infantilised family nicknames such as 'Peggy', 'Girlie', 'Dolly', and women's magazines of the period frequently addressed their female readership as 'little wives' or 'little mothers' in their 'little homes'.[3] Moreover, being 'a lady' was closely associated with daintiness and fragility whilst to become a 'fighter' required reembodiement as 'a tomboy' or 'a cocky lass' and thus a rejection of bourgeois femininity.

In Chodorow's account of mothering, girls remain connected to

femininity via their mothers with whom they can identify rather than separate. Yet this presupposes a fixed and consensual mothering that trans-
mits a coherent sense of female gender identity, and whilst Chodorow
recognises the possible problematics in this trajectory, nowhere does
such an account explain what happens where a working-class girl, consciously or unconsciously, desires the social mobility offered by 'lady-
like' versions of femininity or yearns for the protection and safety
implied in remaining a little girl. For many working-class girls of the
period, consciously to identify with and become like their mothers was
not an aspiration they could feel comfortable with, promising as it did,
disappointment and arduous drudgery, unwanted pregnancies and pre-
mature old age. Less consciously perhaps they were able to insert themselves into forms of femininity, not unlike their mothers', because finally
such forms offered modes of power inaccessible elsewhere. After all
Lizzie's daughter felt 'she could never repay' her Mum – there is surely
a hint here of a recurring cycle and dynamic of power and powerlessness, once again articulated in the language of money and of duty and
obligation. Equally, Margery Crowe married, aged 48, almost immediately after her mother's death. Despite the hostile relations between
Margery and her mother during Margery's childhood and adolescence,
Margery took care of her mother, who became acutely depressed, right
up until her death: 'I wasn't fussed [about getting married] because I
had enough to do without taking on another one. I couldn't do it to her
[get married] and I wouldn't have left her so that was the end of it'.
Margery, despite 'courting' for 20 years, was not concerned to marry
and never wanted children of her own. As Carolyn Steedman has suggested, a different reading of the texts of working-class women's lives
which refuses the myths of working class motherhood, paves the way
for an understanding of how the psychological history of specific mother/
daughter relationships, located in a particular historical and social landscape, might have far-reaching implications for female sexuality
(Steedman, 1992, pp. 119–26).

CONCLUSION – CLASS AND GENDER

When reading autobiographical accounts and oral narratives of childhood in the early twentieth century I was aware of how insistently the
reader was asked to pay attention to the hardship of these early lives,
even where women qualified this with remarks such as 'but we was

happy'. All the accounts I have read draw attention to the hard work, the poverty, the sheer drudgery of daily life before the welfare state and modern technology alleviated some of the worst conditions. Many of the accounts, as I have said, also insist that 'they were happy days'. I do not want to suggest that daily reality did not bring its moments of pleasure or happiness, nor do I want to insist that all working-class women were damaged or unhappy individuals, any more than we would want to make such claims about any group of people. The past really is another country and we cannot know how people actually experienced their daily lives or which aspects of that experience shaped their particular psychological histories. What I am concerned to emphasise is how distorting and patronising it becomes if we insist on viewing working-class childhoods from within those cultural myths which seek to deny the pain, the loss and the damage inflicted upon children as a result of their positioning within both class and gender systems.

Women such as Lizzie, Mary, Mavis, Lily, Nancy and Margery were deprived and excluded as children: their stories insist on that in the constant expressions of envy and resentment towards contemporary life. Sometimes they were treated violently and unjustly by parents equally hurt by the oppressions of poverty and disease; sometimes they found moments of security and happiness in Sunday School outings, street parties, polishing brass till it shone, and later, as adolescents, in the comfort of dreams offered by the cinema or the glitzy glamour of the dance hall. Most of them desired above all to escape the circumstances of their childhoods and dreamt of a better future for themselves and their children (despite their insistence on the 'good old days', all the women interviewed aspired to a better life than that of their mothers). Again we misread working-class consciousnesses if we make easy assumptions about a lack of aspiration or a failure to dream, or if we dismiss those dreams as simply manifestations of a spurious acquisitiveness. The women discussed here may not have perceived education, careers or social mobility via marriage as routes to a better life, but that they wished to escape the conditions in which they were positioned as women and as working class was certain.

'Escaping' may mean two things: it may mean identifying an escape route – getting out – or it can mean finding ways of coping, of 'getting by', that involve escapism in the sense of dream and fantasy. For many women dream and fantasy were lived experiences and can not, nor should be, easily separated off as trivial or pathological. To dream of 'a home of your own' was to fantasise about what was, at this specific historical moment, a materially realisable goal: it must also have been an articulation of profound longings for safety, both financially and emotionally. When Doris Arthurs moved into her new council house in the mid-1930s she and her husband, Jim, 'thought it was a palace', a place out of myth and fairy tale where people lived comfortable and opulent lives as rulers of their world, but also and equally a material object of pride. Doris, whose story will be explored further in Chapter 4, showed me photographs of her middle-class employer's home in the country. This was a mock thatched cottage, the cultural stereotype of pastoral bliss, and one that was adopted by numerous speculative builders in the interwar years. If such images had been available to working-class girls growing up before 1930, it is precisely the kind of 'palace' many might have dreamed of as they shared beds, arduous chores, punishment, grinding poverty and exhausted parents with numerous siblings.

2 A Home of Their Own

Muriel Jones, who grew up in a Birmingham suburb in the 1920s, was often taken by her father to visit relatives in the city centre. Her accounts of these visits are couched in the language of those late-Victorian explorers of the London slums for whom such visits were forays into an alien region (Keating, 1976, p. 14; Walkowitz, 1992, p. 19). According to Muriel 'the houses seemed very queer to me' and 'they used to fascinate me'. Muriel's comments draw on cultural narratives of urban exploration in which the slum areas of large conurbations were constructed in terms of both the horror they aroused and, in equal measure, the fascination experienced in scrutinising them. For the child, Muriel, it was fascination that predominated, the fascination with differences not only of topography and housing but, embodied in this, ways of living. In the 1920s the urban areas of Smethwick and Aston visited by Muriel were a jumble of small workshops and back-to-back housing, criss-crossed by a network of canals and railways lines (Bournville Village Trust, 1941; Briggs, 1952, p. 284). In contrast, Rednal, where Muriel grew up, was a suburb, eight miles from Birmingham's city centre at the end of the new tram line opened in 1924. Bounded on one side by the Lickey Hills, owned and developed by Birmingham Corporation and the Cadbury Brothers as a leisure area for the city's inhabitants, and on the other by the open countryside of Worcestershire, Rednal's only concession to industry was the fast growing Austin Motor Company (Austin Motor Company, 1938; Briggs, 1952, p. 284; Tupling, 1983). However, for the young Muriel the contrast between her suburban childhood in semi-rural Rednal and the crowded noisy environment of the urban terraces was not simply a matter of geography. Equally bewildering to Muriel was the intimacy and blurring of relationship categories engendered in such an environment.

> Well, of course, being so close together they all knew one another and they were in and out of one another's houses. I can even remember calling one of the neighbours 'Auntie' and it wasn't my auntie but she lived across the street and she used to come in, she used to be in the house and I used to call her 'Auntie' but she wasn't my auntie.

Later Muriel recalled that in Rednal people 'kept themselves more to themselves than in the terraces'. Muriel was not from one of those solidly middle-class families who, anxious to escape the increasing horrors of urban living, had settled in the more prestigious Birmingham suburbs of Harborne and Edgbaston in the latter part of the nineteenth century. Her mother was a barmaid and later owned a small tobacconists in Rednal, her father was a nurse at the local hospital: the family had originally come from Tipton, a town north-west of Birmingham in the urban conurbation commonly known as 'the Black Country' because of its concentration of heavy and dirty industry. Muriel's sense of difference from her urban working-class relatives can not be explained simply in terms of the class binarism middle class/working class nor in terms of the cultural binarism that divided the working-class into 'respectable' or 'rough'. Muriel did not describe either herself or her father's relatives in those terms. Although she undoubtedly perceived herself as 'respectable', this did not mean that 'otherness' was understood solely as 'rough', although in part it might be. The difference, as understood by Muriel, was articulated, whatever else it may have signified, as a geographical and spatial difference between homes in inner city terraces and suburban homes in a semi-rural setting. It was within the context of this urban topography and the stories told about it that many working-class women in the first half of the twentieth century sought to define themselves and to construct for themselves hopes and dreams of a better future, dreams that expressed themselves in terms of 'a home of our own'. As Dot Pearce said, 'everybody wanted their own home. I wouldn't have got married without my own home'. This chapter examines how far these desires could be met and explores both the metaphoric and literal meanings working-class women might attribute to the idea of 'a home of our own', as well as the ideals and expectations ascribed to women as homeowners, council tenants and suburban dwellers by a dominant culture.

The 1920s and 1930s saw an unprecedented expansion of house-building both for rent and for purchase. State responsibility for the provision of working-class housing was finally established by the Addison (1919), Chamberlain (1923) and Wheatley (1924) Housing Acts, and a series of subsidies were given to local authorities and private enterprise to encourage the building of homes for lower-income families. 'Homes Fit for Heroes' was a major element of the wider programme of social reconstruction embarked upon at the end of the First World War, and if the reality never quite matched the promise, nonetheless the building programmes of the interwar years made considerable inroads into the housing shortage revealed in 1918 when returning servicemen found themselves faced with housing conditions worse than those they had left (Burnett, 1986, pp. 219–22; Swenarton, 1981). Between 1919 and 1939, 3 998 000 houses were built; 1 112 000 of these were built by local authorities for rent and 2 886 000 by private enterprise (Burnett, 1986, p. 252; Mowat, 1955, pp. 226–31). Speculative building between the wars catered in the main for the bottom end of the market, for those with an annual income of about £200–600 who could afford a small semi-detached, costing between £300 and £800 outside London. Every major city saw an expansion of small semis and villas around its perimeter and along its arterial roads. The dream of owning or renting a modest, adequately designed home in its own garden, away from the crowded terraces of city centres was in the early years of this century a very real possibility for those in regular work.

Burnett observes for these years that 'the home continued to be, as it had in the past, the most important mark of social differentiation and the most significant symbol of social status' (Burnett, 1986, p. 267). It was also, of course, the spatial and symbolic arena of women, the signifier of the feminine and the private, and the primary site of sexual difference and the sexual division of labour. As such the suburban council house and the small semi-detached became cultural and spatial sites where official discourses of gender and class intersected, as well as providing icons around which women's dreams for a better life circulated and a focus for the articulation and assertion of aspirations. At the same time the emphasis of interwar social reform on housing and homes produced yet another arena in which working-class life could be surveyed and probed: council housing required the monitoring of housing officials; suburban semi-detacheds roused the scorn and pity of the educated middle classes; and the new forms of living created by suburbia required new fragments of categorisation to define social gradations.

Housing design articulated the tasks expected of women within the family, what was acceptable as a family and the place of that family in the social system. Thus the meaning of home for working-class women was necessarily assembled from both the proliferation of discourses around housing and its location, discourses specific to a particular historical moment, *and* the psychological and cultural material of earlier life experiences that women brought to their conceptualisations of house and home. I begin by examining examples of the official discourses by which housing reform and its effects were constituted in the first half of this century and then go on to consider the 'voices' of the women (and men) who inhabited the houses and made homes of them.

HOUSING DESIGN AND LOCATION

The ideals that underpinned environmental and housing reforms in the early years of the twentieth century were derived from the vision of social and political reform proposed by Ebenezer Howard and the Garden City movement. The idea of the Garden City as originally envisaged by Howard was not simply a reform of existing physical forms but intended as a vehicle of social transformation in which the principles of cooperation and egalitarianism would find a concrete form in 'a healthy, natural and economic combination of town and country life' (Howard, cited in Ward, 1992, p. 39). Local-authority housing built in the years immediately after the First World War adhered to the basic principles of the Garden City movement as laid down in the Tudor-Walters Report of 1918 (Tudor-Walters, 1919; Townroe, 1924; Burnett, 1986, pp. 222–6). In recommending the location and design of council housing, certain visions of working-class life were being given concrete representation, in particular the ideal of working-class family life, an ideal that was firmly linked to the role of the working-class housewife. The Garden City ideal, despite its origins in a political socialism going back to William Morris, was in its realisation a conservative vision. Its emphasis on the idea of the organic cottage village, rooted in the rural values of an older England, despite being reformulated in the reality of the quasi rural suburb, drew on cultural narratives of the working-class as occupying a specific and rooted place in the social order, a place in which homogeneity, 'community' and harmonious forms of family life flourished. Recently a historian of suburban development has said of the suburban home that it was a 'natural form for ensuring the sanctity of family life' and, of certain suburban houses erected at the end of the nineteenth century, that they were of a

> style not merely bourgeois but feminine, being neatly domesticiated in a manner appropriate to a generation which was at least giving women an opportunity to express themselves culturally (Taylor, cited in Boys, 1989, pp. 48–9).

Council housing and the small semi-detached, erected to (frequently debased) Garden City standards, offered working-class families 'cottage' type homes, with a small fenced-off garden, on the outskirts of large cities and in doing so offered them a certain version of family life that insisted on privacy, seclusion and intimacy. A vision that was both bourgeois and 'feminine' but which, as Taylor recognised, provided women with a cultural space in which they might express themselves as apparently highly valued 'housewives'. Magazines, fiction and particularly the cinema offered many, often competing, versions of femininity, but the preferred image, as peddled by women's magazines as well as educationalists and welfare workers, was that of the competent housewife secure in her suburban home. That this space was ultimately conservative, reproducing and sustaining women's alignment with the domestic and the private, does not negate its attraction for working-class women for whom both the cultural ideal of the housewife and the physical space of the home were emancipatory. Piped water, electricity, separate bedrooms and more spacious living areas were very real aspirations for women who had watched their mothers struggle with lack of space, lack of hot water and the continual dirt contingent upon sharing an environment with industry, vermin and unsatisfactory sanitation.

Before the First World War Clementina Black, an active Fabian and feminist, had advocated cooperative and communal housekeeping, with dwellings clustered around collective kitchens and laundries, and although Black's ideas were directed towards the needs of professional women, the Women's Housing Subcommittee – which reported to the post First World War Ministry of Reconstruction – believed these might solve the problems of working-class housewives. This was to misread the history, the needs and the desires of such women. Black recommended communal laundries, play areas, wash houses and cooking facilities, but the working-class women canvassed by the Subcommittee firmly rejected any form of communal arrangements for housekeeping (Black, 1918; Ravetz, 1989, pp. 195, 197). For working-class women housekeeping had been experienced as, or if still unmarried could be expected to be experienced as, a compulsorily shared activity. Housewives in inner city housing had shared toilets, wash houses, hallways and play areas with other women and their families; women had shared bedrooms, and frequently beds, as well as constricted living space with babies, growing children, elderly parents and sometimes lodgers. It was hardly surprising that dreams of a better future took the form of a house of their own rather than ideals of 'community'.

Mass Observation's 1939 survey of people and their homes found high levels of satisfaction with suburban housing amongst those who had moved from inner city areas as a result of slum clearance. Enthusiasm focused on the house itself rather than the neighbourhood: people appeared not to mind leaving a known locality if the new home offered superior amenities (Mass Observation, 1943, pp. 185–90). It was not simply that the seclusion and privacy of the suburban council house imitated aspired-to middle-class values, though it may well have done, but that it offered both men and women a material symbol of individuality and ownership, even if such 'ownership', based on mortgage payments or rent, was an illusion. A house of one's own could become a home of one's own: a place of comfort, security and privacy; a material object unshared and owned; a cultural expression of individuality and belonging; and a socio-political marker of citizenship in a social system that consistently denied ownership of property or self-definition to 'the poor' and to women. Political citizenship as represented by the suffrage had always remained firmly linked to ownership of property: to be defined as a citizen was to not be defined as 'poor', 'criminal' or 'mad'.

Although this sense of ownership and citizenship was located in a consciousness of class, it was also differentiated along gender lines. Access to housing cannot be understood simply in terms of social status and class mobility – middle-class families have access to superior housing because of income and this in turn reflects social status – but has to be recognised as a highly gendered social practice. In the first half of this century women's access to improved housing was via marriage and a husband's income, except for the few professional women who earned independent incomes or those who inherited property. Middle-class women could expect to gain adequate housing and the comforts that went with this upon marriage. Working-class women's access to housing was either through residential domestic service or again, marriage, although for many poor women marriage did not mean improved housing, especially if they had worked in middle-class homes as servants. Indeed as housewives, working-class women's aim was to rent two rather than one room and this of course was dependent upon income levels. Improved housing for women, and particularly working-class women, was mediated through men, either as housing designers, housing officials or husbands. Where women were involved in house design their role tended to be consultative and as such positioned them as housewives concerned for the health of the family rather than individual women requiring a home (Ravetz, 1989, pp. 187–203).

Moreover, citizenship for women was always posited in terms of their housewifely and maternal role – as one housecraft manual of the period proclaimed, 'take care of the babies and the nation will take care of itself' (*The Motherhood Book*, 1930, p. 752). Women's aspirations for the future were assembled from a nexus of intersecting discourses and possibilities in which the public identity of citizen as well as the private identity of wife and mother were organised around the vision of the suburban home.

The material provision of improved housing for working-class families was produced from a discourse organised around the alleviation of family poverty and ill-health rather than from the needs of women as housewives. At the same time, the ideals of family life enshrined in improved housing were constructed from a discouse predicated on sexual difference and gender roles. So, although women were required to sustain levels of cleanliness and comfort, to maintain the values of private life and to make houses into homes, the material space in which they might achieve this was designed and provided by men. Hence 'ownership' for working-class women might be understood differently from middle-class women *and* from working-class men. I would suggest their sense of 'ownership' centred, less around bricks and mortar, than around the objects *within* the home that made life more comfortable and around family members for whom they were responsible. Owning the constituents of a home is a way of belonging to that home and that family – ownership and belonging are circulating discourses that mutually reinforce each other. As we shall see, 'ownership' and 'belonging' were problematic discourses, beyond the financial mechanics of owning a home, when they concerned themselves with women and their relation to suburbia *as women* rather than as housewives and mothers.

The houses provided through local-authority building and cheap speculative enterprises were, in the 1920s, intended for returning servicemen and the more affluent sectors of the working-class rather than for the poorer slum dwellers. Council house allocation was based on the principle 'that preference shall be given to those who have seen service abroad', and the rented or mortgaged small private house went 'largely to a limited range of income groups – small clerks and tradesmen, artisans and the better-off semi-skilled workers with average-sized families and safe jobs'. (City of Birmingham, Proceedings of the Council, Report of the Housing and Estates Committee, 2/12/1919; Burnett, 1986, p. 238; Merrett and Gray, 1982, Chapter 2; Merrett, 1979, Chapter 4). House allocation was determined by the ability of the husband to provide for his family and his service to his country. Allocation policies placed large families after these criteria; as such the needs of women and their children for more space and better facilities were often not met, or not until the slum clearance schemes of the 1930s, by which time social distinctions organised around suburban housing had become established. For most working-class women aspirations for improved housing were only possible via prudential choice of a husband: a working-class man in regular employment who did not drink or gamble was the route to an improved environment for most working-class women. The design and layout of new suburban homes supported a specific version of family life as represented in allocation policies. Three bedroomed houses with one or two living rooms and a small scullery sustained the growing ideal of the small family who ate and played together, and the rent or mortgage payments demanded, stated clearly the expectation of a male breadwinner in regular work.

One of the design issues fiercely debated in the early 1920s was the provision of parlours in working-class homes and the use of living rooms and kitchens. The Tudor-Walters Report, reflecting the views of Raymond Unwin, was unhappy about providing parlours in working-class homes although it did begrudgingly concede the issue (Tudor-Walters, 1919; Ravetz, 1989, p. 197). The concern focused on 'the danger of improper use of rooms' and in particular where the family might eat. Hence a parlour might become a family living room and larger kitchens might result in families using them as living areas (Tudor-Walters, 1919; Women's Housing Subcommittee, 1918–19, para. 89). This concern with 'improper' use of rooms was rooted in anxieties about hygiene and the spread of infection, but it was also a means of distinguishing the 'deserving' from the 'undeserving' and the 'rough' from the 'respectable'. How a family utilised the space available was a potent visual signifier of that family's social standing, and Seebohm Rowntree's social investigators in York found themselves able to make subtle distinctions between types of council tenants based on the materiality of domestic interiors. Witness these accounts by one of Rowntree's survey investigators:

Description of a Council parlour house occupied by a careful and houseproud tenant. Rent 10s. 6d.

The parlour (12 ft. by 10 ft. 6 in.) has a bow window and is nicely furnished. It contains a brown leather-covered settee and two easy chairs to match, a table, a bookcase, an occasional table in the window and on the floor there is an almost new carpet with oilcloth surround. The family lives in the kitchen, as the w.c. is upstairs it can only be reached by passing through the parlour. The kitchen (12 ft. by 10 ft. 6 in.) is furnished as a dining-room with an oak sideboard, an oak dining-table, two easy chairs and a number of small chairs, a sewing machine and a wireless set. . . . On the wall are a clock and a few framed photographs and coloured prints . . .

and

Description of a Council non-parlour house occupied by a tenant who is poor and has a large family. Rent 8s. 11d.

The front door opens into a small lobby . . . the floor of which is covered with a worn piece of oilcloth, partly covered by a torn piece of rush matting. . . . A door in the lobby leads into the living room (13 ft. 6 in. by about 12 ft.). Clothes lines on which clothes are being aired are stretched across the room, they appear to be a permanent feature. The furniture consists of a painted deal side-board, a deal table covered with brightly coloured American cloth, a horse-hair sofa, much worn, and two easy chairs to match, a few kitchen chairs, a small chest of drawers with a wireless set on the top, a large-size perambulator, and bundles of clothes and oddments in every conceivable spot. . . . The floor is covered with some worn oilcloth, on the top of which are a number of small rugs and pieces of worn carpet (Rowntree, 1941, pp. 236–7).

The signifiers of respectability invoked here include the parlour, the leather-covered and oak furniture, carpets rather than rugs, the sewing machine and the bookcase: all of these connote order, solidity and comfort, and all were of course maintained by women. The reference to 'a careful and houseproud tenant' conflates the domestic upkeep of such a home with the 'owner' (tenant) and in doing so denies the gendered form in which social distinctions between members of the working class were articulated. The second description, placed in contrast to the first, draws upon visual signifiers from a well established legacy for representing 'the poor' and again invokes the domestic work of women in maintaining order, and by implication, comfort. Washing hanging around the room, the large pram, the repetition of 'worn' and 'torn', the American cloth and the horse-hair sofa were intended to be read as suggestive of this family's disorder and impoverished lifestyle. The stated aim was to draw attention to the importance of environmental factors in creating comfortable lives; the implicit suggestion was the social distinctions manifested in type of house and effective household managment within it, which went beyond any simple division of the working-class into suburban 'respectables' and inner city slum dwellers. Both houses described by Rowntree's investigator were in suburban areas of York and the survey took place alongside the slum clearance schemes of the later 1930s when local authority housing, unlike in the 1920s, was targeted at those with the lowest incomes and in the worst inner city housing.

These distinctions between those who were rehoused and those who chose to live on a suburban council estate were transferred onto specific estates. In Birmingham, Allens Cross Farm in Northfield, built earlier in the period, was perceived as more 'respectable' than later estates such as Weoley Castle. In York, Burton Stone Lane, built in the 1930s to house those dispossessed by slum clearance, was, and indeed still is, understood as a 'rough' area. Moreover, those in owner-occupied or rented semi-detacheds in the suburbs were often conscious of differences between themselves and those on council estates. And even before the First World War middle-class observers such as C. F. Masterman and E. M. Forster were deploring the spread of 'red rust' and 'the creeping into conscious existence of the quaint and innumerable populations bred in the Abyss' (Forster, 1910, p. 329; Masterman, 1902, p. 4). Ebenezer Howard's dream of a suburban Garden City may have been envisioned as a means of providing a superior and egalitarian environment for the working classes of late nineteenth century England. In its concrete realisation and in the discourses that surrounded it, it functioned to create a further fragmentation of precisely that social egalitarianism the ideal of 'community' was intended to preserve. What was occurring was a cultural fragmentation of suburbia in which, rather than the egalitarianism envisioned by Howard, new forms of the 'slum dweller' could be discovered, regulated and investigated, via a variety of narratives such as 'slums of the mind', 'the good tenant', 'the good housewife' and 'the neurotic housewife'.

GOOD TENANTS AND GOOD HOUSEWIVES

John Burnett observed of the interwar period that 'house-ownership defined status better than anything else, conferred respectability and responsibility and made a man a fully participant member of society' (Burnett, 1986, p. 277). This link between home and citizenship was the focus not only of policies directed at increasing house purchase, but also of municipal housing policy targeted at returning servicemen and working-class men in regular employment. 'Homes Fit For Heroes' was a specifically gendered message, addressed to those returning from the upheavals of war, but it was also linked to the extension of the franchise in 1918 to all men over 21 (women were not granted the vote on the same terms until 1928). The idea of citizenship incorporated the newly granted right to vote and a recognition of war service. The figure of the 'good tenant', incorporating as it did concepts of home-ownership and the returning serviceman as hero, was important to this discourse of citizenship, interpellating, not only those who purchased their own houses, but also those with council tenancies, as 'fully participant member(s) of society'. As such it appeared to address working-class men and, at times, quite deliberately excluded women. Even the Women's Subcommittee to the Ministry of Reconstruction made this distinction in its report, '. . . whether we are considering their needs from the housewives' and mothers' point of view, or from that of the citizens in general' (Women's Housing Subcommittee, 1918–19, para. 56).

At the same time, however, the ideal of the 'good tenant' incorporated and addressed women implicitly as a (silent and invisible) part of the marital unit that constituted 'the good tenant'. For the ideal tenant, according to housing committee and housing welfare reports, was an amalgam of regular breadwinner, fully enfranchised male and good housewife:

> With regard to the priority of letting houses Rents and Tenants SubCommittee recommended that the tenant is in a position to pay the rent, that the tenant is likely to be suitable from a point of view of looking after and keeping in good and clean condition the house (York City Council, Minutes of the Housing Committee, 17 February 1931).

and

> A further report was considered with regard to a number of applicants who would appear unsuitable as municipal tenants. It was recommended that the Estates Manager should interview these people at

home to encourage the applicants to improve their conditions with a view to a possibility of assisting such cases at a later date if improvement was then noticeable (York City Council, Minutes of the Housing Committee, 18 December 1922).

Incentives to encourage improvement included cookery demonstrations and demonstrations of how to use electricity to best advantage. Such methods as well as the visit of the estates manager or housing welfare officer were targeted specifically at women who, in their home-based role as housewives, provided a captive audience. As discussed above, Rowntree's investigator confidently made assessments of tenants' moral and financial status based on the visual and 'feminine' signifiers of domestic comfort. As such the figure of the 'good tenant' implicitly incorporated both masculine and feminine roles whilst publicly representing itself as male. In doing so an ideal version of working-class marriage was produced in which the marital unit comprised male provider and female housewife, whilst continuing to address the male as 'citizen' and the female as 'housewife'.

As women made 'good' housewives insofar as they served the 'national interest', husbands were encouraged in good tenantry and by extension good citizenship via the provision of gardens. Funds to encourage gardening on municipal estates were often donated by local benefactors, free gardening calendars were given to all Birmingham council tenants and York City Council actively encouraged residents' gardening associations (Burnett, 1986, pp. 234–40; Birmingham City Council, Housing Committee Minutes 7 February 1922, 29 July 1930; York City Council, Housing Committee Minutes, 16 September 1930, 11 January 1933). In 1930 Birmingham City Council ran a Municipal Estates Gardens Competition, which was well-publicised by the local press, where the message that good gardening made respectable citizens was hammered home,

The Lord Mayor who presented the prizes said the two most beautiful things in the world were music and flowers. Many of the municipal gardens in Birmingham were 'colossal' – the tenants producing wonderful results in small room to the delight of themselves and the pleasure of their neighbours. . . . But there were a considerable number who did not take a pride in their gardens. A tenant who allowed weeds to grow rampant was a nuisance to the whole neighbourhood. There were thousands of people who wanted houses and would be only too glad to look after a garden (*Birmingham Post*, 8 November, 1930).

The same report stated that classes in gardening and horticulture were to be started on various municipal estates around the city. Gardening was encouraged as a suitable leisure activity for working men because, firstly, it kept them at home and out of the pubs and provided a space for shared and familial activities. Secondly, it was represented as an activity removed from commerce and economics; as an arena in which working-class men could, it was hoped, share and express the spiritual values of pastoralism the urban slum had denied them. The *Birmingham Mail*, reporting on the 1931 Municipal Estates Gardens competition, eulogised that 'the wonderful results were brought about by gardeners who worked for the love and joy of it and not for remuneration' (*Birmingham Mail*, 22 July 1931). English pastoralism was a potent strand in interwar discussions of citizenship, national identity and environmental reform and functioned to deny the very real economic and social divisions that underlay the suburban ideal of 'rus in urbe'.

Tenants such as D. H. Dodd, who won first prize for his 'rustic arches covered with roses, lily pools with goldfish and running water, and a magnificent display of rock plants, leading up to a miniature well and summer house' (*Birmingham Mail*, 22 July 1931), undoubtedly enjoyed the creativity of gardening. Nonetheless his access to a garden was totally dependent upon his being able to maintain rent payments, which required regular work and good health. Moreover his garden, however lovingly tended, remained under the jurisdiction of the City Council who might, as York City Council did, insist that its tenants cut their hedges twice a year and at no time allow them to grow taller than five feet (York City Council, Housing Committee Minutes, 16 September 1930). As I shall discuss below when considering the voices of those who inhabited these suburban spaces, the discourse of 'good tenant' and the exhortation to this form of suburban pastoralism offered working-class men and women cultural spaces in which they might articulate complex needs and desires at the same time as producing elaborated forms of social distinction, which required constant self-monitoring as well as surveillance of neighbours and which created a framework within which suburbia could be experienced.

Versions of English pastoralism, in which the values of a rural 'Golden Age' might be recreated in the suburban enclaves of the country's polluted and ugly cities, were to be found not only in the socialist ideologies of the Garden City movement but in housing committee minutes, newspaper reports, housing design, as well as in the protestations of a middle-class intelligensia against what they deplored as an increasingly materialistic and urban culture. J. B. Priestley, in his *English Journey* of 1934, follows in the footsteps of Masterman and Forster in condemning the development of suburbia, which he interprets in terms of urban materialism rather than the quasi-pastoralism envisaged by early town planners:

> all it offered me, mile after mile was a parade of mean dinginess . . . the whole array of shops with their nasty bits of meat, their cough mixtures, their Racing Specials, their sticky cheap furniture, their shoddy clothes, their fly-blown pastry, their coupons and sales and lies and dreariness and ugliness (Priestley, 1934/1984, p. 86).

Municipal garden competitions and horticultural classes were offered as a means of combatting the ugliness perceived by writers such as Priestley. The discourses of pastoralism offered to the 'new citizens' of a reconstructed postwar England a role in the creation of a 'decent, civilised life' as 'good tenants'.

Stanley Baldwin, Conservative prime minister throughout the 1930s, consistently represented himself as the paternalistic squire of a mythical rural England, in which urbanisation and industrialisation were simply irritating obstacles to be dealt with as best he could (Miles and Smith, 1987, p. 53). As Alison Light has observed, Baldwin epitomised for the middle classes the cultural ideal of interwar masculinity – the pipe-smoking 'little man' concerned more with his domestic circle, his garden and his private ideals than with heroic exploits or great events (Light, 1991, p. 211). He also captured a version of English domesticity and pastoralism for 'the working man and woman', inviting them to insert themselves into the cultural heritage of the country for which they had fought:

> The wild anemones in the woods of April, the last load at night of hay being drawn down a lane as the twilight comes on. . . . These are the things that make England, and I grieve for it that they are not the childish inheritance of the majority of the people today in our country . . . nothing can be more touching than to see how the working man and woman after generations in the town will have their tiny bit of garden if they can, will go to gardens if they can, to look at

something they have never seen as children, but which their ances-
tors knew and loved. . . . It makes for the love of home, one of the
strongest features of our race and it is that that makes our race seek
its new home in the Dominions overseas, where they have room to
see things like this that they can no more see at home. . . . It is that
power of making homes, almost peculiar to our people, and it is one
of the sources of their greatness (Baldwin, 1926, pp. 7–8).

Baldwin, like housing officials and designers, does not explicitly distinguish the roles of men and women in creating 'home' or 'greatness'.
Like the other discourses I have examined he allows a slippage between
the work of men 'in the garden' and the work of women 'making
homes'. Baldwin's address is to the 'Englishman', a figure in which
gender and class are assumed to be subsumed and under which all
differences might be denied. Baldwin goes onto to address an audience
who 'go overseas and . . . take with them what they have learned at
home' (ibid.) His address was produced via a trope of 'Englishness'
that particularly addressed itself to the cultural figure of the new sub-
urbanite, an identity increasingly open to the more affluent sectors of
the working-class and one predicated upon suburban domesticity – what
Alison Light has called 'a nation of gardeners and housewives' (Light,
1991, p. 211).

The next section will examine one response to suburbia that was very
specifically gendered and that produced another narrative of suburban
life to set alongside the discourses of housing reform and design, the
discourses of respectability and privacy and the discourses of English
pastoralism and good tenanting. If these discourses came together to
produce the 'normative' figures of the domesticated husband tending
his garden with his wife, barely visible, concentrating on the domestic
interior, then Dr Stephen Taylor's detailed aetiology of 'suburban neurosis' tapped into the same discourses to produce the 'deviant' figure of
the 'neurotic' housewife, a figure who for many years was to carry the
blame and the sickness for the apparently spurious gentility of some
forms of suburban living.

'THE SUBURBAN NEUROSIS'

In 1938 Dr Stephen Taylor, a neurological consultant in a London
teaching hospital, published an article in *The Lancet* entitled 'The

Suburban Neurosis'. In this he outlined what he perceived as a new form of mental illness amongst 'less poverty-stricken young women with anxiety states, the majority of whom present a definite clinical picture with a uniform background' (Taylor, 1938, p. 759). Taylor believed that the neurosis he identified amongst the young women who attended his outpatient clinic was caused as much by environmental as by physical factors. The symptoms he encountered time and again were those associated with anxiety states – stomach pain, continuous headache, insomnia, loss of weight and general aches and pains – and in his article he argues that the anxiety and depression of these patients has been caused by the conditions of their lives in suburbia:

> The deep-seated aetiological factors of the suburban neurosis are, no doubt, extremely complex. The stomach which swells represents perhaps an unconscious urge to further motherhood, the sleepless nights a longing for a full sex life. Existence in the suburbs is such that the self-preserving, race-preserving and herd instincts can be neither adequately satisfied nor sublimated (Taylor, 1938, p. 760).

Taylor represents his diagnosis in the form of a case history, a mode of medical and scientific discourse used by both psychoanalysis and social work. In so doing he signals its links to psychology and social casework but also its status as individual autobiography. Case histories were accounts of a specific individual's problem or illness and derived from Freud's reports of individuals whom he had treated via psychoanalysis. Taylor, however, offers a case history of Mrs Everyman, which he subtitles 'The True History', and produces a composite picture, drawn from a variety of cases, of a young mother and housewife, living a bored, lonely and empty existence in her newly acquired suburban home. 'The True History' of Mrs Everyman reads like a novel; it deploys all the devices of narrative, there is description, dialogue, internal dialogue, and a cast of characters from 'hubby' to 'hubby's cousin', who is described as 'that woman'. The following extracts give a flavour of the whole,

> Her parents were respectable, and kept themselves to themselves. . . . All day she added up figures, in the train she skimmed the *Daily Peepshow*, three times a week she went to the cinema, and such mind as school had developed withered and retrogressed. Then love, in the shape of Mr Everyman, came along. . . . So after two years of

saving, and those lovely walks around Box Hill at the weekends, they took the plunge into a small semi-detached hire purchase villa. . . . One day there dropped through the letter-box a circular. It was sent out by the local doctors, and it was all about cancer. . . . Cancer didn't hurt *at first*. Her back was hurting. What if it were? And she was losing weight, too. Hadn't hubby said she wasn't as nice to cuddle as she used to be?

At the end of Mrs Everyman's story, Dr Taylor steps in to 'translate this miserable little story into medical jargon'. His contempt and condescension towards those he describes vies with his concern at their circumstances and his, perhaps, even greater anxiety at the potential political danger, for 'in the latent feelings and strivings of the new mental slum-dwellers, there is waiting a most hopeful field for the teachers of new, and possibly dangerous, political ideologies' (ibid., p. 761). Taylor makes an explicit comparison here with Hitler's Germany and Mussolini's Italy, saying, 'perhaps the success of the totalitarian states with their lower middle classes is due to just such a reasssertion of the "Leader Principle"' (ibid.) The 'false values' Taylor attributes to Mrs Everyman provide a ready soil for the extreme politics of totalitarianism, and for this reason alone the prevention of 'suburban neurosis' should be in the hands of politicians and social workers who could replace isolation and self-sufficiency with community and cooperation. Taylor indicts housing designers, politicians, social reformers and builders for allowing 'the slum which stunted the body to be replaced by a slum which stunts the mind' (ibid.) and, as he perceives it, particularly the mind of the suburban housewife.

It is easy when reading Taylor's article, riddled as it is with class assumptions and a contempt for those he desires to serve, to miss its potentially progressive nature. Taylor's insistence that suburban domesticity is the cause of Mrs Everyman's illness contains the proto-feminist analysis to be made so trenchantly by Betty Friedan and Hannah Gavron in the 1960s, whilst his misogynist diagnosis works to suppress this (Friedan, 1965; Gavron, 1966). Nevertheless Taylor's analysis renders visible the ideological fissure in constructions of domesticity. In focusing on the effects of domesticity, Taylor, in effect, names what Betty Friedan in the 1960s was to call 'the problem with no name', but unlike Friedan, of course, he fails to confront the contradictions his diagnosis makes visible – why if domesticity was a woman's 'natural' sphere did it make her ill? (Friedan, 1965). Taylor was able to avoid the full implications of his position because he articulates it in terms of class and suburbia rather than in terms of gender, despite his representation of 'suburban neurosis' as a specifically female condition:

What wonder that the underdeveloped, relatively poor mind of the suburban woman seeks an escape in neurosis (Taylor, 1938, p. 761).

When Taylor expresses anxiety about the growth of dangerous ideologies it is perhaps not surprising that he does not, or at least not explicitly, mention feminism: in 1938 the perceived danger was totalitarianism and events in Nazi Germany had already proved that anxiety to be well placed. Yet by focusing on women as 'the suburban neurotics', Taylor's analysis of how domesticity could lead to illness provided a space for later feminist analyses of the relation between women's role in the home and their greater disposition to mental illness. That he was able to avoid confronting the issues he raised was due to his attempts to universalise the neurosis as one afflicting 'Everyman' who lived in the circumstances and environment of the suburbs and relating it to an emergent lower middle class, whilst representing this illness in the figure of the 'neurotic' housewife whose material aspirations and 'stunted mind' rendered her both pathetic and dangerous. Bored, isolated, acquisitve and sexually frigid (or in later representations sexually rapacious), she appeared to deny the prevailing norms of female sexuality. This cultural stereotype of the suburban housewife was to be deployed in the 1960s by sociologists anxious to attack what they saw as a growing trend towards acquisitiveness and consumerism amongst the newly affluent and newly housed working class (Willmott and Young, 1962, p. 164). Mitchell and Lupton, describing a 1950s postwar housing estate in Liverpool, noted that:

women also attached importance to symbols of superior status such as the television mast, the outward appearance of respectability and the need 'to keep up with the Jones's (Mitchell and Lupton 1954: 49).

Neither was Taylor's diagnosis a new one: Victorian medics, feminists and writers had debated the effect of a constrained and stifling domesticity on the health of middle-class women, demonstrating how it might lead to hysteria or neurosis (Gilman, 1935; Nightingale, 1928; Showalter, 1987, Chapter 5; Poovey, 1989, pp. 45–6). In many aspects Taylor's analysis produced a reformulation of that predisposition to fragile invalidism that permeated certain Victorian discourses of femininity. In so doing he created a version of femininity that was open to different social groupings: Victorian invalidism was the prerogative of the middle-class woman, 'suburban neurosis' was the prerogative of an increasingly mobile social group, drawn from sectors of the lower middle and upper working class. Women who lived in the slums were, it would appear, immune from the 'neuroses' Taylor describes. Yet the very causes he cites for Mrs Everyman's anxiety were precisely those which inexorably and inevitably dogged the lives of poorer women. Anxiety over money and fear of another pregnancy were never the prerogative of suburban housewives, although in raising them as such Taylor draws attention to the ways in which income, pregnancy and housing were a dissociable triangle in the lives of all women who depended upon a low or irregular income. Taylor was not concerned to challenge the sexual division of labour nor the dominant conceptions of femininity and masculinity; he nowhere suggests paid work outside the home or voluntary outside interests as a solution to 'suburban neurosis'. Indeed he avoids the implications of his diagnosis by suggesting that Mrs Everyman's problems stem from not having enough to do *in the home*:

> as long as the housework, the baby or the sick husband keep the young wife busy, all is fairly satisfactory. But once these cease to occupy her she is left with time on her hands and she starts to think, a process for which she is completely unadapted (Taylor, 1938, p. 760).

Hence women living in the slums, whose daily existence was an unceasing round of tasks dominated by survival and who were rarely left with time on their hands, would, according to Taylor's argument, have been less likely to succuumb to 'neurosis' despite circumstances that might have caused extreme anxiety. The labour-saving devices, smaller families and improvements to housing that transformed daily life and bodily health for so many women were simultaneously rendered problematic and likely to lead to 'illness' – only a surfeit of arduous but satisfying domestic duties would, Taylor implies, prevent the suburban housewife from becoming ill.

The main complaint Taylor makes against the suburbs is that they have promoted a 'false set of values':

The suburban woman has made a fetish of the home. She is aiming at the kind of life successfully led by people to whom books, theatres, and things of the intellect matter. To them, the home is a necessary part of life, but only a part. To her, because she does not see the rest, the home looks like everything, and she wonders why it does not bring her the happiness it appears to bring them (Taylor, 1938, p. 760).

According to Taylor the suburban housewife, unlike her middle-class counterpart, lacks that 'inner life' which sustains domesticity and ensures a balanced moderation in relation to the home. As I shall argue in the next chapter, the idea of an 'inner life' was one that circulated amongst a range of discourses as an expression of class difference. Virginia Woolf used it in her introductory letter to *Life As We Have Known It*, citing as the main difference between middle- and working-class women the middle-class woman's desire for 'Mozart and Einstein' against the working-class woman's need for 'baths and ovens' (Woolf, 1931/1977, pp. xxi, xxviii). Mrs Miniver, Jan Struther's fictional creation of a middle-class housewife, offers a fictional representation of those to whom 'things of the intellect matter'. Returning from her summer holidays, Mrs Miniver finds on her writing table 'a card for a dress-show; a shooting invitation for Clem; two dinner parties; three sherry parties; a highly aperitive notice of some chamber-music concerts. . . . Three new library books' (Struther, 1939/1989, p. 2). The idea that working-class women's lack of an 'inner life' predisposed them to an 'abnormal' relationship to their homes functioned to sustain class differences between women even when (particularly when) working-class women were offered access to the kind of housing and environment previously the prerogative of the middle classes.

The cultural narrative produced by Taylor's account of the working-class woman's aspirations disguises the very real need that underpinned those aspirations for improved housing and those material objects which could make the difference between well being and ill health, order and chaos. It is difficult not to read him as suggesting that the very improvements that made life comfortable for this generation of women were potentially the source of mental illness in the way inadequate sanitation and poor nutrition had caused disease in the slums. As I have shown, Taylor makes a quite deliberate comparision between the 'slum which stunted the body' and the 'slum which stunts the mind'. Neither is it coincidental that in both narratives, whether it be that of urban slum or suburban 'wasteland', it is the woman who carries responsibility. In her rests the potential for improvement through her role as mother yet her body reveals the marks of a 'sick' mind and stands as an icon for a specific social body, 'stunted' mentally as the earlier slum dwellers were stunted physically.

In organising the discourse of suburban neurosis around the figure of the housewife but articulating it in the language of topography, Taylor avoids confronting the gendered implications of his analysis whilst at the same time producing a gendered narrative that functions to maintain social boundaries at a historical moment when such boundaries were under dispute. The figure of the 'neurotic housewife' serves to maintain barriers between women, as well as between women and men, by constructing women's relationship to their homes in terms of 'sickness' or 'health' – between the woman who makes 'a fetish' of her home and the woman who treats it with balanced moderation. By locating the 'sickness' in, and blaming it on, suburbia Taylor is saved from examining the reasons why women might 'fetishise' their homes and the relation of this to the system of domestic service, which constructed different meanings of home for different groups of women, or its relation to the poverty and want from which suburbanites were escaping.

Whilst domestic service will be discussed further in a later chapter, it is enough to point out here that social relations between women, which had in part been structured via the institution of domestic service, were becoming considerably more fluid with the emergence of daily 'helps' and a decline in residential domestic service. The suburban housewife, not dissimilar to the Victorian governess, occupied a position in which she belonged neither with the servants nor the ladies, neither with the slum dwellers nor the Mrs Minivers. Positioning the 'neurotic housewife' against the normative figure of the middle-class woman who understood the 'right' meaning of home and the poor slum woman whose struggle for survival exposed her to the ministrations (and regulation) of middle-class charity and philanthropy, reinforced the inextricable and complex network of social relations that structured women's relations to the home. This juxtaposed positioning constructed distinctions between women whose relationship to the home, once raised above the level of survival, became 'deviant' because rooted in 'false values', and women whose relationship to the home was 'normal', constituted as an expression of love, freely given, and guaranteed by its association with 'things of the intellect' rather than material objects. The suburban housewife was problematic for an imagination such as Taylor's, in which the economic underpinning of certain ways of life was consistently avoided and denied, revealing as she did precisely the material basis on which domestic comfort and well being was possible.

Moreover, in the interwar period the figure of the 'suburban neurotic' was sexually ambiguous. Female sexuality for working-class women remained located firmly in maternity; for middle-class women the work of post-Freudian sexologists represented female sexual expression and pleasure as located firmly within heterosexual conjugal relations but requiring full expression if 'neurosis' was to be avoided (Holtzman, 1983, pp. 39–51; Jeffreys, 1985; Weeks, 1989). Taylor's Mrs Everyman is neither fully maternal nor able to lead a full sex life and her body quite literally reveals the signs of her 'abnormality' – 'pendulous flabby breasts'; 'poor abdominal muscles'; her clothes 'hang on her rather as a covering than as something to be worn'. The 'neurotic housewife' functioned as a cultural icon of all that was 'abnormal' in suburbia and in doing so sustained the barriers between women that were rooted in relationships to domesticity, the home, the private and the house. Hence the problem of women's economic dependence as a social group per se and as dependent upon each other via their relations to homes and housework was avoided by a discourse that insisted the problems of 'neurosis' and domesticity lay not in the structural relations of the sexes, but in the individual woman's relation to her sphere, a relation that, precisely because it was individual, could be pathologised and thus reformed via medication, psychology or community work. Equally, it is precisely in the act of 'discovering', naming and exposing what supposedly preexists that the idea of 'suburban neurosis' is given concrete form and with it a new form of 'deviant' femininity.

SUBURBAN VOICES

I want now to turn to the voices of the suburbs' inhabitants and to explore how far they reveal traces of the official discourses that have been discussed and how far they were able to adapt the prevailing discourses of suburbia, gender and class to produce meanings that articulate their specific and complex experience. First I will examine a correspondence that took place in the pages of the *Birmingham Mail* about municipal housing and its tenants and then I shall discuss accounts of suburbia by some of the women interviewed.

The *Birmingham Mail* for 20 July 1931 published a letter, signed 'Caveat Emptor', in which the writer urged the Housing Committee to reconsider their allocation policies. 'Caveat Emptor' (let the buyer beware), who was a prospective municipal housing tenant, writes:

> I am no snob (on a rental of 45s. 7d. per week!) but personal knowledge of other estates and reports of friends living on or having doings with same are in agreement that the great drawback of accepting a house under the Corporation is the tremendous possibility of undesirable neighbours. . . . The Estates Committee make many and strict enquiries into all our circumstances before enrolling us on the register, and their visitors can adequately sum up the type of folks with whom they deal. Surely it should not be impossible, therefore, for people who have some regard for the decencies of life to be granted the privilege of living beside one another, and not, as so often happens be thrust among persons of vastly different manners and tastes (*Birmingham Mail*, 20 July 1931).

In the following week the *Birmingham Mail* published six responses from municipal tenants agreeing with 'Caveat Emptor' and no responses that challenged or disagreed with the original letter. The *Birmingham Mail* for 22 July 1931 also carried a report of the Municipal Estates Gardens competition and the edition for 25 July 1931 reported on 'City Housing Situation', in which it was suggested that house building in the city be reviewed 'lest, the supply exceeding the demand, the city be left with a very heavy liability'. Thus the concern of 'Caveat Emptor' and the other correspondents was publicly located in a wider concern about city housing, 'good' tenanting and the economic 'problem of providing dwellings for workers with small incomes' (*Birmingham Mail*, 25 July 1931). In publishing this correspondence the newspaper allowed the voices of the city's municipal tenants to be inserted within the official discourse of housing and to appropriate those voices for the production of a public, consensual version of municipal tenanting and respectability.

All the letter writers drew on the language of respectability, a language I have already shown was deployed by housing investigators and officials. The repetitive use of words and phrases such as 'decent-class', 'decent-living', 'clean-living' and 'respectable' assumes a tacit understanding between reader and writer as to precisely what they signify; an understanding that relies on juxtaposition with polarised phrases such as 'uncouth', 'coarse', 'undesirable types' and 'the type of person who

...' Such words and phrases circulate with signifiers such as the parlour (two of the writers consider their problems with 'uncouth' neighbours to have been the result of living in a block of non-parlour type houses) and street gossiping to produce an assumed relationship of understanding and sympathy between reader and writer. Equally, 'Caveat Emptor's' use of a Latin tag was presumably intended to emphasise, not so much a public school classical education as self-education, revealed through a close knowledge of English phrases and their usage, which again signifies respectability. It is tempting to read these letters as simply examples of a spurious gentility and social aspiration. All the letter writers condemn the 'coarseness' of neighbours whose 'gossip', 'jeers' and refusal to adhere to the tenets of good tenanting are felt to be deplorable:

One has only to look at some of the gardens (at the back) and the windows (at the front) to imagine what the inside must be like (*Birmingham Mail*, 23 July 1931).

The adoption of a formal, and at times slightly pretentious style suggest an unwarranted snobbery.

However snobbery was not an overcoat of attitudes to be slipped on and off at will, it was a response to social experience and a form of consciousness, produced from the cultural materials available at any specific moment, in which that experience could be articulated. The writers of the letters not only reveal a desire to maintain certain social distinctions but also an overriding sense of misery and frustration. All the letters use a language of unhappiness that exceeds the formal and controlled language of the discourse of respectability in which much of the writing is couched, for example, 'your life is one long misery . . .', 'mothers driven to desperation', 'perpetual humiliation' and neighbours who have 'made life almost unbearable'. One writer concludes:

I have had hardships, sorrow, hunger, but never have I been so unhappy as since becoming a municipal tenant (*Birmingham Mail*, 24 July 1931).

All the writers used pseudonyms – 'Another Sufferer', 'Reserved Tenant' – and whilst this will be returned to in a moment in relation to gender, for now I want to make the point that for these working-class writers public articulation was a violation of that reserve and restraint which signified their respectability. Hence their desire for anonymity can be understood as both a need to protect themselves within their own environment and a need to protect a safe space in which they might articulate their very real sense of misery and resentment. For these letter writers the privilege of a council tenancy was very closely associated with the newly granted franchise and for some with their war service. 'Reserved Tenant' alludes directly to her husband who, 'with many more fathers, fought in 1914 for his country'. A council tenancy was not simply about improved housing, although that was important, but it also signified a sense of belonging as a full citizen to a society, which in the past had denied its working-class both political rights and the dignity of self-definition. 'Ownership' of a council house, because it was dependent upon official assessment of worth via highly regulative allocation procedures, conferred a certain status as a 'good' tenant and housewife: to maintain that identity was paramount; to feel it threatened was to envision a negation of such self-definition and to fear loss of that newly acquired sense of belonging. When 'Tenant' writes,

> It is most heartbreaking to one who takes a keen interest in the beauty of his home and garden, to find litter and filth of all kinds continually strewn about – chip-potato papers and empty beer bottles thrown defiantly into one's front garden, merely because it has the appearance of being well-kept (at considerable expense and hours of labour); privet plants pulled up in one garden and thrown into the next (or stolen), fences and gates chalked with obscene words, to say nothing of thefts from back gardens (*Birmingham Mail*, 24 July 1931)

it was not simply an attempt to imitate the discourses and values of middle-class observers of the poor but was also an expression of frustration and resentment at a world in which obeying the rules of virtuous tenanting and citizenship not only brought no reward but resulted in the destruction of the concrete and outward symbols of that citizenship.

As already observed, all the letter writers used pseudonyms and identified themselves according to emotion ('Frankly Fed Up', 'Hadsome', 'Another Sufferer'); local identity ('Brummy'); or their relation to their home ('Tenant', 'Reserved Tenant', 'Caveat Emptor') rather than by sex or class. One of the writers refers to her husband but it is only possible to speculate about the others. However, given the details of daily life reported in some of the accounts and the articulation of profound feeling, it is interesting to speculate how many of the writers were women. This might be borne out by the use of pseudonyms, which was of course a well-established tradition amongst women writers wishing to remain anonymous. Working-class women conventionally used oracy, in the form of private conversation and gossip, to express and communicate personal feelings, their life stories and their social experience and might not have considered the public space of the newspaper an appropriate or seemly place in which to make their voices heard. It is possible that 'respectable' housewives as well as 'good' tenants, cut off from gossip and personal conversation, by their commitment to the values of respectability, could well have felt themselves impelled by the strength of their misery to insert their voices into a public discourse from which hitherto they had both excluded themselves and been excluded. Certainly the concern over children hearing bad language and the sense of being the object of 'unspeakable gossip' and 'all kinds of scandal' might well suggest the writers were women.

In deploying self-definitions organised around locality and housing, the letter writers contest the dominance of gender and class as necessary and inevitable modes of self-identity. What is significant for my purpose is the extent to which these writers draw on the official discourses of respectability and suburbia in order to produce social distinctions that allow the construction of a self-dignifying identity around the definitions of 'good' housewife and tenant whilst locating this, at least temporarily at the moment of writing, outside the boundaries of gender but within notions of citizenship. In order to achieve this, of course, self-definition depended upon identification of a polarised 'other' who could be made to carry the displaced or denied aspects of experience that threatened the, as yet, fragile consciousness of belonging and ownership articulated in citizenship. As discussed, political citizenship was, at least until 1928, a male prerogative. Yet I would suggest that if the writers of these letters were women then they bear witness to the ways in which working-class women might adapt the official discourse of 'good' tenant, in which was subsumed their own identities as housewives, in order to expropriate the associated identity of 'good citizen' for themselves.

We will now turn to the women I interviewed in order to explore how the discourse of respectability and suburbia was experienced in the lives of those who inhabited the new council houses and semi-detacheds. The letter writers occupied a public space and deployed traces of the official discourses of housing; it is in the social practices of individual actors that it becomes possible to consider the variety of ways in which these discourses might have been understood and experienced.

As argued at the beginning of this chapter, Muriel Jones, a first generation suburban child, defined herself against those who inhabited the urban streets and terraces of Birmingham. Muriel's mother was a restless, energetic woman whose childhood had been spent helping out in her mother's pub in the Black Country, an area dominated by the small workshops of the metal trades and notorious for its 'roughness'. Once married and settled in Rednal with four children she turned her energies to small business, buying two semi-detacheds, one of which she converted to a tobacconist's shop and the other she rented out. According to Muriel she 'did pretty well out of it', amassing a moderate amount of capital, which was passed to her children, and eventually buying a large detached house on the Lickey Hills. Muriel's mother voted Conservative all her life but her behaviour and attitudes were far less easily categorised:

> There were some people who used to have what they called strap. You know they say 'we'll pay you on Friday'. Anyway if they went longer than a fortnight she'd be round there 'Right you owe me some money'.

> Where did they come from, the people who owed money?

> Usually the council cottages. . . . And she used to get quite a lot from these cottages who owed her money. But she wouldn't let them do it too long and if they continued with it she'd say 'Right don't come in my shop again' and she'd have a row with them. I've seen her row outside on the street because people whould argue with her and she'd say 'Right, OUT!'

Arguing and fighting in the streets was one of those behaviours which distinguished the 'rough' from the 'respectable', but Muriel's mother continued to deploy the social and business practices of an older way of life in her new suburban environment, gossiping and arguing over the shop counter and in the streets. However she was equally concerned that her children should acquire both social accomplishments and a secondary education. Muriel and her sister both had piano lessons, Muriel also learnt the violin and her sister took ballroom dancing lessons, and Muriel's mother insisted Muriel should sit for a scholarship to the local grammar school (which Muriel failed). Yet according to Muriel her mother was not 'snobbish', 'she didn't mind who we mixed with, she was a very friendly type of person, and she didn't like wrong things'. Hitting or fighting with weaker or smaller children was something she classified 'wrong' and she would be very strict about bullying or other kinds of social injustice.

Equally, Alice Wilkes and Lizzie Smith both self-identified as 'decent' and 'respectable' women. Yet Lizzie had an illegitmate child and her husband was violent and abusive towards her and the child, until finally, after a particularly unpleasant fight between father and son, she 'cleared him out'. Lizzie's account of her life on a York council estate stresses her role in the community of the estate – she was called upon to lay out the dead, to minister to wasp stings and to help out generally at times of trouble. Alice's husband was a soldier who never returned after the Second World War: Alice spent all her married life with her mother in a council house on the edge of York. She worked long hours as a general help in a city centre hotel and her two daughters were cared for by a neighbour. Alice's mother, like Muriel's mother and like Lizzie, was not averse to settling issues via argument and fighting. When the health visitor called to see Alice after the birth of her first child, Alice's mother 'chased her out', shouting 'don't come here talking books and that, if you burned your finger, would you run for a book to find out what you ought to do. Get out!' Moreover Alice's children were allowed out in the streets until 8.00 pm in the summer, which according to 'respectable' standards was unacceptable – children playing in the streets was one of the complaints of the letter writers above, who presumably saw in such practices traces of that life in the slums they were anxious to distance themselves from. Such attitudes were reinforced by medical and educational experts, who 'discovered', along with 'suburban neurosis', the figure of the 'unslept child' whose 'careless parents . . . resort to the easy excuse that it is useless to put children to bed by daylight' (school medical officer for health, cited on p. 25 of Hygiene Commitee of the Women's group on Public Welfare (1939–42), *Our Towns*). A Board of Education handbook categorised the effects of inadequate sleep as malnutrition, lassitude and 'mental fatigue' and recommended at least twelve to fourteen hours sleep a night for children up to adolescence (Board of Education, 1933, p. 24).

Neither Alice nor Lizzie fitted the cultural stereotype of the 'good housewife' deployed by the discourses of housing and welfare, yet both women felt themselves able in producing narratives of their lives to define themselves as 'respectable'. In part this was due to the changing geography of urban housing and the possibilities for self-definition opened up by suburbia. Both women were relocated to suburban council housing as a result of slum clearance schemes in York in the 1930s, and whilst they transferred certain social practices from their urban environment, they perceived themselves as having materially improved their lives as a result of the transition from the slum streets, and felt able to use the opportunities provided by this transition to appropriate certain aspects of the cultural ideals of suburbia and respectability to their own circumstances.

Lizzie, for example, took considerable interest in her garden, growing flowers and vegetables, and judges today's tenants as 'riff raff' because of their refusal or inability to care for their gardens: 'I mean *our* gardens were all done beautiful. . . . I had all bulbs down the side and the [bird] bath and flowers all way round, and then in the front garden I had a standard rose tree'. Lizzie, who would undoubtedly have been judged 'coarse' and 'uncouth' by the Birmingham letter writers, on account of her premarital pregnancy, her violent marriage and her succession of extremely menial jobs (at one time she was a 'step lady', the lowest form of domestic service)[1] was able to adapt certain aspects of the figure of the 'good tenant' for her own purposes. Her situation as main provider for herself and her two children may have enabled this. With her name on the rent book and her creativity in the garden she appears to have adopted the male position in the composite figure of the 'good tenant', and in doing so was able to represent herself to herself as a respectable citizen rather than as dispossessed poor, which is almost certainly the way she would have been represented in the official discourses of housing and welfare.

Mabel Matthews and Dot Pearce bought their own homes in suburbia when they married in the 1920s. Dot felt that purchasing a house rather than renting was what distinguished her from her parents – 'Our parents lived in rented houses, I never lived in a rented house' – but she continued to rent out rooms to lodgers, a practice that was, of course, forbidden to council house tenants and that was in official eyes associated with the overcrowding of slum areas. Although insisting that purchasing a house was a signifier of respectability, Dot only partially linked this to 'keeping yourself to yourself' or with ideals of familial privacy, as her willingness and enjoyment in renting rooms was evident in her account. Whilst she almost certainly took in 'visitors' in order to make ends meet, there was perhaps a sense of power in her status as landlady, gained from her knowledge that she was providing for others what her family had once required. Like Muriel's mother, she does not appear to have suffered the isolation, boredom or lack of mental stimulus cited by Stephen Taylor as causal factors in the development of 'suburban neurosis'. Yet her desire for a home of her own, her small family (she had two children with a large gap in between), her self-evident pride in keeping her home clean and her husband's occupation as a small shopkeeper placed her very precisely in Taylor's composite category of potentially 'neurotic housewives'.

The difference between Dot's narrative of her life and Taylor's narrative of the 'neurotic housewife' is organised around perceptions of empowerment and powerlessness. Taylor's Mrs Everyman is represented as an object of scrutiny, caged in her small semi-detached, powerless to change or direct her life, which is entirely dependent upon husband, education, builders, social reformers and other external agencies. Dot in contrast, represents herself as an acting subject in her own story. Dot's parents had run a small tailoring business before the First World War and her sense of herself, in the same way as Muriel's mother, was organised around the idea of 'being in business'. Hence for Dot, as for Muriel's mother, suburban life was experienced as offering opportunities for self-empowerment and stimulus through 'businesses' such as renting rooms and running a small shop, and whilst Dot undoubtedly enjoyed her role as housewife, having a day for each household task, she does not appear to have been obsessive in the sense of Taylor's diagnosis – 'the suburban woman has made a fetish of the home' (Taylor, 1938, p. 760).

Mabel met her husband Ernest through the local Conservative association, to which their parents belonged: Mabel's father was a fishmonger and her mother had been a cook. Of all the women interviewed Mabel was the only one to marry into the lower middle class. Her husband was a weights and measures inspector for the local authority and they were, by dint of careful saving, able to buy a small detached house when they married in 1933. Like Dot and Muriel's mother, Mabel was able to take advantage of the opportunities offered by the development of suburbia: whilst continuing to help her father in his fishmonger's shop, Mabel taught herself to play the piano so as to be able to give piano lessons and she recalled how busy she was at this time:

I used to rush around doing the housework, down to the shop, and then come back up in time to have a wash and change for 4 o'clock teaching, and I had a break for tea and then I went on teaching until about 9.00 o'clock.

Mabel had a sense of identity based on her position in the suburban community and on her social class, but she also evidenced an ambiguity around the distinctions engendered by the suburban organisation of social life. Mabel fostered a child from the local children's home and recalled the party she allowed Pauline to hold, which was attended by children from the local council estate. Mabel's own children were 'dressed normally like children', but the children from the council houses had

> those dresses with frills and vests underneath that the sleeves came down here, they were obviously dressed up for a party and perhaps navy blue knickers under, well our two kept on giggling . . . and I thought 'little snobs' – oh, I was furious with them, children can be cruel.

Despite her recognition that her own children were 'cruel', she was herself uncomfortable with such a visible rendering of class difference, as her recourse to the standards of 'normality' suggests, and her later observations articulate an acute sense of uncertainty and guilt around the distinctions formalised through geographical space:

> the whole idea of having a foster child out of a home is to make her one of the family and Pauline had to go right across to the school which served the council estate, knowing nobody and all our children with all their friends just across here. Well, of course, the result was very bad because, without being snobby, the council estate, when it was first built, it brought all the people and I don't know where from, but just as good as anybody else, but the children seemed to be poorer. And you couldn't get her to sound her aitches and of course going out to the council estate school didn't help.

The geographical location of schooling and housing within the suburbs continued to be organised around categories based on social distinctions, whilst at the same time representing itself as a distinctive and polarised opposite to the inner city slum. Those, like Mabel, Dot, Lizzie and Alice, who chose to live or found themselves rehoused in the suburbs constructed their sense of identity not simply from the cultural narratives around gender and class but also from the official discourses of citizenship, housing policy and reform as well as the less public but well-established discourses of respectability that circulated, reformed and recirculated within their own social groups, via, for example, public expressions such as those of the Birmingham letter writers. However, despite (because of) their interpellation as 'respectable' or 'rough' by prevailing discourses, women such as Muriel, Lizzie, Alice and Dot were able to contest the polarisations inherent in such definitions in their juxtaposition of these dominant cultural narratives with the psychological and cultural material of their earlier and current life experiences.

'A home of one's own' whether it was privately rented, purchased on a mortgage or a council tenancy *was* different from renting rooms. It was officially represented as an icon of citizenship and proffered a sense of ownership and belonging; as a social and political ideal it created a space in which working-class men (and by extension their wives) were invited to reimagine themselves as 'fully participant members of society' and it provided those material comforts lacking in so many childhoods. In doing so it made available a cultural space in which working-class women might expropriate or adapt such reimaginings, focused as they were on the home, for their own self-dignifying purposes. Yet, as Stephen Taylor's article suggests, the emotional price might be high – a woman's relation to her home was never simply a material one. 'Home' was the place where a woman was expected to find her 'true self'. It was assumed to be the locus of her emotional life and her sexuality, the heart of her 'private' life. Yet in the early twentieth century the home became, as never before, a public spectacle, open to the scrutiny of a whole range of observers, visitors and commentators. Middle-class women retreated into their 'rich inner lives'; working-class women 'kept themselves to themselves'. The next chapter examines the ways in which women's 'private' lives were constructed, represented, scrutinised and hidden within the actuality and concept of 'home'.

3 'Keeping Yourself to Yourself': Private Lives and Public Spectacles

The cluster of behaviours and attitudes implicit in the idea of 'keeping yourself to yourself' has often been read as signifying a spurious respectability, a respectability perceived as particularly evident amongst the socially aspiring and frequently explained as specifically engendered by the growth of suburbia, the emergence of consumerism and the break-up of the extended family and community networks associated with urban street cultures (Willmott and Young, 1962, p. 164). Stephen Taylor cites 'keeping yourself to yourself' as a cause of 'suburban neurosis':

> Few who have not worked or lived in the suburbs can realise the intense loneliness of their unhappy inhabitants ... Lack of individual enterprise, shyness and bashfulness prevent calling and the striking up of friendships. It is respectable to keep oneself to oneself (Taylor, 1938 p. 760).

The Birmingham letter writers of the previous chapter defined themselves in terms of 'reserve' and 'keeping ourselves to ourselves', attributes that were seen as essential to achieving respectable status but that could also be read as expressions of a profounder disappointment and resentment against a world that consistently failed to reward the virtues it insisted upon. If the idea of a 'home of one's own' provided a space in which to articulate desires for material ownership and social belonging via narratives of citizenship and 'good' tenanting, then 'keeping yourself to yourself' offered the possibility of constructing and believing in a psychological subjectivity in which it was equally possible to 'own' and indeed 'keep' a sense of unique identity – an inner self in which the 'core' or 'essence' of personality could be located.

The idea of an 'inner' self is an historically specific construction related in its twentieth century conception to the Enlightenment concept of the unique, autonomous individual: 'a conscious awareness of the singularity of each individual life' that is 'the late product of a specific

96

civilisation', by which is meant Western societies since the Renaissance (Georges Gusdorf, cited in Friedman, 1988, p. 34). As Friedman (and others) have recognised, this model of the autonomous, self-defining individual is fundamentally inapplicable where 'the self, self-creation and self-consciousness are profoundly different', as in the case of 'women, minorities, and many non-Western peoples' (ibid.)

For those who have conventionally been the object and rarely the speaking or writing subject of the moral, medical, scientific and religous discourses in which public articulations of private identity are constructed, the late nineteenth and twentieth century bourgeois model of an 'inner' self, organised around and 'discoverable' in the autonomous imagination and in personal relations, takes on a very different meaning. Working-class housewives rarely entered public discourse as speaking subjects, they even more rarely produced autobiographical accounts giving voice to the 'real' woman. As such working-class women were defined publicly by others, and as such they were defined either according to the geographical space they occupied (as we saw in suburbia) or their sexuality was represented as a polarised division between maternity and 'deviance': good mothers and housewives or feckless whores.

The emergent discourses of the early twentieth century, in which an active female sexuality replaced the Victorian model of passive modesty, were addressed quite specifically to middle-class women. For example Marie Stopes, whose *Married Love* advocated sexual pleasure as essential to a woman's emotional and psychological fulfilment, made it clear that she was addressing primarily 'our educated classes' (Stopes, 1918, p. 25). In these circumstances it makes sense to consider the ways in which 'keeping yourself to yourself' offered possibilities for escape and protection from the insistent intrusions of middle-class observers (both male and female) anxious to produce certain versions of working-class life and of femininity. Emotional thriftiness offered a cultural model that allowed women to define themselves as respectable and thus to retain their personal lives, their sexuality, as 'secret', in resistance to the consistent concern amongst medics, educationalists, welfare workers and social commentators of the period to 'expose' it.[1]

Virginia Woolf, as observed in the Introduction, struggled with an acute awareness of the class divisions that separated women: for her, as for many educated women, class consciousness organised itself around what she perceived as the one-dimensionality of working-class women's subjectivity and the complex, multi-faceted, 'inner' lives of middle-class women such as herself. Hence if we are to understand the ways in which a more complex consciousness was experienced and expressed by working-class women, it is important to unravel not only the encodings embedded in the terms 'respectable' and 'rough', 'private' and 'public' as they were understood by women of all classes but also to recognise the sometimes contradictory, sometimes overlapping, and hence fluid and flexible meanings that might be produced around concepts of relationship and private identity. Indeed it seems likely that the private and the personal would have been understood in very different ways by women whose psychology and experience were shaped by the combatative childhoods discussed in Chapter 1. Emotional thrift was as much a way of preserving an embattled psyche as was material thrift for ensuring physical survival. Women who grew up understanding the need to be a 'fighter'; who understood their human identity as well as their gendered identity as constantly under threat; women who knew how quickly and easily the brutalities and deprivations of poverty could endanger a hard-won sense of belonging as a citizen, a tenant, a home owner, were unlikely to squander their inheritance in emotional excess any more than they would be likely to indulge in financial extravagance.

When I asked Muriel Jones if the people in suburban Rednal were friendly, despite not 'popping in and out of each other's houses', she recalled, as did a number of the women interviewed, that neighbours talked over the fences of their gardens, in the local shops and would help out at times of sickness or difficulty. Muriel's responses suggest ambiguities around concepts of 'friendliness' and 'privacy':

> They were friendly [in Rednal]. I think they were less friendly, they kept themselves more to themselves than in the terraces. They were friendly during the war. Everyone knew one another during the war. They seemed a bit inclined to, . . . they didn't want people to know what was in their house, sort of thing.

Moreover the naming of relationships was important in understanding the boundaries and expectations of such relations, and this understanding was built to some extent on environment. Muriel's concern with calling a neighbour 'Auntie' was directly linked to the inner city street culture she found so alien: '. . . being so close together they all knew one another and they were in and out of one another's houses'.[2] The contradictions articulated here and the problems of defining degrees of communality and privacy suggest the ways in which women's understanding of these ideas could be historically and geographically specific: 'they were less friendly . . . in the terraces . . . they were friendly during the war'. Feminist theories of female psychology have argued that, in contrast with men, women's sense of self is relational and organised around and within a constant awareness of others: the isolated individual positioned against his social world, the masculine self of post-Renaissance thought or the Rousseauean confession in which 'characters and events exist only to become part of the landscape of the hero's self-discovery' are not models of selfhood with which women are necessarily comfortable (Mason, and Hurd Greed, 1979, p. xiv; Gilligan, 1982). Women, it has been argued, tend to perceive themselves in complex relational associations to others that render dichotomised categorisation and polarised judgements of self or others difficult to sustain:

[o]ur studies of women's psychological development began with listening to women's voices and hearing differences between the voices of women and men. Privileged men often spoke as if they were not living in relation with others – as if they were autonomous or self-governing, free to speak and move as they pleased. Women, in contrast, tended to speak of themselves as living in connection with others and yet described a relational crisis which was inherently paradoxical: a giving up of voice, an abandonment of self, for the sake of becoming a good woman and having relationships (Brown and Gilligan, 1992, p. 2).

Muriel's unease at attempting to define or categorise her relationship to neighbours suggests the ways in which she understood these relations as shifting within temporal and spatial parameters, but also suggests her need to articulate this fluidity and make sense of it – a need that is refused by the prevailing and available narratives of the self and other, either then or now. As will become apparent later in this chapter, at one level Muriel 'knew' the personal relations she was involved in; at another level – that of prevailing behaviours and dominant beliefs – she also and equally 'knew' which relationships counted within her class and culture if she was to fulfill her identity as a 'good woman'. Calling a neighbour 'Auntie' when she was not an aunt was to privilege deference, prevailing notions of relations between the generations and the polite behaviour expected of 'good' girls, above the actual lived relationship. Hence the reserve inherent in the idea of 'keeping yourself to yourself' was never simply about the physical privacy of the suburban street. It was, as I have intimated, both a social attitude and a psychological imperative organised around the cultural narratives of working-class women's relationships with public and private spaces, relationships and discourses.

This chapter examines whether the ways in which prevailing ideas about street and home, public and private, produced and imagined specific subjectivities within which working-class women were inscribed and thus invited to contemplate themselves. The early twentieth century saw the emergence of 'welfarism' and the development of an increasing number of official bodies concerned with the health and welfare of the working class. Health visitors, social scientists, welfare and housing workers, as well as educationalists, youth workers and writers were constant observers and recorders of working-class life. In particular, in line with a growing concern for infant and family welfare, women in their roles as housewives and mothers became the objects of detailed scrutiny, their stories, their needs and their aspirations spoken for them, often by middle-class women for whom work in social welfare offered new professional and career opportunities (Lewis, 1980; Davin, 1978).

'Keeping yourself to yourself' involved, as the phrase suggests, a relationship with a private self that might be distinguishable from another 'public' self. Hence this chapter also raises questions about how the class and gender systems in operation at a specific historical moment produced multiple and contested identities around ideas about the private and the public. In this context I shall explore how the women interviewed understood and articulated ideas about private identity, how these ideas related to social necessities and precisely what was at stake in aspiring to the emotional thrift required of respectability. In such circumstances 'privacy', public space, the idea of an 'inner' life and the relationships and conditions that sustain these subjectivities might come to be understood differently by women from different classes and, as Muriel's comments suggest, by women in different material and historical circumstances.

As suggested, this raises questions about the internal dynamics of a consciousness in which not simply class and gender, but also age, environment and family position interact to produce understandings about the distinctions and blurrings between the public and the private. 'They', in the life stories of the women interviewed, frequently and simultaneously signified the public world of power and authority as vested in teachers, employers and welfare workers; families who were perceived as less respectable; and potential male partners – 'you go to the pictures and you meet 'em and that's it'. 'They' might constitute a whole public world of 'otherness', which required negotiation in order to construct the distance it was deemed necessary to maintain between those 'inside' and those 'outside'. 'They' were also of course parents, husbands and family members whose position could be understood differently in different circumstances – sometimes representatives of authority and the public world, sometimes intimate and companionable 'fighters' against the impositions of the outside world. In such circumstances negotiations to assert the boundaries between public and private, 'them' and 'us', were never complete. This mental landscape produced anxiety, uncertainty and resentment alongside a concomitant need to control and fix the limits and nature of relations with others, both privately and publicly.

'Keeping yourself to yourself' articulated a need and a desire for certain forms of privacy in the face of constant attempts to regulate the lives of working-class women by innumerable 'theys'. 'Keeping yourself to yourself' might also have been a means of contesting the subjectivities offered to working-class women at a time when, as we shall see, they were frequently interpellated as either over-burdened victims, stoical insensitives or sexual predators; actors in narratives whose iconography was drawn from the well-established and well-rehearsed sources of dominant culture. Emotional thriftiness created a space in which, rather than finding themselves always and already inscribed in the narratives of others, women might resist the inevitable exposure and scrutiny of such inscription, by refusing that most bourgeois of possessions – 'a rich inner life'.

PUBLIC PLACES

When Winifred Holtby opened her book, *Women and a Changing Civilisation*, with the words 'during the autumn of 1933 I rode one evening on the top of a 'bus from Rottingdean to Brighton' she was not only beginning with an anecdotal example but signalling a certain position as a woman to her readership (Holtby, 1934, p. 1). Riding on the top of buses was, in the late nineteenth century, a characteristic of 'advanced' women. 'New women', such as the novelist Olive Schreiner, displayed an 'agility in gaining the tops of omnibuses' as well as talking and laughing in the street 'quite naturally' (Walkowitz, 1992, pp.

63, 69). By 1934, of course, riding alone on the top of a bus or laughing in the street was no longer seen as quite such shocking behaviour for 'respectable' women. Nonetheless, in including this detail Holtby draws attention to the freedoms women had gained in their access to public spaces. Financial independence, increased job opportunities, educational opportunities and the mobilities occasioned by the First World War had made women visible as never before in the public spaces of all large cities. City buses and trains were no longer the strictly gendered (male) space of their Victorian counterparts: women out shopping, women travelling to and from work and schoolgirls all used transport networks to travel independently and extensively around urban and suburban areas. For many middle-class women this physical independence and geographical mobility was in itself exhilarating; their insertion into the public places previously belonging to men – public transport, the school, the university, the office, the street – was to change the meaning of those places and to result in a blurring of the distinctions associated with each (Brittain, 1933; Swanwick, 1935). The emergence of innumerable women from the domestic space of the home and their entry into public places hitherto reserved for men, disrupted 'the public/private division of space along gender lines', a division that was essential to maintaining a gendered map of the social order (Walkowitz, 1992, p. 23).

The language of space however is not only gendered it is also organised around cultural understandings of class. Charles Booth's journeys with his investigators around London in the 1880s were represented in 'a complicated but well-established moral and visual semiotics' (ibid., p. 34). Certain streets could be identified as 'rough' or 'respectable' according to a range of visual signifiers. According to these codings, 'respectable' areas were characterised by quiet streets, closed front doors, clean doorsteps, shining brasswork and a lack of *public* interaction either between family members or between neighbours beyond social civilities. In contrast 'rough' areas revealed themselves by noise, dirty windows, lack of curtains, children playing in the street, women 'popping' in and out of each others' homes, gossiping in the street, and arguments between neighbours, between family members and between mothers over children (Keating, 1973, p. 596; Roberts, 1973; Ross, 1985).

Equally well established through the work of social commentators such as Charles Booth, Henry Mayhew, Charles Dickens and the art of the engraver, Gustave Dore, was the identification of the East End of

London in particular, but all territories of the urban poor as a 'dark continent', 'an abyss', a place of terror and fascination, peopled by 'outcasts', and 'hotbeds of vice, misery, and disease' (Keating, 1976; Dyos and Wolff, 1973; Walkowitz, 1992). Social investigators used and reused the language of 'otherness' and pollution to describe their explorations of 'darkest England'. For example the concept of 'the abyss' is deployed repeatedly – the following titles were all published in the first decade of the twentieth century; *The People of the Abyss* by Jack London (1903), *From the Abyss* by C. F. G. Masterman (1902) and *Glimpses into the Abyss* by Mary Higgs (1906). George Sims, writing in 1889, began *How the Poor Live* as follows:

> In these pages I propose to record the result of a journey into a region which lies at our own doors – into a dark continent that is within easy walking distance of the General Post Office . . . the wild races who inhabit it will, I trust, gain public sympathy as easily as those savage tribes for whose benefit the Missionary Societies never cease to appeal for funds (cited in Keating, 1976, pp. 65–6).

As Muriel's account, which began the previous chapter, suggests, this iconography had by no means disappeared as a way of organising and understanding social distinctions in the twentieth century. Indeed Eileen Elias, writing in 1978 of her middle-class South London childhood in the early part of this century, deploys the cultural stereotypes and iconography of nearly a hundred years ago to articulate her childhood consciousness of 'otherness':

> There was horror and want in the streets – I caught glimpses of barefoot children, heard angry voices shouting outside the pubs at night, listened to talk of murderers and burglaries, and people still spoke of Jack the Ripper, and of notorious Charlie Peace, arch-criminal of the last century, who had lived only a few streets away. But our little home was inviolate; our station in life the most desirable that could be imagined. Nothing could touch our own safe family (Elias, 1978, p. 14).

When 'the poor' inserted themselves into the public spaces of the middle class – the office or the suburbs – they had to negotiate and reorganise their consciousness of such space around these visual and moral metaphors. Working-class women (respectable or rough) had always occupied public spaces, moving around the streets of their locality as necessary, and had learned to negotiate an identity that included, repudiated or ignored the identification of street and walker as 'prostitute'. Unlike their middle-class counterparts, working-class women in the years after the First World War did not experience a *new* freedom in their ability to move around the city. Rather the boundaries that had circumscribed their environment were extended. Edith Stewart recalled how, as a young adolescent in the 1920s, she was able to see three different films on a Saturday after work by using the excellent tram service over Birmingham, and Mavis Kitching observed that:

> You could go miles and miles [over the city] and nobody'd harm you. As long as you was in by nine o'clock you could go where you liked.

Mavis's comments contrast with those of Eileen Elias in her apparent unconcern about the sexual and violent dangers that might await a young woman travelling independently around a large city. Mavis expresses a safety in the city streets akin to Eileen's safety in the home. Yet of course this is ambiguous: as Eileen's references to Jack the Ripper highlight, there always was (and is) the possibility of sexual and violent assault in city streets and working-class women have more often been the object of that violence, in part at least, precisely because they *were* at home in the city streets in a way middle-class women were not.[3] Equally, the emergence of respectable working-class women into the spaces previously reserved for middle-class men (and their chaperoned wives) – the shopping street, the office, the cinema/theatre, the park – constituted a transgression of those cultural boundaries which organised the social order around gender and class distinctions and produced, in time, a geographical relocation of the boundaries of each and, as I have argued with relation to suburbia, a reformulation of the social distinctions visually encoded by geographical space.

Distinctions between suburb and city might, as already suggested, manifest themselves in the visual images of their nineteenth century inheritance, yet as the comments of Mavis and Muriel suggest, distinctions between street and home, outside and inside, public and private spaces were far less fixed in working-class imaginations, and certainly so when contrasted with Eileen Elias's polarisation into private haven/ public nightmare. A good example was that of the Monkey Run. Common to most towns, the Monkey Run was a certain street where young men and women would congregate to jostle and flirt with the ultimate purpose of pairing off (Thompson, 1975; Roberts, 1984, p. 71). Monkey Runs had their own rituals: groups of men and women would parade up and down in same-sex pairs, viewing each other. After a while a flirtatious remark would be made or conversations might start and then the man and woman would walk up and down the street together. At the end of the evening the man might ask for a date. The point seems to have been that the whole business of starting a courtship should be *publicly* enacted in front of one's peers. In this sense the bourgeois belief in the significance of the sexual relationship as the locus of 'inner' identity was disturbed: courtship took place not in the 'privacy' of the home, where its ultimate expression and significance would be located in marriage, but in the public arena of the street – a transgressive space where, in other contexts, 'private' desire and commercial dealings met in the figure of the prostitute. Representations of working-class female sexuality had been and continued to be organised around public space – the street, the cinema, the dance hall were all dangerous places where working-class women were positioned as both predator and victim. In this way the post-Enlightenment and bourgeois model of an 'inner life', expressed primarily through sexuality and personal relations, was ambiguous and problematic for working-class women: visibility in certain public spaces defined their sexual role as 'deviant', with the only acceptable and respectable expression of their sexuality located in maternity and the home, itself never free from the scrutiny and attempted regulation of the proliferating external agencies of welfarism.

However the destablisation of these categories could work back into the private sphere of the middle classes. In 1939–40 thousands of children were evacuated from deprived industrial areas to rural or suburban villages and towns. The arrival of these children in suburban homes was often a source of extreme concern and anxiety. The children of 'the poor', who went to 'board school' and dropped 'their aitches' and had 'dirty faces' and no shoes (Elias, 1978, p. 15), were objects of compassion and philanthropy certainly, but as such were much easier to make sense of when encountered in the public spaces of school, welfare clinic or their own homes. According to the Women's Group on Public Welfare, a number of the families who received evacuees 'were extraordinarily intense and bitter' at the 'inadequacies' of young working-class mothers, whom they identified as 'dirty, verminous, idle and extravagant' (Hygiene Commitee of the Women's Group on Public Welfare, 1939–42, pp. 3–4).

This intensity and concern reveals the ambivalence middle-class women felt towards the objects of their concern when these women and their children left those *public* spaces and discourses in which they could be spatially and morally imagined (and thereby understood) according to a well-established collection of cultural codes and narratives, and entered the *private* homes of their benefactors. Under these conditions of intimacy the, always fragile and uneasy, relationship between middle-class women and 'the poor' became publicly visible in the most private arena, and in becoming so contested the compassionate and philanthropic public accounts of welfare workers. According to the Women's Group on Public Welfare, women receiving evacuees complained that the mothers

> could not hold a needle and did not know the rudiments of cooking and housecraft, and that they had no control over their young children who were ... dirty, verminous, guilty of enuresis and soiling both by day and night, ill-clad and ill-shod, that some had never had a change of underwear or any night clothes and had been used to sleep on the floor, that many suffered from scabies, impetigo and other skin diseases, that they would not eat wholesome food but clamoured for fish and chips, sweets and biscuits, that they would not go to bed at reasonable hours, and finally that some of them were destructive and defiant, foul mouthed, liars and pilferers (Women's Group on Public Welfare, 1939–42, pp. 3–4).

Anxiety was contained insofar as working-class women occupied certain geographical and occupational spaces – the home as wives and mothers, the street as prostitutes and the middle-class home as domestic servant, but not as guest or family member. Hence the relations between certain groups of women organised themselves around significations of 'public' and 'private' space produced from a well-established legacy of cultural iconography that itself sustained the gendered and class-based assumptions about home, sexuality and private life upon which it was built.

PUBLIC VOICES

If late Victorian England perceived London's East End as a home-grown alien country, 'the dark continent' of Freudian femininity and 'otherness', the 1920s and 1930s witnessed a transfer of this vision to those areas suffering the acute deprivation of slump and depression. The 1930s in particular were marked by an expanding literature on social issues, much of which focused on the industrial areas of mass unemployment – South Wales, the North East, Lancashire and York-shire (Mowat, 1955, pp. 480–531; Stevenson, 1984, pp. 321–2). Social investigators followed in the paths of their Victorian counterparts. Young men such as George Orwell and Tom Harrisson were ready to go amongst 'the poor' 'living in poor quarters, wearing rough clothes' mixing in all aspects of working-class life, in order to report on 'the condition of England' (Mowat, 1955, p. 530; Hoggart, 1965, p. v.; Orwell, 1937). The male social investigator played out the role of the adventurer whose 'disguise' allowed him to 'penetrate' the 'labyrinths of little brick houses blackened by smoke, festering in planless chaos round miry alleys ...' (Keating 1976, p. 16, Orwell, 1937, p. 52). In doing so social investigators constructed a literary and imaginary land-scape of class that built on the social imagination of their Victorian forefathers, '[i]t was not only the dirt, the smells and the vile food, but the feeling of stagnant meaningless decay, of having got down into some subterranean place where people go creeping round and round just like blackbeetles, in an endless muddle of slovened jobs and mean grievances' (Orwell, 1937, pp. 18–19; Walkowitz, 1992, pp. 15–40).

Orwell, like many of his educated contemporaries, grappled with a class consciousness rooted in the physical body of the working-class man:

> Very early in life you acquired the idea that there was something subtly repulsive about a working-class body; you would not get nearer to it than you could help. . . . The smell of their sweat, the very texture of their skins, were mysteriously different from yours (Orwell, 1937, p. 130).

This sense of physical horror was contained in a series of denials and suppressions that enabled male observers to construct 'the poor' as a collective body whose interests could be served via political action, rather than individualised and actual bodies whose rescue might well entail getting 'nearer to it than you could help'. If Orwell's anxieties and struggles with his understanding and sense of class took the form of repulsion from the physicality of the *male* working-class body, his attempts to transcend and escape his prejudices focused on the *female* body and the private sphere. In *The Road to Wigan Pier* Orwell's ambivalence about the individuals whose lives he recorded and wished improved via socialism could be suppressed by 'gazing' on the female body or the family interior and constructing them as icons of, respectively, working-class suffering and working-class warmth and solidarity. Orwell's famous description of the young woman unblocking a drainpipe on whose face, Orwell reads, the hopeless, passive despair of a whole social group, or his idealised account of winter evenings in the prosperous working-class home, are offered from the position of a voyeuristic spectator, whose distance from the spectacle he invoked enabled a suppression of its actual physicality as well as the range of possible and potential meanings thus generated (Mulvey, 1975, 1981; Orwell, 1937, pp. 20, 118; Walkerdine, 1990, pp. 196–7). The ambivalent attitudes of investigators, observers and philanthropists towards the objects of their concern, articulated as above, as repulsion for the individual but compassion for the group, were not of course the prerogative of educated males. Such ambivalence was apparent in the responses of middle-class women (see above with respect to evacuee reception responses). However the personal as well as the political agenda was different for female welfare workers, and their understanding of their relationship to 'the poor', and particularly towards its women, was articulated differently.

Middle-class women in the late nineteenth century, and increasingly by the interwar years, had mobilised the opportunities created by the growing concern with social welfare to insert their voices into the discourses of social investigation. Welfare and charity work was an extension of the philanthropic role allowed the Victorian gentlewoman and as such provided an arena in which many middle-class women were able to claim a public space and a public voice, for, as Thane argues, the 'experience of women in philanthropic organisations of the conditions of poor women created an early link between the women's movement and welfare' (Vicinus, 1985; Thane, 1991, p. 102; Walkowitz, 1992, pp. 52–9). By the 1920s and 1930s women – as investigators, welfare workers, health visitors and writers – were regularly contributing to the multiplicity of voices attempting to define and regulate working-class life through welfare work and social survey. Yet, importantly, such women articulated their understanding of their role as investigators and charity workers as being different from men's, and claimed for themselves as women a specific social role:

They [Labour women] argued that a male-dominated state had ignored grave social problems, and therefore the state needed the experience and values of women at its centre if it was to respond to the needs of all of its citizenry (Thane, 1991, p. 102).

Moreover women were less concerned than their male counterparts to be invisible or disguised spectators of urban deprivation. Although they deployed many of the well-established archetypes to make sense of despair and poverty, they perceived themselves as active agents, not only in the moral lives of those they observed, but also in their dealings with that very physicality Orwell recoiled from. Hence the introduction to the Women's Health Enquiry Committee's *Working Class Wives* (1939) states:

It was the wisdom and foresight of unofficial pioneer workers which led the way to our Maternity and Child Welfare Service; it seems fitting and proper that the voluntary effort of women deeply con-cerned to bring greater happiness to other women less fortunate than themselves should point out this gap in our social services, and should contribute many *practical* suggestions for the remedy of ills which, once recognised, we must all deplore and desire to remove (Spring Rice, 1939, p. xviii, my emphasis).

Female welfare workers in the 1920s and 1930s were able to assert an authoritative voice in the discourses of social welfare by their claim that, as women, they had themselves experienced and were willing to become involved in the domestic and practical side of working-class life and poverty as opposed to simply being observers. A district nurse, writing of her life amongst the families of agricultural workers, explic-itly invoked her access to women's domestic duties as significant for offering advice and guidance:

I find the best time to talk to the mothers is when I am bathing her baby; we go in every day for a fortnight after the birth, it is so much easier to tell her things gradually and talk things out together; we can do a lot with a young mother and she is generally very anxious to learn (Spring Rice, 1939, p. 67).

This claim that, as women, welfare workers could transgress the public/ private boundaries of working-class life and that it was precisely in the domestic sphere that, as women, they might instigate the improvements necessary for a healthy citizenship, legitimated and enabled women's claims to a place in those professions concerned with social welfare. The medical officer of health for Aberdeen stressed in his report for 1916–21 the links between women's role in running a home and their 'place' in welfare schemes: 'the requirements . . . that are wanted in a good housewife . . . will equip a woman for house and family manage-ment, and for a place in the public administration of health schemes' (Professor M. Hay, cited in Peretz, 1989, p. 23). Margery Spring Rice wrote that working-class women 'lead private and often very solitary lives; their work is unpaid and unorganised' (Spring Rice, 1939, p. 18). She goes on to observe that

> members of parliament . . . do not see what is going on in the small dark unorganised workshop of the home. Men and young people who work in large communities and in the political limelight of the fac-tory, the railway or the mine, have time and energy and opportunity to make their voices heard (Spring Rice 1939, p. 18).

And of course it was precisely by women in 'the small dark unorgan-ised workshop of the home' that the physical needs of the working class family were met: Orwell's 'great sweaty navvy' in 'his discol-oured shirt and his corduroy trousers stiff with the dirt of a decade' was a practical and physical reality for many women (Orwell, 1937, p. 130). Equally, as observed below, the nursing of wounded and crippled ex-servicemen inevitably fell to their already over-burdened wives.[4] Pro-viding practical remedies, 'baths and ovens', electricity, fresh air and adequate space were the very issues women – often drawn, as in the case of the Women's Co-operative Guild, from different social classes, as feminists, as welfare workers and as politicians – campaigned for (Woolf, 1931/1977, p. xxi; Thane, 1991, p. 94).

Under these circumstances, where, it was believed, time, money and education prevented working-class women from speaking for them-selves, women such as Margery Spring Rice and the Women's Health Enquiry Committee reasoned that if reforms were to happen it was imperative that they speak *for* and interpret the women whose stories and injuries they recorded. Hence the stories the committee collected from working-class women were mediated through and framed within the voices of their middle-class observers, many of whom, despite claims for skills and expertise based on a common identity as women, were enabled to follow such a career precisely because they had chosen not to be housewives and mothers. In the 1981 Virago edition of *Working Class Wives* (Spring Rice, 1939) the voices of working-class women are only reached after four introductory pieces and an impressive list of the Health Enquiry's membership. Even then they are mediated through reports from district nurses and health visitors, from which the book was compiled. The effect was to produce an account of these women's lives that stresses their (generally) uncomplaining stoicism, their deference to the help and guidance offered by 'experts' and their devotion to their families. What was constructed was a working-class identity that fits a well-established iconography of 'the deserving poor'. This in turn legitimated the authority and expertise enjoyed by female welfare workers, for whom their work amongst 'the poor' provided a sense of identity in the public world without disturbing their commitment to the values of the private sphere. This sense of value and dignity achieved via a public deployment of the maternal values of the bourgeois home was well expressed by a district nurse writing of the families with whom she worked:

I find them all wonderfully friendly and so pleased with a visit; even if they have no intention of taking my advice they generally seem to want me to come and soon tell me if they think I have left them too long without a visit. It is wonderful how one finds out, and without asking, their joys and troubles, all their aches and pains, all their hopes and family histories; they expect advice about baby's rash; what to do with Granny; Father's false teeth; Johnny's boots which will wear out; teach Father to make a custard, a milk pudding, barley water; how to cure a rough skin, falling hair; Lily's love affairs; the pump is out of order; rain comes into the bedroom, a pattern for a vest; improvise a cot for the new babe; show Mary how to knit herself a new jumper . . . and so on and so on (Spring Rice, 1939, p. 68).

However the self (as well as public) legitimation of her role as expressed by the visitor above, depends precisely on a mental landscape in which 'the poor' could be imagined, not in Orwell's vision as iconic or repulsive figures, but as childlike innocents or stoical victims of life's hardships – deserving, deferential and grateful. In order to sustain such imaginings it was imperative that envy, resentment or belligerence on the part of the women visited or observed should remain unrecorded and invisible, and thus denied. Where anger does surface in the testimonies constituting *Working Class Wives* it is set alongside contrasting accounts, which are highlighted for their cheerful acceptance of difficult conditions and which thereby negate the 'bitterness' expressed (ibid., p. 71). Again, one woman's story, characterised as 'unnecessarily disgruntled', is dismissed as exaggerated on the ground that she 'was a nursemaid before marriage, wherein perhaps lies the explanation' (ibid., p. 72): the assumption being that her job as nursemaid had given her expectations beyond what was reasonable for her class. If *Working Class Wives* rescued working-class women from the iconicity or caricature thrust upon them by Orwell's account, it nonetheless reconstructed them as one-dimensional figures, playing out a single role as struggling housewife and mother.

The expanding welfare services of the early twentieth century focused much of their concern on the health and well-being of infants and children. In the 1920s there were 2054 welfare clinics run by voluntary organisations and local authorities, and health visitors had been appointed in approximately 200 towns; by 1938 the number of clinics had increased to 4585, with over half run by local authorities who also employed 5350 health visitors (Gittins, 1982, p. 51; Thane, 1991, p. 104; Peretz, 1989, p. 22). Health visitors and district nurses, who were always female, entered working-class homes in order to provide advice and guidance on infant care, child rearing, hygiene, cooking and housewifery. Although in theory the health visitor's area included all social classes, in practice her expertise was assumed to be targeted at the poor. Her brief was to teach women 'the art of looking after children' and to supersede the 'bad' advice of grandmothers, whom it was believed continued to pass on their own 'ignorance' (Lewis, 1980, p. 61; Peretz, 1989, pp. 22, 23). Working-class women, once taught the rudiments of hygiene and a nutritious diet, would, in their roles as wives and mothers, produce a healthy and stable citizenry. How far this prevailing discourse of welfare provision was accepted by those in charge of its practical implementation is impossible to know. Miss Singer, a health visitor in York in the 1930s, recalled the indifference and sometimes abuse she encountered from those she visited, but was not unduly concerned. Whilst hoping that the women she visited would accept her suggestions, she seems to have accepted as reasonable their resistance (York Oral History Project, CN32). Thane cites *The Labour Woman*:

The mother of a healthy baby of some six months old told the present
writer that . . . she felt that no doctor or nurse knew the whole story
and she began to wonder how many mothers with three or four
children, all of them healthy, actually kept to the rules to which they
listened so politely (cited in Thane, 1991, p. 103).

The concept of 'maternal ignorance' provided a space in which working-class women *as* women, rather than members of the working-class
family, could be considered and their needs examined, even if such
challenges tended to emphasise women as mothers, with reforms focusing on the health and well-being of the child (Banks, 1986). Furthermore, positing the working-class housewife as a significant figure in the
nation's welfare offered opportunities for women to insert themselves
into the public discourse of citizenship and thus to make political demands for social improvements on the basis of their identity as citizens
rather than as 'the poor'. Eleanor Rathbone refuted 'maternal ignorance' as the fundamental cause of ill health, as did the Women's
Health Enquiry Committee, and insisted that social policy and welfare
provision should confront the underlying reasons for infant mortality
and disease (Rathbone, 1924). The 'new feminism' of the interwar
years argued for family allowances, birth control and adequate housing
in order to support women in their roles as mothers. Yet as a result the
feminist discourses, which emphasised concern for the working-class
woman as mother, could find themselves allied to eugenicist debates in
which 'the lower classes' were perceived as 'polluting the purity of the
best British stock by their reckless multiplication' (Hall, 1978, p. 15).

This tension between the interests of gender and class in middle-
class women's relations with their working-class counterparts and in
the identities available to poor women is well illustrated in the work of
Marie Stopes. Marie Stopes, unlike Margery Spring Rice, Eleanor
Rathbone and the women in the Labour Party, did not espouse feminist,
radical or socialist politics, neither – as she admitted – was her work
primarily concerned with working-class women. Conservative and eugenicist in her writings on population and reproduction, nonetheless
Stopes responded warmly and sympathetically to many of the thousands of letters she received from working-class women:

I sympathise with you very much for having lost your children and
desiring that you should have another one. I think, however, from
what you tell me that there is something a little wrong inside that

wants clearing up and that once you are treated properly, you should be pregnant again. . . . Do not be afraid of the Welfare Centre, they are there to help, and if the first Welfare Centre does not understand your case, find another one (Hall, 1978, p. 32).

Stopes' mission as a sexual reformer and the major impulse behind her work were, as she proclaimed in *Married Love*, born out of the experience of her first marriage:

In my own marriage I paid such a terrible price for sex-ignorance that I feel knowledge gained at such a cost should be placed at the service of humanity (Stopes, 1918).

Thus, whilst Stopes' personal experience as a woman enabled her to speak to 'humanity' regardless of class, nonetheless her understanding of herself as belonging to the class with 'a sense of responsibility', rooted in conservative politics and Christian beliefs, revealed itself in a complete lack of knowledge of the day-to-day realities of working-class life (Stopes, cited in Weeks, 1989, p. 190). Her birth-control work was directed, as she admitted, at 'our educated classes', and despite the concern and warmth of her replies to working-class enquirers she fervently disassociated herself from women such as Nurse Daniels, who had been dismissed from her job as a health worker for attempting to disseminate contraceptive knowledge and advice to working-class mothers (Stopes, 1918, p. 25; Weeks, 1989, p. 191).

The multiplicity of 'voices' encountered in Stopes' work testifies to the multifarious and contradictory positions from which she constructed the interacting relationships of gender and class. As part of her 'service to humanity', individual women of all classes could be sympathised with and personally supported in the difficulties that beset them as a result of their specific reproductive and physiological functions. However, as members of a specific social group, 'the C3 population', women could only be addressed as potential producers of 'innumerable tens of thousands of stunted, warped and inferior infants' and were thus denied access to information and advice that might have alleviated some of their problems (Stopes, 1920, cited in Weeks, 1989, p. 190).

Stopes wrote personal letters of sympathy and understanding at the same time as publicly withdrawing support from Nurse Daniels and at the same time as advising new mothers to rest in bed for six weeks after a confinement, an idea that would have appeared so impractical as to be laughable to most working-class women. These contradictions could be held together, if not reconciled, by shifting perspectives from gender, to class, to 'humanity', and by separating the forms in which Stopes articulated her perspectives. It was in her letters that she spoke to women personally as women, and in her published books that she expressed her more public politics. Letters have always been a way in which women have shared their personal lives and their intimacies, and Stopes' attempts to transgress this public/private boundary by personally disseminating *A Letter to Working Mothers* in 1919 were met with hostility. For us today, the play of voices in her work and the separations of form that allow these voices to speak simultaneously offer insights into the ways a middle-class and conservative woman negotiated the conflicting demands of gender, class and 'humanity'. In doing so, as Weeks suggests, Stopes removed birth control from its associations with radicalism and 'free love', and made contraception palatable to wider sections of more conservative thought (Weeks, 1989, pp. 191, 192). This in turn was to benefit working-class women as birth control clinics were established and doctors became more willing to offer contraceptive advice. On the other hand, of course, Stopes' construction of the poor as 'stunted, warped and inferior' reinforced and reinscribed differences between women, differences predicated upon the regressive discourses of social Darwinism.

The point I am making is that whilst female social investigators and welfare workers were concerned to regulate as well as help working-class women, this cannot be understood simply in terms of middle-class scrutiny or voyeurism. Educated women such as Margery Spring Rice, Eleanor Rathbone and Marie Stopes were genuinely concerned at the plight of the poor, and whilst they recognised the benefits of appropriating to themselves as women a public voice on such issues (Stopes rather more than most was an inveterate self-publicist), they devoted this public voice to alleviating what were real social issues. Yet the politics of all their endeavours could only be experienced within their own consciousness and imagination; a consciousness that was formed from the cultural and social expressions of class as well as gender. The politics of middle-class feminists and welfare workers, whether from the left or the right, were devoted on the one hand to encouraging working-class women to adopt what they perceived as the normative behaviours of middle-class life; on the other hand they were equally concerned to maintain the distance necessary to sustain their own class position. The dynamic thus generated made it possible for educated women to insist on the importance of material factors in the domestic life of the working-class family – income, food, clothing, furniture, medicine – whilst in the next breath condemning working-class women for living their lives too much in the material world and failing to nurture 'a rich inner life'. Pearl Jephcott, writing in 1943, expressed her belief that after the war working-class young women must be

> people who draw on deeper sources of satisfaction than those which material possessions can provide, but who, at the same time, are determined that when gay clothes, electric dryers, tennis courts and hiking holidays are again available, they shall be shared equally among those who need them (Jephcott, 1943, p. 169).

This polarisation of 'inner' life and material necessity shaped the ways in which educated women as well as their male counterparts were able to understand the lives of the poor. The cultural narratives thus produced circulated and amplified versions of 'the working-class housewife' that, over time, produced a moral distinction between her need for material comforts and her *desire* for such objects. In these stories, when need became desire, the possibility of a spiritual, 'inner' life was reduced. Yet of course, by maintaining the circulation of narratives that refused the working-class housewife an 'inner' life, the distance between those who 'desire Mozart and Einstein' and those who desire 'baths and ovens' could be sustained (Woolf, 1931/1977, pp. xxi, xxviii).

PRIVATE SPACES

We return to Muriel Jones' difficulty in expressing her understanding of the distinctions between privacy and friendliness:

> They were friendly [the people in Rednal]. I think they were less friendly. . . . They were friendly during the war. Everyone knew one another during the war. But they kept themselves more to themselves than in the terraces. They seemed a bit inclined to . . . they didn't want people to know what was in their house.

It is significant how she uses the pronoun 'they'. 'They' signified 'others', people who are not simply not 'me' but not 'us'. In almost the next breath Muriel goes on to talk about 'we', by which she means the members of her immediate family – in other contexts she uses 'we' to signify her friends at school and later, as a young woman, her work-mates. The flexibility of allegiances that her use of pronouns suggests is significant for understanding the way in which she perceived herself both in relation to the shifting social groupings she occupied – at any one time these might consist of family, schoolmates, female friends and/or workmates – and in relation to those outside these groupings; a frequently unspecified 'they', whose membership was never fixed. For example, family might in one configuration be understood as 'us'; in another, where parents were invoked as authority figures, the same family members might be configured as 'they'. Moreover 'they' could equally refer to those (that is, parents, teachers, welfare workers) who held and sometimes withheld necessary information and knowledge – 'they told us nothing' (about sex and reproduction); 'they just gave you instructions' (supervisor at the laundry where Muriel worked) and, in doing so, offered certain versions of femininity. 'They' might equally signify an undifferentiated 'public' that did not fall into an easily named category such as 'family', and in this sense 'they' could refer to males when they were perceived in a sexual context rather than as companions, playmates or, and this is significant, husbands: '*They* were all men up there (at work) and I was inclined to be very bashful in those days', as opposed to 'When I was about 16 or 17 I can remember a group of *us* and the boys dug holes in this field and then covered the holes over with grass'.[5]

For Muriel the world was divided into those who provided a sense of belonging and safety and those who might wield power through their possession and use of knowledge withheld from or unknown to Muriel. Yet, as the above suggests, the boundaries of this division were never fixed, hence her anxiety and ambivalence about calling a neighbour 'Auntie'. 'Them' in working-class culture has often been taken to signify middle-class officialdom and authority as opposed to the pronoun 'us', which encodes a sense of a cohesive group based around a consciousness of class (Hoggart, 1958). However Muriel's usage is far more fluid than this class polarisation suggests, and articulates the sense in which identity as working class and as a woman was organised around fluid and shifting relationships that were as equally concerned with age, family position and sexuality. Negotiating the network of power effects thus created often required a refusal of relation and connection in order to sustain the behaviours expected and necessary in order to identify as a 'good woman'.

Muriel learned early the importance of 'making your own way' in a world where certain kinds of knowledge were shrouded in mystery, withheld or metered out in small measures. When Muriel, like many of the women interviewed, insisted that 'we didn't *know* anything', she referred not only to knowledge of her sexual and physiological functions but also to a wider knowledge about the material and psychological realities of life as a working-class women at a specific historical moment. Learning to 'know' what older working-class women knew meant recognising the importance of reserve, restraint and thrift, both economic and emotional. It also meant learning to stand up for yourself and learning how to be a 'fighter'. Equally, it meant 'forgetting' desires for intimacy and connection and learning to understand these as 'immature' and 'silly'. As one woman commented, 'we didn't know anything at all, we just picked it up as we went along'. This sense of 'having to stand on your own feet' and 'make your own way' coexisted with an equally powerful sense of conforming to what was expected of you. Recalling leaving school and starting her first job, Muriel observed:

> You didn't just go and look for a job yourself . . . the parents usually went with you. It was expected and they said 'we'll go and have a look at this job' and Mother said 'Yes I think that'll be alright' and you just went. You didn't have any say in it and I don't think you expected to.

Independence and dependence were the poles between which women such as Muriel constructed a sense of themselves. On the one hand recognising the need to assert themselves in order to negotiate dignity from their social position, whilst at the same time appropriating and adapting the cultural narratives of respectability from which they might construct an acceptable sense of identity. 'Keeping yourself to yourself' was one way in which 'making your own way' and conforming to expected behaviours might be achieved.

Asserting yourself as yourself was also one of the ways in which working-class women contested cultural narratives and stereotypes that diminished them both as women and as working class. Muriel, as the youngest in a family of three boys, recalled that until she started work at 14 her family always referred to her as 'Girlie', thus naming her according to her sex and family position. It wasn't until she started work that she was able to insist on being called by her 'proper' name:

I was always called 'Girlie' right up till I started work and then I said 'I'm not going to let anyone call *me* that. Anyone doesn't call me by my right name I'm not answering' and I wouldn't, I wouldn't answer anyone who didn't call me Muriel!

Mary Porter, whose stepfather was a chemist and affluent enough to employ a maid of all work, remembered that 'we always had a maid and we always called her Peggy. No matter which one we had she was always called Peggy'. Dignity, self-sufficiency and reserve were ways of insisting on an individuated identity and resisting imposed subjectivities that represented such women as collectively 'girls' or 'maids'. In such circumstances 'keeping yourself to yourself' was about protecting and sustaining a beleaguered self from the range of inscriptions offered by the numerous forms of authority (parental, heterosexual, welfare, educational) that attempted to regulate identity and behaviour.

Gladys Hutchings spent her childhood in the city streets and terraces of pre-First World War York. She was the middle child of seven, two of whom died in infancy, and there was never very much money despite her mother's frugality and thrift. When Gladys married Fred in 1929 his secure job as a grocery assistant allowed them to buy one of the new semi-detacheds in the suburbs of York. When asked if people were friendly on the new estate Gladys replied:

We all knew that if anybody wanted anything we would have all helped – there was a friendly atmosphere. But there was not the running in and out of everybody's houses. We felt we had come up one.

Gladys had left behind what she perceived as the less evolved, chaotic, unrestrained life-style of the city streets 'to move from the background, not that it wasn't a good one . . . there was so much love, to something just that little bit better'. This was not simply understood as geographical and material progress but also as psychological growth. Gladys' reference to 'running in and out of everybody's houses' suggests childlike, less mature behaviours that have been put aside for the rational and mature dignity of 'a friendly atmosphere' in the privacy of the suburbs. This draws on and in doing so challenges those narratives which, for example in the district nurse's account above, interpellated 'the poor' as childlike dependants. It was not only 'popping in and out', gossiping and living more publicly on the streets that Gladys believed signfied less-evolved behaviours. Like many of the women I interviewed, Gladys believed in restraint, caution and common sense and repudiated sentimentality or excessive emotion as 'soppy' and immature. Common sense, like 'the facts of life' was one of those things you learned the hard way; as Dot Pearce said, 'common sense, it all boils down to common sense in the end'. Common sense dictated that keeping your private life to yourself was prudent: the public and relatively more relational nature of life in the city streets (as they perceived it) was, as women such as Gladys and Dot well knew, easily invaded and defined by authorities and 'experts' in the form of police, teachers, welfare workers and health visitors, as well as by the moral standards of the street community.

Gladys and Dot also knew that the focus of social and moral attention was the home and their role as upholders of its moral values as well as its material comforts. One of the potential but unspoken rewards of a home of their own was a degree of freedom from the critical surveillance of authority, whether in the form of parents, 'experts' or local gossip. As a consequence women such as Gladys and Dot were concerned to invest considerable time and energy in protecting both their emotional and physical privacy – they had 'grown up' and the marker of this was their emotional thriftiness; their insistence on the right to authorise their own identity; and a demand that this self-sufficiency be awarded appropriate recognition.

That they were able to do so was due to the historical moment and the cultural legacy they inherited. Women, like Dot and Gladys, could not 'operate as autonomous cultural actors, as interrogatory voices existing outside of power or outside the system of cultural production' (Walkowitz, 1992, p. 244). The possibilities for self definition were generated in the whole process of cultural dynamics which, as we have seen, produced and circulated representations of gender and class, power and powerlessness, authority and sexuality, and in which all social actors participated. Writing in *The Psychological Care of Infant and Child* the behavioural psychologist, John Watson, advised parents on the 'sensible way of treating children':

Never hug and kiss them, never let them sit in your lap. If you must, kiss them once on the forehead when they say goodnight. Shake hands with them in the morning. Give them a pat on the head if they have made an extraordinarily good job of a difficult task. Try it out;

in a week's time you will find how easy it is to be perfectly objective with your child and at the same time kindly. You will be utterly ashamed of the mawkish, sentimental way you have been handling it [sic] (Watson, cited in Newson and Newson, 1970, p. 429).

Alison Light has suggested that this retreat from intense emotion, this refusal of 'sentiment', which began in the 1920s as a radical challenge not only to the imperialist project that ended in the carnage of the Great War, but to those modes of sexual difference which underlay nineteenth century thought, could become a withdrawal into the isolation and 'safety first' of private life (Light, 1991, pp. 210, 211; Giles, 1993, p. 245). And I would add, as in Watson's vision, could result in an attempt to negate those very sexual differences perceived as constituting the core upon which the formation of 'self' rested and whose representation had been so volubly produced, disseminated and circulated by Victorian culture. In this scheme masculine heroics, as suggested earlier, could be rewritten as optimism and endurance and reimagined in the figure of the cheerful housewife; a figure whose counterpart was the 'little man', more concerned with his family, his home, his garden and his locality than with great public events.

Whilst, as Light has shown, the increased attachment to a certain form of self-sufficient private life in the years between the wars was represented as the values and behaviours of the middle classes, the significance and value given to the role of the housewife in this vision of a privatised and desexualised home life created a cultural space in which working-class women could expropriate the self-definition 'housewife' as a means of asserting their own relationship to an acceptable form of femininity (Light, 1991; Giles, 1992, 1993). Indeed it was precisely those skills so long practised by many working-class wives which were now being celebrated as 'true' femininity. The competent, cheerful manager of a small house and family without the help of servants was a preferred version of womanliness: the skills of home-making were revalued as 'housecraft' and 'domestic science', and the housewife was offered social status as a quasi professional worker in a skilled occupation. Coupled with a general disavowal of excessive emotion and 'sentiment', these cultural ideals produced a space in which women such as Gladys, Muriel and Dot could both assert a dignifying public identity and an internalised comfortable subjectivity as mature, restrained and self-sufficient housewives. In doing so there was the possiblity of transcending or, at least, leaving behind those forms of working-class female identity in which the experience and lives of women such as themselves were variously inscribed as childlike dependency, overburdened stoicism or closer to 'nature' and 'the animal'. However, as I shall argue, these attempts to participate in and thereby contest the prevailing cultural narratives of the period were never wholly successful nor completely achieved.

SEXUALITY AND PRIVACY

Victorian culture produced and circulated a multiplicity of discourses that attempted to define not only what constituted sexuality but where, when and with whom sexuality was acceptable (Foucault, 1978; Weeks, 1981/1989, 1985; Walkowitz, 1992). Central to this debate had always been the question of female sexuality and female sexual pleasure. The Victorian ideal that claimed female sexuality as synonymous with motherhood and otherwise non-existent was never comfortably complete and in the years leading up to the First World War was seriously challenged by feminists and 'freethinkers'. As Jeffrey Weeks has observed, there was 'a new zeal in defining and categorising sexuality' from the 1880s onwards (Weeks, 1989, p. 21; Bland, 1986; Walkowitz, 1980). The feminist politics of prostitution, the sensationalism of the 1888 Ripper murders, the newspaper scandal of W. T. Stead's 1885 exposé of child prostitution, 'The Maiden Tribute of Modern Babylon', and the development of theories of human sexuality via Havelock Ellis and Freud, *inter alia* produced the historical conditions in which discussion on and elaborations of human sexuality were very firmly part of the social and cultural agenda and, as Laqueur has noted, always rooted, as all discussions about sexuality are, in discussions about gender 'norms' (Laqueur, 1990, p. 11). Attempts to define sexual 'norms' and acceptable sexual practices focused on identifying new forms of conjugal heterosexuality not necessarily linked to procreation, and on specifying 'dangerous' sexualities as 'free love', same-sex relationships, prostitution or commercialised sexual relations and, after the First World War, 'frigidity', repression and permanent (heterosexual) celibacy (Walkowitz, 1992, pp. 5–6).

This reforming zeal continued throughout the early twentieth century with the popularisation of Freudian theories and the emergence of an 'expert' discourse on sexuality, voiced by a growing band of sexologists, who owed much to the work of early pioneers such as Havelock

Ellis and Edward Carpenter. In 1921 the first World Congress on Sex Reform met and was to lead in 1928 to the establishment of a World League for Sexual Reform. Although Marie Stopes and Norman Haire, chairman of the British section of the League, may have disagreed over issues of birth control, both were agreed that sexual harmony was important to a stable marriage and that sexual expression by both sexes (within marriage) was essential to, if not the core of, a sense of self-identity (Weeks, 1989, pp. 197–224).

This privileging of conjugal sexuality as the core of identity was a specific formation of Victorian bourgeois culture that found its full flowering in the years after the First World War with the emergence of sexual reform and its association with the most profound forms of self-expression. Marie Stopes wrote in elevated and lyrical terms of the fulfilment awaiting the sexually educated couple, and even those with a less cosmic view of the significance of sexual pleasure emphasised its centrality to a satisfactory private life:

> No matter what difficulties and troubles beset a married couple, if their sex life is harmonious in every way they will have a basis strong enough to overcome most obstacles (Edynbury, 1938, p. 176).

Although Ellen Holtzman has argued that many middle-class women insisted that, despite sexual disappointment, their marriages were happy, nonetheless the *ideal* of 'modern' marriage as firmly rooted in sexual pleasure produced a discourse in which to identify as someone's wife was to acknowledge a sexual relationship in a way that would have been unthinkable in the nineteenth century. The 'inner life' of bourgeois individualism was closely linked to and might be expressed via the deep feelings aroused in a sexually harmonious heterosexual and married relationship.

Edward Griffith's *Modern Marriage and Birth Control*, like Marie Stopes' *Married Love*, combined the religous and spiritual language of Christianity with the new insights provided by psychoanalysis and science to produce a discourse that presented married love as the highest expression of a spiritual self-identity (Griffith, 1938; Stopes, 1918). The foreword to Griffith's book warns that '[t]his book should not be read by those with Victorian minds, for it is outspoken on subjects that Victorians did not, and do not, mention' (Griffith, 1938, p. 11). *Modern Marriage and Birth Control* goes on to insist that married sex:

[q]uite apart from any reproductive purpose ... is essential to two
people who are in love with each other, and who desire a completely
satisfactory life. Thwarted and misused, it leads to disharmony and
unhappiness; developed and practised, with knowledge and apprecia-
tion, it grows until it ultimately provides for the couple who practise
it a happiness which it is almost impossible to describe. ... It is a
mystery which has to be learnt and understood, and the more we
learn about it, the more mysterious it becomes. Rightly used it is one
of God's greatest gifts; wrongly used, it is man's greatest curse
(Griffith, 1938, p. 22).

Dr Griffith's book, published as a Left Book Club edition by Gollancz
and therefore available only on subscription, had by 1938 gone into its
eighth impression. The Left Book Club, founded by Victor Gollancz in
1936, published works that addressed serious social issues of the day
from a left-wing perspective and by 1937 had a membership of 50 000
(Stevenson and Cook, 1979, pp. 75, 139). It opened up a market for
progressive and radical thought that confronted not only unemployment
and foreign policy but also issues such as birth control and 'modern'
sexual relations. As a result of its left-wing leanings, the Club was at
times under surveillance by Special Branch officers reporting to Scotland Yard (ibid., p. 226). Griffith's view of marriage, located within
this broad sweep of 'progressive' thought, whilst potentially radical for
women in its insistence on sexual pleasure for both partners and its
support for birth control (the appendix gives a full list of voluntary and
municipal clinics where birth control advice was available and is cau-
tiously sympathetic to the issue of legalising abortion), ultimately continues to locate sexuality within heterosexual marriage and a conservative
theology.

Whilst female reformers such as Janet Chance, Marie Stopes and
Margaret Llewelyn Davies were concerned, on one level, that meaning-
ful sexual relationships in marriage should be available to all women,
as women, this concern was undermined by an equally compelling belief
that it was as housewives (not wives in the sense suggested above) and
mothers that working-class women required help, advice and reforms
(Chance, 1931; Stopes, 1918; Llewelyn Davies, 1931). It was, as we
have seen, in their roles as mothers that working-class women were
most frequently represented and addressed in these years: where any
other form of working-class sexuality was discussed it was nearly always in terms of its problematic nature. As Jeffrey Weeks has argued,

these years saw the emergence of the psychologically based concept of 'sex delinquency', which included 'all forms of extra-marital sexual intercourse, from the crude practice of commercial prostitution through various degress of promiscuity to isolated cases of "sex adventure", or the anticipation of marriage relations' (Rolfe, cited in Weeks, 1989, p. 222). Where 'delinquency' was identified in girls it was always sexual and more often than not associated with those public spaces frequented by groups of working-class girls – the cinema, the dance hall and the street:

> it is no longer an indication of the absence of moral sense if an acquaintance made at a dance hall or cinema should ripen into friend-ship . . . even though such casual acquaintances may sometimes become partners in extra-marital sex relations (Rolfe, cited in Weeks, 189, p. 207).

Youth workers saw the solution as providing clubs and interests for working-class adolescents whose greater geographical freedom sup-posedly rendered them particularly susceptible to the temptations of 'sex delinquency':

> The girls who hang round the doors of the cinema or who sit about on the grass at the entrance to the aerodrome are losing their sense of proportion. They are becoming stale about men before they are women themselves (Jephcott, 1943, p. 133).

Official discourses linked sexual relations in working-class life either to motherhood or to adolescent promiscuity. In doing so the emerging cultural narrative of female sexual pleasure as a source of a satisfying private life was sealed off from working-class women who were of-fered instead stories of sexual danger or addressed as potential sexual predators.

Under these circumstances it was not easy for working-class women to find a way of inserting themselves into the prevailing discourses of personal identity defined as sexual. Personal identity for these women was shaped by the cultural representations available to them and adapted to fit comfortably with the social and historical conditions of their lives. Moreover, pregnancy both within and outside marriage was a constant anxiety for working-class women. Lack of adequate contraceptive ad-vice for married women and the fear of social stigma for single women rendered sexual intercourse a dangerous, rather than pleasurable, activity for working-class women. Aspirations for a better future could be seriously jeopardised by an extra mouth to feed or a premarital pregnancy. Even where husbands were 'careful and considerate', euphemisms for withdrawal and abstinence, fear of too many pregnancies and their consequences in terms of poverty and ill health was all-pervasive for women who had watched and experienced their mothers coping with large families. The transports of sexual delight exhorted by Stopes and Griffiths were less likely to appeal to women for whom 'being swept off your feet' was a fate too dangerous, however seductive, to contemplate for a consciousness formed from poverty and social exclusion. 'Keeping yourself to yourself' meant not only acquiring a self-sufficiency and independence in relationships with the public world of neighbours, welfare workers and authority figures, but it also signified a self-sufficiency and restraint in the most intimate and private relations.

Gertie Harris told me the story of her courtship as an example of the dangers of 'being swept off your feet'. Born in York in 1905 Gertie was the eldest daughter of a large family. Gertie's father was physically violent, was often drunk and rarely earned enough to keep her and her four siblings. Her mother took in washing and Gertie herself undertook a variety of casual jobs – such as hat trimming – for neighbours once she was old enough. Gertie loved dancing and became an expert ballroom dancer, entering and winning championships throughout Yorkshire. Her father disapproved of dancing and forbade her to dance, but Gertie, aided by her mother, would slip out when he was drunk or asleep and attend the dances she loved. Her enjoyment was a mixture of excitement, danger, the pleasures of potential romance and the glamour of the dance hall, as well as her pride in exercising her dancing skills:

> I was having a marvellous time and the men after you and you get to dance if you was a good dancer, and I was rather a pretty girl in them days, a lovely figure and everything, a lovely bust, and you could get dance band leaders [to dance with you] and I remember once Victor Sylvester's brother . . . and there was Sid Fay, the trumpeter, and Bobby Martin on the drums. You could go out with any of them!

When Gertie's regular boyfriend was sent overseas at the outbreak of the Second World War, Gertie continued to go dancing and eventually met Bernard. Bernard was ten years younger than her, and according to Gertie's account, good-looking, charming and a wonderful dancer. He 'swept her off her feet' and within three weeks she had written to her regular boyfriend of fifteen years, ending the courtship, and had married Bernard. Her parents were angry and disapproving of Bernard: they refused to attend the wedding and the ensuing estrangement was never fully mended, despite Gertie's care of her mother in her later years. After the birth of their three children, Bernard continued to go dancing and proved to be an unreliable provider. Gertie continues to castigate herself rather than Bernard for the disappointment of her marriage:

> Well, he [the boyfriend she dropped] would have made a good husband but I somehow didn't want to settle down. I was a fool when I look back, but as long as I could dance it didn't matter, all that mattered was going dancing and being dressed up and folk saying 'you look lovely tonight'. This is all that my life was, it was silly, it was a silly life, it was living in a cloud because you have to come down to earth . . . and I did – with a bang! We stayed together but things didn't . . .

Gertie presents her story as exemplifying her lack of caution and restraint – one moment of 'silliness' could lead to a lifetime of regret. Certainly, Gertie's story seems to illustrate the warnings of middle-class observers who saw in dance halls the dangers of an 'over-stimulated' sexuality and desire for romance:

> The dance hall offers the company of young people, an opportunity for rhythmical movement, a very considerable measure of emotional excitement, and, again, makes little demand on the dancer's mental capacity. The syncopated music, *Let There Be Love*, *Heart to Heart*, *You and Your Kiss*, the lowered lights, and the excitement of all the new contacts mean that for many young adolescents, the sex instinct is being over-stimulated at precisely the age when this should be avoided (Jephcott, 1943, pp. 124–5).

The dance hall, like the Monkey Run, was a place where young people might meet future partners. It was also one of those public spaces, like the urban street, which came under the scrutiny of middle-class observers, whose anxiety to 'expose' the sexual secrets of working-class life ensured their 'discovery'. For working-class girls such as Gertie, however, the dance hall offered a space in which dreams of romance, pride in a skill and excitement might be enjoyed whilst, simultaneously, allowing women the possibility of controlling the extent to which they involved themselves with men, via the respectable discourse of 'keeping yourself to yourself', which could be deployed to keep sexual danger and attraction at a distance. Gertie understood her 'mistake' as one of lack of prudence rather than one of excessive sexuality and she continues to castigate herself for what she calls her 'silliness'.[6]

Betty Walker, like Gladys Hutchings, moved out of the city streets to a new council house in the suburbs when she married. She and Ted deliberately limited their family to two children, because, as she said, 'Ted didn't want a big family, he wanted us to be *companions* to each other ... and so we did our best to regulate to what we could afford and cope with and it worked to a certain extent' (my emphasis). Betty also expressed forcibly her views on sexuality:

> all this promiscuity [today], I can't accept it. You earn your happiness, they have a jaundiced idea of what they can get away with today. Because when you were young, you were taught to keep a reserve, have restraint ... my attitude is that respect comes before love. If you respect each other well the other follows but if you don't respect them, well ...

Reserve, restraint, respect were the values that framed Betty's idea of private life; love was something to be earned, emotional thriftiness ensured this, and sexual pleasure was something likely to be punished (Betty believed that AIDS is retribution). Certainly, 'keeping yourself to yourself', emotionally and physically, fitted with contemporary discourses that constructed the 'modern' housewife as sensible, unemotional and prudent, and therefore offered a dignifying identity to those whose lives had been short on that quality. Moreover, 'keeping yourself to yourself' in sexual terms fitted neatly into the discourses of respectability and 'delinquency', within which the sexuality of working-class women was defined, and at the same time ensured the small family an outward sign of an inward respectability. As a Lancashire housewife commented:

> My own opinion is that people wish to have a small family on account of public opinion which has now hardened into custom. It is

customary – and has become so during the last twenty-five years or so – to have two children and no more if you can avoid it. A family of five or six children loses in prestige and, some think, in respectability (Mass Observation, 1945, p. 74).

Yet, as Betty commented, it only worked 'to a certain extent'. Betty and Ted had two children, with a long gap between, and their life together, as Betty represented it, had been harmonious and contented. She and Ted had had their own interests – he played cricket and Betty sang in the church choir – and she had enjoyed bringing up her two boys. However she wonders now if she would have liked more children and sees herself as having been 'selfish' in only having two, despite her insistence that Ted had only wanted two children. It is possible to speculate that 'selfish' in this context meant an unwillingness to engage in frequent intercourse: she commends Ted for being 'considerate', a euphemism for sexual abstinence, in order to limit their family. Betty also recalls the opportunity she had to go to work in London in order to train more fully as a photographer's assistant, work she gave up in order to earn more at Rowntrees, the chocolate factory. Her sons, she told me, accuse her of being 'a perfectionist' and 'over strict', and because of the considerable age difference between them they have never been close as brothers.

There is a sense of loss in Betty's account that is never overtly articulated (she 'keeps herself to herself') but expresses itself in regret for lost job opportunities, the lack of a close relationship with her sons and possibly with Ted, and a nostalgia for the pleasures of her childhood, which she represents as a time of community and closeness. Reserve and restraint may have worked to suppress sexual desire, and yearnings for a fuller life could be rationalised as 'selfish', but such internalisations were never complete. Betty's considerable energy and creativity (she enjoyed and enjoys drawing) found a possibly less than satisfactory outlet in the zeal with which she kept house, a zeal that was celebrated and encouraged by certain discourses of private life addressed to women and men in which wifehood and housewifery become conflated: 'happy and lucky is the man whose wife is houseproud . . . who likes to do things well, to make him proud of her and her children' (Housewife, 1939, cited in Weeks, 1989, p. 205). According to Betty, Ted 'liked his home to be comfortable, he liked to see it nice, he was proud of his home'.

The psychological internalisation as well as the social practices of 'keeping yourself to yourself' required that women saw *themselves*, as well as being seen, as sexual actors in limited and one-dimensional roles. Identifying as a 'housewife' rather than a wife allowed women to displace the sexual aspects of the conjugal relationship (which inevitably led to pregnancy) and to construct themselves solely in terms of their relationship to the material and the practical. As already discussed, the regulation and scrutiny of working-class women at this time consistently invited them to construct selfhood from a mass of material signifiers – dirt, disease, cleanliness, home, food, clothing – and to ally themselves with a suitably 'motherly' (and working-class) version of the home as the locus of material comfort rather than an expression of emotional, sexual or spiritual conjugality. In thus allying themselves, working-class women confirmed certain middle-class beliefs that a rich spiritual life was the prerogative of the educated. Hence middle-class observers were enabled to continue seeking signs of and deploring the lack of an 'inner' life in the psyche of the women they scrutinised, whilst working-class women continued to resist surveillance and probing by evasion, by 'keeping themselves to themselves' and by hiding their 'secrets'. The result was a greater and greater proliferation of cultural narratives that attempted to explain and fix this unknowable 'other' – 'the working mother'; 'the sex delinquent'; the 'good housewife'; the childlike, dependent young mother; the 'gold digger whore'; cheeky factory girls and so on.

Many of these narratives, of course, transgressed class boundaries and were primarily gendered in their attention to sexuality. Nonetheless the public focus of these discourses was nearly always organised around class: middle-class adolescent girls or housewives were far less likely to be the object of detailed scrutiny. The role of spectator or observer was classed as well as gendered: one of the hoped for rewards of suburban respectability was to be freer of surveillance *and* to become a surveiller of others. Hence Gladys, Dot and Betty defined themselves in terms of what they were not and in doing so both participated in prevailing discourses of respectability and produced further discursive fragments. They identified themselves as working class but not 'rough'; they had 'come up one'; they were different from those above and those below; neither did they perceive themselves as sexually active – 'goings on' were attributed to the upper classes or to 'common' people. Even Gertie, who momentarily transgressed these boundaries, later came to define herself within the terms of these discourses – 'I was silly', that is, sexually aware, immature and uncontrolled.

However, if respectability required that emotional intensity and sexual expression became 'secrets', the price of this safety and privacy was high. Intensity over children, sexual passion, close friendships with other women, intimacy of any kind could threaten prudence and reserve and hence the articulation or practice of such emotion was necessarily displaced and oblique, paralleled for some, like Betty, with a profound sense of loss of relationship. Gertie too reveals a sense of loss when she tells me that whenever she watches 'Come Dancing' on the television 'the tears trickle down my face', and Mabel Matthews expresses a similar loss with regard to her children:

> In some ways it's lovely today because mothers and daughters are so close and things, and children are closer because you talk and things. Well, we never discussed a thing with our children.

That the price of emotional thrift was high is testified to in the nostalgia invoked by all the women interviewed for 'the good old days' of childhood. It is surely not insignificant that in all the accounts of childhood the emphasis is on relationships and community, on shared activities, on communal outings and a sense of closeness. Given the grim and limited childhoods experienced by many interviewees, these 'good old days' have to be read as contradictory and fantasised versions of a profoundly desired memory. Yet this is not to deny their equal significance in the making of identity: such fantasies speak of a deeply desired past, no less unimportant because never fully achieved. Such fantasies of 'the good old days' articulate at some level that which a commitment to emotional thriftiness and necessary prudence has rendered unspeakable and perhaps forever lost: the desire for intimacy and connection and an emotional neediness that has had to remain suppressed and unassuaged.

4 Servant and Mistress: The Case of Domestic Service

In her introductory letter to *Life As We Have Known It* Virginia Woolf recognised the profound division that existed between women who could 'stroll through the house and say, that cover must go to the wash or those sheets need changing' (Woolf, 1931/1977, p. xxiv) and women who actually undertook the physical tasks of washing, ironing and cleaning, either in their own homes or in the homes of other women. For Woolf, the divisions she identified between those who kept servants and those who carried out the tasks of servants were too great and the gulf thus separating such women was, for her, unbridgeable in anything but the most superficial way. Equally Celia Fremlin, an Oxford graduate who found employment as a domestic servant during the 1930s in order to understand better the 'servant problem', concluded, in similar fashion to Woolf, that the social differences between women made any kind of friendly or informal relationship between mistress and servant impossible (Fremlin, 1940, p. 158).

This sense of an unbridgeable gap between women of different classes arose from and was sustained by the system of domestic service, which had been one of the most powerful institutions in the structuring of social relations between women throughout the nineteenth century. Despite the changing nature of domestic service in the first half of the twentieth century it nonetheless continued to provide a means of expressing and maintaining differences between women within the middle-class home – 'the very heart of "private life"' (Light, 1991, p. 219). I drew attention in the Introduction to the ways in which the signifiers of class difference between women organise themselves around the domestic, the home and the private life – 'servant', 'mistress', 'lady', 'woman', and, as Light has pointed out, it is terms coined directly from the rituals of domestic service that are still used to tease working-class girls with ambitions – 'little madam', 'her ladyship' (ibid., p. 220).

Before 1950 women of all classes would have been touched at some time in their lives by the system of domestic service, either as employers or servants, or as the daughters, grandaughters, nieces or sisters of employers or servants: the 1901 census records 1 691 000 females under the category 'domestic service' or 40 per cent of the employed female

132

population (Burnett, 1976, p. 140). Moreover, through marriage and intergenerational contact the experience and consciousness of former domestic servants might be transmitted to a wider family network (McBride, 1976, p. 120). Residential domestic service finally collapsed after the Second World War but, I would argue, its ramifications for women's sense of themselves in relation to their domestic role and the place and value of that role in society more generally were far-reaching. Ideas about the value and worth of home-making and house-wifery; about authority within the home; and about appropriate class and gender behaviours and attitudes within and to the home were shaped, sustained, sometimes resisted and frequently made sense of via the cultural narratives and social experiences of domestic service.

The positing of a dynamic and fluid relationship between self and society such as that provided in the work of Giddens and Foucault (see Introduction) is useful for a more complex analysis of the ways in which social relations between women, such as those which obtained in the system of domestic service, might be worked out, experienced and narrated in the lives of individual women, without recourse to concepts of static and impositional power. The ways in which women of all classes in the early twentieth century constituted themselves in relation to the structures of their society were shaped by the patterns of relating suggested by cultural forms and specific social groups. One of these patterns was the system of domestic service, which proposed differential modes of understanding and experience for mistresses and servants, but equally suggested different forms of relating between women within the system, between women not within the system of domestic service and between men and women positioned differently to the structures of domestic service.

Many domestic servants, whilst recognising the exploitative and subordinate nature of their occupation, did not perceive themselves only or always as powerless, although at times they may have done so. Rather they viewed their relations with their employer as presenting opportunities in which they might interpret their position in ways that were self-dignifying and positive through the exercise of variously chosen individual acts of competence, defiance and even, as we shall see, affection. Furthermore, women who employed domestic servants did not always view this function as an exercise of power: it was as equally likely to be understood as a burden and a responsibility that could place middle-class women at the mercy of their servants. Women who employed servants might express these anxieties through fantasies of powerlessness as well as through articulations of their authority or lack of it.

This chapter will consider various articulations of the experience of domestic service and its significance in constituting specific identities within the interpretive framework just established. It is therefore intended to focus on the relationships of women as they were understood, expressed, enjoyed, resisted and challenged through the structures of domestic service at a specific historical moment when the social relations underpinning domestic service were in a state of flux. First, it is necessary to examine the historical landscape in which women's experience and understanding of domestic service was located in the first half of the twentieth century. From there I shall move to considering the desires and fantasies expressed via narratives of domestic service; fantasies that formed themselves around notions of the home, the servant, service and which, whilst implicating class and gender subjectivities, were not reducible to either one or both of these social relations but were also constituted around issues of age and historical moment. To this end the chapter concludes with two stories that concern themselves centrally with domestic service: one by Doris Arthurs, who worked, when young, as a servant for the Lord Mayor of Birmingham and as a daily non-residential 'help' after her marriage and the birth of her only child; the other, *Rebecca*, by Daphne Du Maurier in which the figure of the terrifying and sinister housekeeper, Mrs Danvers, articulates, I would argue, the deep-seated fears and fantasies that could attend the practice of servant-keeping. Both stories articulate fantasies of power and powerlessness specific to the historical moment that they recall.

DOMESTIC SERVICE IN THE EARLY TWENTIETH CENTURY

The Victorian system of domestic service reached its apogee between 1851 and 1871. As the middle classes grew in size and wealth the number of domestic servants increased out of proportion to the population as a whole, with the largest increases occurring amongst the most specialised branches of service such as nursemaids, housekeepers and cooks (Burnett, 1976, p. 138; McBride, 1976, p. 112). By 1951 only 724 000 females were categorised as 'indoor domestic servants' and most of these would have been general servants (Burnett, 1976, p. 142).

Although the demise of domestic service is often taken as having occurred between the wars in England, before the end of the First World War middle-class grumblings could be heard on the subject of 'the servant problem'. Vera Brittain, returning home on leave, recalled that the 'universal topic of maids and ration cards now completely dominated the conversation' (Brittain, cited in Beaumann, 1983, p. 107). Even before the end of the nineteenth century observers had commented on the unwillingness of young women to enter domestic service and proposals were made both to improve the conditions of domestic service and to encourage women to enter it (Glucksmann, 1990, p. 244; *How to Improve the Conditions of Domestic Service* by a Servant, 1894: Booth, 1903). Moreover, the weakening economic position of some middle-class families from the 1880s onwards and a growing desire to privatise domestic life may have resulted in a decline in the demand for domestic servants, although such a drop in demand never matched the lack of residential servants to hire and numerous initiatives in the interwar years by successive governments, both Conservative and Labour, failed to recruit to the occupation (McBride, 1976, p. 67). In 1923 the Ministry of Labour reported on the 'Present Conditions as to the Supply of Female Domestic Servants', recommending a variety of means by which young women might be encouraged to enter domestic service; domestic training centres and junior instruction centres encouraged unemployed young women to enter the occupation; elementary schools offered a full programme of domestic training in housewifery, cooking and infant care for working-class girls; and in some areas local committees were established to regulate conditions of employment.

Nonetheless the older patterns of residential domestic service continued to change. The exact point at which domestic service began to decline and the reasons for this have been the subject of some debate. Pam Taylor argues that as late as 1931 23 per cent of employed women were engaged in domestic service and that its final demise was halted until after the Second World War; others have argued for the First World War as the watershed, with a gradually diminishing pool of servants up until 1939 (Taylor, 1979, pp. 121–39; Burnett, 1976, pp. 135–42; McBride, 1976, pp. 111–16). The latter position sees the increased census figures for 1931 as a localised response to the depression rather than evidence of long-term trends (McBride, 1976, p. 112; Burnett, 1976, p. 141; Glucksmann, 1990, p. 246). However, despite debates over timing, what is indisputable is the sense of crisis and middle-class anxiety over 'the servant problem' manifested in government initiatives, in the fiction of the period and in localised attempts to urge young women into service. As I shall argue, it is probably more fruitful to consider this anxiety in terms of the changing nature of service and its implications for social relations between women rather than simply in terms of its absolute decline.

Whilst there is no doubt that the system of residential domestic service in its nineteenth century conception changed over the first half of the twentieth century, I would argue that the attitudes, ideas and beliefs that underpinned domestic service reshaped themselves into reformulated concepts of 'service' and employment, both inside and outside the home but always organised around tasks associated with homemaking, comfort and housewifery. In other words it very much depends what was meant by the term 'domestic servant': the 1931 Census records 1 926 978 'persons engaged in personal service', of whom 1 332 224 were classified as 'indoor domestic servants', 127 647 as 'laundry workers, washers, ironers, manglers, dry cleaners' and 140 146 as 'charwomen, office cleaners'.

From the late nineteenth century onwards the large middle-class home staffed by a hierarchy of servants was giving way to the prevailing norm of the interwar years – a general maid who might be expected to cook, clean and care for small children, and who would certainly be expected to do 'the rough' work of step cleaning, coal carrying, scrubbing and general cleaning. By the early twentieth century the changing composition of the middle class from entrepreneurial business families to the families of salaried professional workers meant a decline in the income available for the forms of conspicuous consumption associated with the Victorian middle classes in their heyday. Moderate-income middle-class families were unlikely to be able to afford more than 'a daily', whilst many lower-middle-class families (many of whom would have been the new suburbanites) might only be able to afford occasional 'charring help' or a 'step lady' (Glucksmann, 1990, p. 251; Elias, 1978, p. 31).

'Servant-keeping' was still a signifier of social status but its forms were changing: far fewer families employed more than one maid and far fewer families employed large numbers of live-in servants. Personal service in the form of hairdressing, clothes valeting and beauty treatments were taking place outside the home; smaller families required fewer nursery staff; and the increasing availability of labour-saving devices enabled middle-class women on moderate incomes to maintain their own homes with a minimum of servant help. Nonetheless, for many women some form of personal and domestic service to more affluent women and their families was a central experience of their lives, as daily helps, as maids in private boarding schools and private nursing homes, as hairdressers, as cleaners and charwomen in hospitals and hotels as well as private homes, as laundresses, as waitresses, as step ladies and as shop assistants. Many women as young girls had experienced the social relations attendant upon the system of domestic service through helping their mothers with washing, ironing and cleaning for better-off families. Lizzie Smith, for example, recalled, as a child, helping her mother scrub the steps and front paths of the prosperous homes of York's professional families: she spoke of these families with deference and respect whilst recalling the pride and dignity both she and her mother felt in being able to 'serve' such families. Service for Lizzie was not understood nor experienced as oppressive and exploitative. Like many ex-servants she created an alternative set of positive values through which to interpret her experience.

The first half of the twentieth century witnessed not only a change in the forms of domestic and personal service, but a related shift in the 'official' status and value of service. By the 1920s there were few residential male servants except in the most wealthy and aristocratic households; domestic service was almost completely a female occupation, unlike in the eighteenth or early to mid-nineteenth centuries when to be a gentleman's valet was a position of some importance and the employment of male servants was a very real possibility for the wealthier middle classes. Employment of male servants was throughout the eighteenth and nineteenth centuries a mark of high social status and the sons of artisans or farmers could find a respected social position in such employment. William Tayler, for example, was the son of a yeoman farmer. In the mid-nineteenth century he received a salary of 40 guineas a year and his diary reveals him to be literate, intelligent and respected by his employers, to the extent of treating him to a visit to the theatre (Burnett, 1976, pp. 175–85).

By the 1920s and 1930s residential domestic service in a private home was, except in the wealthiest households, to be a maid-of-all-work and such employment generally went to young women of school leaving age with little education and few opportunities for other employment. Girls from families hit by the interwar depression, girls from orphanages and girls from the 'depressed' areas of Wales and the north-east, where there was little female employment even at times of prosperity, made up the pool of residential maids, often migrating to the new centres of affluence in the Midlands and south-east, to seaside and spa resorts, and to the residential areas of large cities such as Birmingham and London, which were less affected by depression and unemployment.

Whilst the number of young women aged between 15 and 25 entering residential domestic service was declining, this was accompanied by an increase in the number of older women, aged 40 and over, entering domestic service on a non-residential, daily basis, often part-time, as cleaners and 'charwomen'. The census for 1931 records 140 146 women categorised as 'charwomen', 9.9 per cent of the whole 'servant class', and this figure almost certainly underrepresents the numbers actually thus employed (Census, 1931, pp. 112–16). 'Charring' was frequently undertaken in order to supplement family income and its part-time, daily nature fitted well with childcare and home commitments; as such it must often have gone unreported to census enumerators. Like the general maid, the charwoman was often represented as a figure of ridicule and condescension. The 'Mrs Mop' of numerous novels and films was an elderly version of the adenoidal young maid found in many fictions of the period. Despite attempts by various agencies to reformulate them as skilled, quasi-professional occupations, signalled most notably in the appellation of 'housecraft' to the subject as taught in elementary schools, both forms of domestic service were frequently represented in the public media as unskilled and undervalued female occupations. Whilst the fictional conventions and cultural discourses for representing male servants emphasise an equality of intelligence, wit and resourcefulness between man and master, mid-twentieth century representations interpellated female servants as comic and often unattractive figures. It is only necessary to contrast P. G. Wodehouse's Jeeves with the numerous housemaids of Agatha Christie's detective fiction to see the difference.

However the increased visibility of domestic service as employers' discourses of anxiety continued to construct both the occupation and its employees as a 'problem', made possible changes that not only altered the forms of service but shifted the relations around which these forms were organised. The growth in non-residential domestic service placed domestic service employment on the kind of contractural basis of other waged labour. Daily cleaners agreed to work a set number of hours for a set payment and, unlike their residential counterparts, they could stipulate specific times when they were not available. Employers could no longer assert moral custody over their servants, neither could they easily regulate the activities of their servants outside working hours, and the practice of wages in kind, in the form of board and lodging, was no longer applicable. Professional and affluent women who previously would have employed servants increasingly expected to perform domestic tasks with the aid of new technology and appliances whilst poorer women were drawn out of the private economy of the domestic household into factory or public sector employment. Women who in the previous century would have swept their employers' carpets were now producing the components that would provide their erstwhile employers with vacuum cleaners. Working-class women, of course, had always performed their own domestic labour: in one sense the changes taking place in the conditions under which middle-class women experienced domesticity brought the two classes closer in relation to the task of maintaining and sustaining the domestic sphere. As Glucksmann has observed:

> The difference between the two classes became more one of the relative size of their income and the greater relative purchasing power of the middle class, rather than of one class employing the other. Both middle and working classes became integrated into the circuit of capitalist consumption in the same way. These trajectories of the two classes were linked through the shift of women out of domestic into capitalist employment which reduced the pool of potentially available domestic servants, and in turn stimulated commodity purchase on the part of the middle class (Glucksmann, 1990, p. 254).

The effect of the changes in domestic service resulted in long-term changes in the relations between middle- and working-class women, providing spaces in which it became possible to challenge the injustices of the system at the same time as more deeply embedding the divisions in self-identification between those who did their own washing and those who had it done for them:

> It is singularly hard on the women of us that, just when the workers' wages are pushed right down to the fodder level and below, there should be such ingenious and delightful devices put on the market for easing kitchen labour. . . . As I say excellent. But only the women who don't do their own washing can afford it. A splendidly arranged world, isn't it? (writer in *Daily Herald*, 3 February 1922, cited in Bourke, 1994, p. 69).

Despite the increasingly contractual and non-residential nature of domestic service such employment was of a particularly servile and dependent nature, experienced directly in day-to-day contacts and manifested through expected behaviours and attitudes. Servants were called by a common Christian name such as 'Peggy' or 'Mary' and maids were expected to wear a uniform, consisting of dress, apron and cap, which, though never formalised in the way nurses' uniforms were, was tacitly accepted as standard across the country. Obedience, deference and invisibility were the qualities demanded of residential servants; most young women entering domestic service learned not 'to chime in with the conversation or smile or let on you were interested at all. You had to keep sort of strong-faced. I was always getting in a row about that' (cited in Taylor, 1979, p. 134).

Every girl growing up in the first half of the twentieth century would have been touched in some way by the psychological and cultural manifestations of an all-pervasive system of personal and domestic services rendered by one group of women to another; a system that paralleled and intersected their experience and understanding of their own family relations, focusing as both relations did on authority/deference and organised around those material and economic factors which constituted different understandings of the concept of home for different groups of women. Fourteen year old girls, whether from affluent or poorer homes, were subject to the authority of older women as, for example, mothers, mistresses, teachers, nannies, youth workers or matrons in boarding schools.

Such relationships were organised around age but were also constantly striated by the asymmetries of class. A young middle-class girl could find herself at times in a position of subordination to an older servant, as for example in the relationship of a young charge to a nanny; young working-class girls experienced relations of authority and deference with their mothers, which prepared them for similar relationships as domestic servants (Taylor, 1979, pp. 126–30). It was conceivable that a woman could move across a range of these relationships during her lifetime: for example, a young working-class girl might move from an authoritarian parental home to become servant in a middle-class home; later she could marry and become, via a degree of social mobility, the mistress of a maid-of-all-work. Keeping a servant was a rigid index of social and economic status and defined precisely the kinds of home that a women might experience at different times in her life as daughter, servant, mistress, wife or mother. Rowntree, in his

1901 survey of York, drew the boundary between the working and the middle class at the point of servant-keeping, even to employ one general maid or 'skivvy' was to signify membership, albeit at the lower end, of the middle class:

> The investigation did not extend to the servantkeeping class, and necessarily did not include domestic servants living away from their homes. Indeed the keeping or not keeping of domestic servants has in this inquiry been taken as marking the division between the working classes and those of a higher social scale (Rowntree, 1901, p. 14).

As a result of the social and historical changes that have made such practices and significations more or less obsolete, it is difficult for us to understand the ways in which domestic service regulated and organised certain forms of consciousness between women. Giddens distinguishes between practical knowledge and discursive knowledge, that is, between the tacit knowledges that allow people to 'get on' with their daily, routine lives and those 'second order' or discursive knowledges that are used by social actors to narrate and describe daily activities (Giddens, 1984, pp. 4, 7, 284). 'Getting to know what actors already know and have to know to "go on" in the daily activities of social life' is, of course, made harder when historical circumstances mediate that understanding, and any analysis of women's accounts of domestic service as either maid or mistress has to bear witness to the difficulties of hearing those tacitly understood knowledges from a distance of more than fifty years (Giddens, 1984, pp. 284). Nonetheless, even if we may not know, we are not debarred from judicious imaginings based on close attention to the iconography and language of oral and written accounts. What then did women know and understand about domestic service and how might they use this knowledge in order to make sense of social relations between women and of their own relationship to the idea of home and domesticity?

'THE SERVANT PROBLEM'

In April 1929 Virginia Woolf recorded in her diary:

> I am sordidly debating within myself the question of Nelly, the perennial question. It is an absurdity, how much time L and I have

wasted in talking about servants. And it can never be done without because the fault lies in the system (Woolf, 1977, p. 220).

For Woolf, talking about servants was 'sordid', 'absurd' and a waste of precious time. Yet she accepted her dependency on domestic help as inevitable and unchangeable: 'the fault lies in the system'. Servantkeeping was essential in Woolf's view, firstly because she would have been unable to write without domestic help. Indeed, as Quentin Bell explains, even for the affluent the 'processes of cooking and cleaning were incredibly laborious, messy and slow' before the easy availability of refrigerators, electricity, processed and frozen foods, and constant hot water; 'in these circumstances someone must be perpetually at work if any kind of comfort or cleanliness is to be maintained' (Bell, 1972, p. 55). Secondly, because to be in a position to talk about 'the servant problem', however 'absurd', was, of course, to be distinguished from 'the servant class'. Thirdly, because the ministrations of servants were, at least in part, materially responsible for enabling the privacy that Woolf felt to be essential to her imagination and her writing: 'I must be private, secret, as anonymous and submerged as possible in order to write' (cited in Gordon, 1984, p. 5).

This consciousness in which a right to privacy and service coexisted with a sense of difference and division was produced and expressed from and through cultural narratives of comfort and well-being whose central icons were the middle-class domestic hearth and the hands, fantasised as invisible but somehow always worryingly visible, which maintained privacy, order and plenitude:

> So there we were and rooms were clean and tidy, the meals were cooked and served, orders to shops were delivered on time and there were at least three posts a day, all based on our being at the top end of the class structure (Mitchison, 1979, p. 28).

For women such as Virginia Woolf and Naomi Mitchison a significant and powerful element of self-identity was produced from the very heartland of 'private' life – the middle-class home. They were able to identify and recognise themselves as belonging to a specific social group via their insertion in a domestic order that, whilst their responsiblity, required only that they be there to enhance and supervise it. Both Mitchison and Woolf were feminists who in other places attacked the worst excesses of certain versions of bourgeois Victorian femininity –

Woolf attacked the disabling and paralysing effects of 'the Angel in the House' and Mitchison wrote openly about the possibilities of sexual pleasure for women, both within and outside marriage (Woolf, 1931; Dyhouse, 1989, pp. 179–80). It was not that either were unaware of the exploitations and exclusions of class; Mitchison was deeply concerned with working-class housing in the 1930s and Woolf, despite her general ambivalence towards political activism and her condescending tone, was in broad sympathy with the aims of the Women's Co-operative Guild (Dyhouse, 1989, pp. 186–87; Woolf 1931/1977; Barrett, 1993, pp. xliii–xlix). Mitchison, recalling her girlhood, comments 'Dusters, soap, soda? These belonged to another world', and it was this consciousness of being separated from the world of household chores and daily drudgery that produced a specific sense of self in these women. Their relation to the domestic was not understood in terms of physically *doing* housework nor even in terms of practical homemaking, but in terms of their authority (or lack of it) in supervising via servants the production of meals and the maintenance of cleanliness, and in organising a certain degree of privacy for themselves in which they might, as Woolf expressed it, seek 'the synthesis of my being' perhaps via writing, politics, or other self-fulfilling activities (Woolf, cited in Gordon, 1984, p. 7).

Although the activities in which Woolf and Mitchison engaged were broadly feminist and, with Mitchison, socialist, this desire for and understanding of the home as a private space in which they could, as women, carry out the roles and responsiblities expected of them, whilst maintaining some time and space in which to sustain a degree of independence was not the exclusive property of a socialist or radical imagination. Woolf recognised her need to 'kill' that self-denying readiness to be available to all-comers if she was to find any route to self-determination – the search for privacy and solitude in which to 'be oneself' has been a consistently articulated need of middle-class woman (Woolf, 1931).

The First World War had loosened those Victorian conventions which prevented middle-class women from moving freely around their environment or undertaking paid work; the emotional and educational needs of child-rearing were not yet perceived solely as the responsibility of middle-class mothers; and the drudgery of housewifery could still, despite servant shortages, be relegated to cooks, parlourmaids and general maids. Middle-class women before the Second World War were well placed to enjoy a degree of autonomy from marriage, motherhood and housework that had not been available to their mothers and was to prove impossible for their servantless daughters of the 1950s and 1960s – middle-class women in the 1930s could find autonomy, dignity and 'that retreat into self-containment which has often been a woman's vision of paradise' within the well-ordered routines of domestic life (Light, 1991, p. 127).

Nettie Holland, the wife of a Lancashire solicitor, employed a maid-of-all-work and her only daughter attended boarding school from the age of 9 or 10. Nettie supported her husband as Lady Mayoress, read and entertained friends in 'her' drawing room, played golf and tennis frequently, and travelled to Europe regularly with her husband. She would have been horrified to be identified as a feminist and equally horrified to hear her life regarded as exploitative or demeaning: to the end of her life she upheld her belief in 'separate spheres' but did not perceive this as limiting or degrading. That she was able to understand and experience her life and herself as dignified and self-determined was due in no small part to the historical circumstances in which she found herself: 30 years later in the 1950s her highly educated daughter, Dorothy, struggling with two small children and no help in the home, became acutely depressed and ultimately alcoholic.[1]

As Alison Light has argued, the *Mrs Miniver* column, which appeared in *The Times* from 1937 until 1939 and that later became a best-selling book and an Oscar-winning film, caught the British and American imaginations and articulated the desires and pleasures that middle-class domesticity of the period, in all its conservatism, spoke to (Light, 1991, pp. 113–55). In her fictional recreation of the domestic life of a middle-class wife and mother of three children, Jan Struther draws on the same iconography of domestic comfort and parallels the language of human invisibility deployed by Mitchison above, in order to place her central figure, Mrs Miniver, very precisely as not only a wife and mother but, and this would be tacitly understood by her readers – one of those practical knowledges – as a mistress of servants:

> She arranged the fire a little, mostly for the pleasure of handling the fluted steel poker, and then sat down by it. Tea was already laid: there were honey sandwiches, brandy-snaps, and small ratafia biscuits, and there would, she knew, be crumpets. Three new library books lay virginally on the fender-stool, their bright paper wrappers unsullied by subscriber's hand. The clock on the mantelpiece chimed, very softly and precisely, five times. A sudden breeze brought the

sharp tang of a bonfire in at the window. The jig-saw was almost complete, but there was still one piece missing. And then, from the other end of the square, came the familiar sound of the Wednesday barrel-organ, playing with a hundred apocryphal trills and arpeggios, the 'Blue Danube' waltz. And Mrs Miniver, with a little sigh of contentment, rang for tea (Struther, 1939/1989, p. 3).

The meals that are prepared and waiting, the fire that only needs poking for the 'pleasure of handling the fluted steel poker' and the orderliness of the whole scene, build up to that final act upon which the foregoing depends – Mrs Miniver 'rang for tea', and in that phrase Struther represents her protagonist's unmistakable and supremely confident consciousness of herself as a married woman, as middle class and as the mistress of servants. It is the same subjectivity that Woolf recognised, albeit less comfortably and confidently, when she identified herself as one of a class who could 'stroll through the house and say, that cover must go to the wash' (Woolf, 1931/1977, p. xxiv). The chapter from which this is taken and which opens the book is entitled 'Mrs Miniver Comes Home', and whilst literally true – Mrs Miniver is returning from holiday – it also functions metaphorically to suggest a return to that domestic space in which she is 'truly herself' as mistress of her own household, its comforts and her privacy and where, summoning domestic help by the ringing of a bell, articulates precisely the social relations she expects to experience with women from a 'lower' class. As Light has observed, 'the home has been arranged all for her: it is her "space" and no one else's' (Light, 1991, p. 127).

Mrs Miniver has no apparent problems with her servants, they remain, for the most part, nameless and invisible and thus her dependency upon domestic help for her specific lifestyle and self-definition is rendered 'natural' and self-evident. The narrative of *Mrs Miniver* explicitly works to construct the relationship between mistress and servants as one based on mutual respect, interdependency and informality, and to elide its material basis as waged labour. Yet the invisibility of the hands that prepare meals, clean the home, make up the fires and wash clothes continually draws attention to both the power and powerlessness of the domestic servant. The emphasis placed on the comforts of home keeps the reader constantly aware of how dependent Mrs Miniver is on servants to provide these, whilst the invisibility of these servants reinforces their 'place' in the hierarchical structures of the middle-class home. Mrs Miniver's domestic comfort and contentment depends upon the work of servants, yet these servants remain one-dimensional for the most part, rendered visible only as comic characters or illustrations of a moral point. Mrs Miniver is confident and comfortable in her middle-class domestic identity and part of that comfort expresses itself in her ability to conduct 'modern' relations with her servants. Struther's depiction of the aimiable Mrs Burchett, represented as the archetypal Cockney charwoman, is potentially democratic, allying mistress and servant in their 'zest for life', and Mrs Miniver's relatively informal relations with her servants are based on similar personality assessments. Despite the lack of complexity or individuality attributed to the servants, this attempt to relate to her servants as people rather than faceless automata suggests more egalitarian and 'modern' forms of understanding the mistress/servant relationship.

Molly Hughes, a schools inspector and examiner, was widowed with three sons. She chose to manage without domestic help not because she rejected the system of domestic service but, as she tells her brother, Tom, because

> I am alone for long stretches of time, when Vivian and Barnholt are at Oxford, and Arthur is at school all day, so there is not much wear and tear or meal-getting. . . . As for the ordinary servant in the house, Tom, my experience has been either that they are young and you have to look after their health and their morals; or that they are old, faithful, and blameless and at last boss you entirely. And it's so hard to get rid of a saint (Hughes, 1940/1979, p. 59).

Like Struther's Mrs Miniver, Molly Hughes values her domestic privacy as the space where she can be most herself. Her autobiographical narrative is extraordinarily similar in many ways to that of Mrs Miniver. It is the story of an 'inner' life expressed via the daily incidents of work and family life, but both work and family, even her three sons, are firmly placed in relation to her own independence and her desire for a domestic privacy – which she perceived as nourishing that 'rich inner life' – that was so significant in the accounts of middle-class women of this period. Her attitudè to domestic help has to be understood in terms of this desire for privacy. Molly feels neither the need nor the obligation to undertake the responsibility and loss of autonomy that accompanies 'servant-keeping', as articulated through her specific consciousness as a middle-class and, in many ways, highly conservative woman. Yet, like Nettie Holland and Mrs Miniver, she appears to have achieved freedom from the excessive demands of family life, which included the responsibilities and anxieties of servantkeeping; a freedom that eluded so many middle-class women and that so often, in the first half of this century, expressed itself in terms of relationships with recalcitrant, tyrannical or intrusive servants. The desire for privacy, to be free of the constant and continuing demands of others, was (and continues to be) a central plank of feminist politics, but it did not necessarily and inevitably articulate itself as a rejection of domesticity nor in the terms of a radical feminist discourse.

Brought up to expect help with domestic tasks and brought up to understand maturity as becoming mistress of their own household, the issues and problems middle-class women perceived and experienced around 'servantkeeping' were never simply those of practical domestic organisation. The anxieties felt were deeply rooted in self-identity and organised themselves around the dynamics of power and dependency. Many middle-class women in the early twentieth century, unlike Mrs Miniver, expressed considerable concern about the shortage of 'good quality' servants, about their own inability to supervise and manage servants, and about the changing nature of their relationship with the servants. The 'servant problem' runs through Virginia Woolf's diaries as a constant theme. The 'Nelly story' is Woolf's attempt to grapple with both her need for domestic help, her frustration at being thus dependent and her clear-sighted awareness of the changing nature of the mistress/servant relationship:

> In Bloomsbury the domestic servants were not offered the servile status of the Victorian age, but neither had they the businesslike employer/employee relationship which can be established today between the 'daily' woman who 'helps' and the woman who is 'helped'. They were part of the household, in a sense a part of the family, but they were also independent human beings, equals with feelings to be respected. Ideally, hopefully, they were friends. But how many of one's friends are there whom one can see daily, who are dependent on one for a livelihood, who hold one's comforts in their hands, and with whom one is never bored or cross? (Bell, 1972, p. 57).

And how much might that deeply desired privacy be threatened by daily contact with servants who could no longer be conceptualised as invisible hands or a series of 'Peggys' or 'Marys' but instead were to be perceived as 'friends', as 'independent human beings'? In E. M.

Delafield's *The Way Things Are* the heroine Laura feels herself to be at the mercy of her servants:

> Gladys was twenty-six and Laura thirty-four. Gladys was the servant of Laura, paid to work for her. She had been at Applecourt only six months, and it was highly improbable that she would remain for another six. Nevertheless, it was Gladys who, in their daily interviews, was entirely at her ease, and Laura who was nervous (Delafield, 1927, p. 31).

'Servant-keeping' is represented here, unlike in *Mrs Miniver*, in terms of power relations that are in part rooted in the economic nature of the relationship but that also stem from the shifting nature of the relationship in the first half of the twentieth century. Laura recognises that her economic relationship with Gladys should ensure that dependency works one way; that Gladys, happy to have work and a wage, will act in a deferential manner to her employer. Yet Laura is well aware that it is she, the mistress, who finds herself constantly in a conciliatory position, deferring to Gladys and anxious to keep her. Laura, unlike Mrs Miniver, could never confidently set off to 'the red-brick jungle which is known as "the Buildings"' in search of a charwoman (Struther 1939/ 1989, p. 29). Delafield's *The Diary of a Provincial Lady* constructs a wry and self-deprecating humour from the struggles of 'the Provincial Lady' to order her domestic environment by alternately wooing and placating her servants:

> March 10th – Still no house-parlourmaid, and write to ask Rose if I can go to her for a week. . . . March 11th – Rose wires that she will be delighted to put me up. Cook, very unpleasantly, says 'I'm sure I hope you'll enjoy your holiday, mum'. Am precluded from making the kind of reply I should *like* to make, owing to grave fears that she should also give notice. Tell her instead that I hope to 'get settled' with a house-parlourmaid before my return. Cook looks utterly incredulous and says she is sure she hopes so too, because really, things have been so unsettled lately. Pretend not to hear this and leave the kitchen (Delafield, 1930/1984, p. 43).

Writings such as Delafield's and Woolf's articulate a very real concern that, whilst more friendly, egalitarian relationships between mistress and servant are to be desired as an ideal, such ideals are impossible on a day-to-day basis where the dynamics of power are constantly in play. Moreover at another level such ideals, by definition, contradict the middle-class woman's equally powerful desire for privacy, which, as Molly Hughes recognised, very precisely relied on not recognising the human claims of servants. Both Woolf and Delafield perceive that economic power and moral tyranny can no longer serve as the basis of mistress/servant relationships whilst simultaneously recognising that it is precisely the economic relationship that permits an acquiescent servant class and allows them to rely on domestic help. Laura (and others like her) perceive themselves as in thrall to servants who only enter domestic service when there is no other employment. In particular this inability to retain a traditional mistress/servant relationship is imagined not only as a domestic problem but as a threat to a vital and constituent element of an integrated consciousness and subjectivity. To be accused of being 'ruled by her servants', as Laura is in *The Way Things Are*, was to attack the very basis of a middle-class woman's sense of identity, rooted as it was in her ability to control, organise and create a harmonious domestic and private life both for her family and, as I have argued, for herself.

'Home' for middle-class women was inextricably linked to their role as mistress in the household – marriage meant not only companionship, love and children but the attainment of a considerable degree of authority and domestic privacy. Middle-class marriage for women in the early years of this century signified companionship, dignity, privacy and autonomy. It meant being in a position to give orders and in this sense allowed them to escape the frequently limiting and deferential behaviours expected of single young women in their mothers' homes. Even those women, like Vera Brittain, who, as a result of financial independence, found themselves in a position to challenge normative expectations of domesticity did so from within a cultural and social system that invited women to define maturity and adult status primarily according to the married ideal. Despite a perceived shortage of 'good' servants and the constant anxieties of dealing with servants, even feminists such as Vera Brittain failed seriously to attack the system of domestic service or to do without it. On the contrary, Brittain argued for increasing recruitment to domestic work as long as employers and employees were encouraged to value it as a worthwhile and skilled occupation (Brittain, 1928, p. 31).

The pervasiveness of 'servant-keeping' as a significant element of the middle-class psyche went hand in hand with a distaste for 'dusters, soap, soda', which 'belonged to another world' (Mitchison, cited in Dyhouse, 1989, p. 107). The routines, drudgeries and daily tasks involved in maintaining a home were considered unbecoming for middle-class women. Chopping food, washing, scrubbing and polishing were perceived as distasteful tasks and as such the activities of 'lower-class' women. No respectable housewife would be found doing her own washing before the advent of washing machines unless she was forced to by penury. In such instances her inability to employ 'help' was a marker of her declining status. Eileen Elias recalls the strategies adopted by her mother when the family finances no longer permitted a residential maid:

> Mother was determined, however, that though the family prestige had been shaken, the running of the household should go on as smoothly as before. Nobody should ever guess that this was a servantless house. Shining white table napkins and cloths appeared, beautifully and painstakingly laundered, on our tables as before; the clothes were all immaculate; the rosewood piano top shone with polish; the brass knocker on the front door gleamed like gold, though I guessed Mother had to get up at the crack of dawn to do the cleaning of it, before anybody was about to notice her. The only household task with which she had any help at all now – and everybody along the road employed help for this, for no self-respecting housewife would ever be seen on hands and knees in the street – was the cleaning of the front steps (Elias, 1978, p. 31).

It was no accident that step cleaning, floor scrubbing and other physically arduous and dirty tasks were called 'the rough'; in doing so they became associated with those whose place on the social scale rendered such tasks 'suitable work'. It was not simply that prosperous married women expected and attempted to define themselves as employers of servants, benign or otherwise, but that their understanding of the actual tasks undertaken by servants functioned to maintain a distance not only from those who undertook such tasks but from the tasks themselves. When early twentieth century advertisers wished to sell labour-saving devices and when women's magazines of the 1920s and 1930s extolled the virtues of the servantless and labour-saving home, they manifested a tacit recognition of the social nuances of housewifery, and targeted their appeals at the 'house*keeping*' woman or celebrated housework as a scientific, 'modern' and quasi-professional occupation. Women's magazines focused on personal care, cooking, sewing, interior design and childcare rather than on how to whiten steps or scrub a scullery floor. Thus, those tasks which were potentially creative – cooking, decorating, sewing – were highlighted as acceptable and indeed fulfilling activities, whilst 'the rough' remained unspoken – degrading work, hidden and suppressed in these respectable and 'modern' conceptions of housework.

Moreover it was not insignificant for the production of practical knowleges that in the larger household certain servants associated with specific tasks had easier accessibility to their mistress than others. Lady's maids, cooks and housekeepers enjoyed a high status in the servant hierarchy and this manifested itself in direct, unmediated contact with the lady of the house: parlourmaids, step-ladies, laundresses, kitchen maids – all those who actually scrubbed, washed and polished – were refused direct access to their employer and could only approach her indirectly via a more senior servant (Burnett, 1976, pp. 143–53). When reduced incomes and a shortage of labour diminished the number of servants per household, the maid-of-all-work and 'char' found herself engaged to undertake the 'rough' but equally found herself with direct access to her mistress. Middle-class women, for whom the hierarchy of service had previously acted as a distancing screen, found themselves in unmediated contact with those who undertook the dirtiest and 'lowest' of household tasks. It was one thing to expect a less formal, friendly relationship with a 'genteel' lady's maid, quite another to engage in an egalitarian working relationship with a fourteen or fifteen year old adolescent, or even an older woman such as the ubiquitous Mrs Burchett, especially when such women were employed to do 'the rough'. Furthermore, read metaphoricaly, the intrusion of 'the rough' into the drawing room of middle-class sensibility further threatened the desire for a 'rich inner life' and emotional privacy, which precisely required the suppression and exclusion of 'the rough' and 'the low' for its sustenance.

'THE MISTRESS PROBLEM'

Far from perceiving themselves as 'a problem', women who entered domestic service desired to be seen as valued and respected members of society. As a parlourmaid witness to the 1923 Committee testified,

I do not believe any girl minds the work. They do mind being ridiculed. I have suffered untold misery by the name 'only a servant'. Invitations out state 'Be sure and do not let it be known you are a domestic. We should not like our friends to mix with servants'. It is the snobbery of our own class (cited in Burnett, 1976, p. 142).

The changing nature of domestic service in the years after the First World War meant that the occupation was, as observed above, devalued and deskilled at the same time as young women were being exhorted by school, labour exchanges and sometimes their own families to enter it. However hard various agencies worked to dispel the myth that domestic service was a low-skilled occupation, working-class women refused to perceive it as anything other than low-status, 'I knew that once I had donned the maid's cap and apron I would become a menial, a nobody, mindful of my place, on the bottom shelf', and 'I would now have to submit to the badge of servitude – a cap and apron. . . . I started on the long road that only ended in 1940 – a sixteen years' sentence' (Foley, cited in Burnett, 1976, p. 227; Rennie, cited in ibid., p. 236). The association of domestic service with young women who could find no other employment, or who came from orphanages or from depopulated rural areas, resulted in female servants being perceived as 'low' or 'stupid' by both the cultural narratives that interpellated them and, as the comment above testifies, by those in more apparently prestigous working-class occupations.

Yet for working-class women entering domestic service either as maids-of-all-work, daily 'helps' or charwomen the specific historical circumstances under which they did so enabled and indeed appeared to legitimate complaints against the system by servants. The shortage of servants and the change to non-residential domestic help meant that middle-class employers had to reconsider the conditions under which they employed women: tyrannical regimes were now negotiable and, as we have seen, some middle-class women felt they were being ruled by their servants. This fear appears unfounded when the stories of ex-servants are read. Even the most angry and rebellious servant became adept at suppressing overt resentment, outright challenges to authority were rare and the nature of the work made organised attacks by employees difficult if not impossible. Despite the concern expressed in numerous quarters about the conditions of domestic service and the reluctance of young women to enter the occupation, there was never any serious collective attempt on the part of working-class women to organise for better conditions or to use the increased visibility of domestic service on the social agenda to oppose its fundamental premises. Resentment at the rituals of domestic service, which eroded individuality and reduced the servant to faceless anonymity, were far less likely to surface in overt rebellion or organised resistance: attacks on the system were individualised, subversive and covert rather than openly confrontational.

The refusal of young women to enter domestic service when other employment was available was an example, as was the huge turnover in jobs. Even before the First World War the long-serving faithful retainer of cultural stereotyping was a lot less common than a succession of general maids, cooks and charwomen, which was the experience of many employers. Few women stayed in posts longer than two or three years and often left earlier than this. The reasons given were to seek better conditions, to seek a higher position on the occupational ladder and to leave domestic service for other occupations (McBride, 1976, pp. 76–98). Doris Arthurs, Jean Rennie and Winifred Foley changed jobs frequently in the search for a reasonable conditions and wages:

> I decided to get another job to better myself. This time it was in Cheltenham, that aristocrat of towns, where in the 1920s everybody who wasn't a servant was a somebody. . . . Again I was to be the only maid, and still at five shillings a week, but I thought I was making headway into a more sophisticated and plentiful world. In fact the only thing I found more plentiful was the work (Foley, 1974, p. 140).

Doris Arthurs was born in 1908. She left school at 12 and immediately entered domestic service. Prior to her marriage in 1932 the longest she had stayed in a job was three years and the shortest six weeks. She left her job as a nursemaid to take an apparently lower status job as a housemaid because her employer's expectations of how much work she could do were excessive. Moreover, as a housemaid, she was employed in the home of the Lord Mayor of Sutton, a more prestigous employment, she believed, than nursemaid to a suburban family. In 1929 Jean Rennie sought work via a domestic agency 'and they gave me about ten jobs to go and see. I wanted a kitchen-maid-with-scullery-maid job, and very soon I found one that I liked' (Rennie, cited in Burnett, 1976, p. 244). Thus whilst the conditions of domestic service were often tyrannical and demanding, young women were able to retaliate in a plentiful job market by moving to another job and felt justified in continuing to seek a more ideal employment. There is very little sense in any of the accounts of ex-domestic servants of the 'faithful retainer' commitment and loyalty to specific households that women employers longed for, although, as Winifred Foley's account suggests, a degree of loyalty to an employer might conflict with self-interest at the most inappropriate moments.

However the power inherent in the ability to up and leave was a limited one, despite apprehensions to the contrary on the part of mistresses. The mobility of domestic servants was dependent upon receiving a 'good character', without which it was almost impossible to secure alternative employment. There were no formal sanctions requiring an employer to provide 'a character' and withdrawal or refusal of a reference was a powerful weapon to prevent servants leaving or to complicate the search for another job (McBride, 1976, p. 73). Jean Rennie qualified for entrance to university and later became cook to a firm of London solicitors. In 1955 she wrote her autobiography, *Every Other Sunday*, detailing her experiences of domestic service. Jean consistently questionned the servant/employer relationship and saw no justification for the system of domestic service. Nonetheless she draws back from an exchange with a tyrannical cook and her 'rebellions' are covert and pass unacknowledged, if not unnoticed. As she observes, 'obedience was deeply rooted in my character': to openly challenge the system of authority and power rooted in the mistress/servant relationship was, as she recognised, to risk losing both job and reference. The shortage of domestic help meant jobs were plentiful, but both servants and mistresses knew the importance of a good reference. The lack of formal training and standardised qualifications in the occupation meant that employers were dependent on 'the reference' or a 'good word' from another middle-class woman as a means of selecting potential employees, and this informal networking amongst middle-class women gave them considerable power, despite their concerns to the contrary, over the hiring and firing of domestic help.

Domestic servants, such as Jean Rennie and Winifred Foley, who resented their economic dependence and the deference expected of them found ways of resisting and subverting the system whilst steering clear of outright challenge. Jean's employer placed a half-crown and a spread out pack of cards under the billiard room rug in order to test both Jean's honesty and her thoroughness in cleaning under the rug. Jean, incensed by this imputation of dishonesty and carelessness, glued the cards and the money to the floor and covered them with the rug. Nothing was ever said openly to her but she believed that her actions 'branded [me] as a rebel, and that was a dangerous thing to be in 1924' (Rennie, cited in Burnett, 1976, p. 242). Dangerous not because she would be unable to find other work – she worked in numerous places during the 1920s and 1930s – but because 'of the awful consequences of "not getting a good reference"' and the ways in which an employer could make her daily life difficult (ibid.)

Winifred Foley's first job was as general maid to a ninety year old widow in the Cotswolds. Winifred's account of this time represents her employment as a story of conflict and power (Foley, 1986, pp. 132–9). Young women such Winifred and Jean were very well aware at a practical level of the dangers of open rebellion, but were equally concerned to assert a sense of dignity and self-worth in a system of social relations that consistently worked to deny autonomy and self-definition. The sense of outwitting a 'cantankerous old tartar' evidenced by Winifred has to be understood as part of a wider working-class consciousness in which hoodwinking authority was understood as a legitimate means of redressing the injuries of an unjust social and economic system. From the start Winifred's account asserts the shrewd sharpness of the fourteen year old country girl who outwits her ninety year old employer,

'Get up, you lazy creature, it's gone 9 o'clock!' she would fume, digging me in the ribs for all she was worth. 'The clock must 'ave stopped last night, ma'am,' I lied, and turned the hands back on the clocks downstairs before I got her up. She often complained how quickly the evenings drew in (Foley, cited in Burnett, 1976, p. 232).

The relationship between Winifred and her employer continues in Winifred's narrative as one of deception, duplicity and suspicion, with the old lady represented as being determined to get good value for her money and Winifred, equally determined, to resist too many obvious exploitations. When Winifred gives in her notice, the old lady throws it on the fire; when Winifred insists, the old lady 'gave me a sort of bribe, a fine wooden needlework casket with a sampler in it which she had worked at the age of six' (Foley, 1986, p. 139). In the end Winifred is rescued by her elder sister who persuades her to run away, leaving a note for the old lady, and presumably losing her reference. The elder sister 'teaches' the fourteen year old Winifred that concepts of loyalty or service could be directly opposed to self-survival in the world of domestic service:

> 'I can't come,' I wailed, 'she's got nobody to take my place.'
> 'Nor likely to, you sawney hap'orth, as long as you be muggins enough to stop 'ere. Where's your things?' (Foley, 1986, p. 139).

The sense in these accounts by ex-servants of an intense struggle for autonomy is rendered more difficult, and at times even painful, because of the lack of the formalised distancing mechanisms usual to the employer/employee relationship. Where service was residential and where no other servants were kept, the relationship between mistress and maid could become intense and highly personalised despite its economic basis. Winifred Foley was expected to sleep in the same bed as her ninety year old employer, whose night fears kept Winifred from her own bed, and Lilian Westall recalled working for a 'wealthy but unhappy woman who had grown dependent on servants and was incapable of looking after herself' (Westall, cited in Burnett, 1976, p. 220).

In such situations domestic servants might find themselves negotiating a range of contradictory understandings and feelings about their relationships with their employers. On the one hand they could recognise the economic base upon which their relationship depended, the potentially exploitative nature of the system within which they were structually positioned, and therefore the necessity for those small victories of covert resistance that sustained pride and dignity. On the other hand they could find themselves pitying, liking, even defending the mistress whom survival demanded should be constructed as 'the enemy'. Winifred Foley found herself protecting her employer from 'maid-pinching' when attempts were made to entice her to other employment behind the old lady's back, despite her own attempts to hoodwink her employer. Lilian Westall found herself pitying and supporting the unhappy widow she worked for in London, a situation that led to her being 'plagued with telegrams when I was at home asking me to drop everything and go up to the flat to help out at unexpected dinner parties' (ibid.)

For those like Jean Rennie who worked in larger households employing numerous servants, such contradictory definitions of their position were less likely: the servant hierarchy in such households sustained and produced the emotional distance between mistress and servant that was essential to the maintenance and regulation of the social relations between women. However by 1918, and certainly in the 1920s and 1930s, the one-maid household was a far more likely form of domestic service for young women entering the occupation. The National Union of Women Workers noted as early as 1900 that 60 per cent of the 'servantkeeping classes' kept only one servant and another 20 per cent kept two servants (cited in Dyhouse, 1989, p. 109).

Hence the 'problem' of domestic service for servants might be expressed in terms of covert and small victories against the potential and actual exploitation and tyranny of their employers. Hoodwinking and outwitting a mistress was rooted in secrecy and suspicion; overt deference might hide powerful feelings of resentment and hostility that found articulation in oblique resistances. The single-maid household, with its unmediated relationship between maid and mistress, enabled such power dynamics to be fought out, not in the arena of wages and conditions, but in the area of personal relations – many small wars of attrition and manipulation must have been won and lost on the battlefield of domestic service. Accounts such as those of Winifred Foley are articulated in terms reminiscent of the advice given by women's magazines on how to handle husbands, of which the following is an extreme example:

> By a constant series of little deceptions the tyrant is led to believe that his measures are carried out, whereas, in point of fact, they are quite properly ignored (Housewife, 1890).

Strategies for resisting domestic tyranny were targeted at authority: the practical and emotional lessons learned in service might well be transferred to the equally intimate arena of working-class marriage, where economic survival could depend on the ability to outwit and 'handle' bullying or feckless husbands.[2] In such circumstances self-definition was achieved via duplicity and suspicion: authority, in whatever form, was 'them' and hence available for hoodwinking and deceit. Yet, as Doris Arthurs' account below demonstrates, whilst the structures of social life determined such divisions, the circumstances of history in which specific relations occurred could equally and simultaneously allow Doris to reconstruct and represent her experience as a source of fulfilment and pride.

DORIS ARTHURS AND 'REBECCA'

This final section will examine two stories in which the relationship between mistress and servant provides a central focus. My intention is to draw attention to the ways in which women of different classes might make sense of the relations of domestic service and the forms available in which to articulate their understanding and knowledge. As argued above, the early twentieth century witnessed dramatic changes in the nature of domestic service, which were to lead to its final eclipse in its nineteenth century form after the Second World War. Changes in domestic service, in the relations between employer and servant, meant fundamental shifts in the ways people of different classes perceived and understood each other. This was particularly true for relations between women of different classes, for whom the system of domestic service had long regulated and organised the ways in which such relationships might manifest themselves in both social practices and cultural expression. Daphne Du Maurier's romantic fiction, *Rebecca*, articulated, as critics have noted, the acute anxieties of a threatened middle class at a specific historical moment when the security of an older social order appeared in jeopardy (Light, 1984; Bromley, 1986).

What has been less commented upon is the way in which that anxiety organised itself around 'the servant problem'. Doris Arthurs told her life story to me in 1987. Despite the semi-structured approach of the interview, time and again Doris ignored my questions about her home life in the interwar years in order to tell me about her relationship with her employer, Jessie. For a long time I resisted 'hearing' the significance and importance of this relationship for Doris, concerned as I was with home and family rather than employment. Nor did I feel comfortable with the apparently deferential and admiring account Doris gives of her employer: I wanted overt evidence of resistance to the oppressions of class and gender inherent in the system of domestic service. I wanted to 'discover' the kinds of rebellion practised by women like Jean Rennie and Winifred Foley. My resistance testifies to my own consciousness, embedded as it is in the quest for 'truths' and teleology, which demands and needs one way of seeing and understanding the world I inhabit. Doris insisted I pay attention to *her* understanding and experience even if it did not fit the picture I was attempting to assemble. Both Doris's story and *Rebecca* testify to the vastly different ways in which women may articulate and understand their relationships with each other: if we are to understand how women have made sense of their lives and 'got by' we need to pay attention to *all* the stories we hear and *all* the forms in which those stories can be told. Above all we need to resist the impulse to create new hierarchies of knowledge by evaluating the stories we hear in terms of our own preconceptions, beliefs and preoccupations. Jane Flax has warned that, just as our current gender arrangements create men who have difficulty in acknowledging relations between people and experiences, they produce women who have difficulties in acknowledging differences within relations. In either gender, these social relations produce a disposition to treat experience as all of one sort or another and to be intolerant of differences, ambiguity, and conflict (Flax, 1987, p. 640).

Rebecca and Doris's story are very different: separated in their telling by 50 years and in the purpose for which they were produced. Nevertheless it is possible and indeed necessary that they should be juxtaposed. In so doing they might speak to our understanding of differences and the multi-layered, interconnecting, but ultimately unsynthesisable determinants of culture, behaviour, psychology, economics and history from which individual as well as collective subjectivities are produced.

Rebecca was published in 1938. Alison Light has said of it that it was 'a romance about respectability' and a reworking of romance for those 'superior' readers who 'despised the Barbara Cartland school of romance' and the sentimental 'gush' of a previous age (Light, 1991, pp. 158–66) The narrative tells the story of a young, middle-class woman who, whilst acting as a lady's companion, meets and marries the enigmatic Maximilian de Winter, owner of Manderley, a large country house in England's West Country, and of the mystery that surrounds de Winter's first wife, Rebecca. The narrative concerns the heroine's struggle for maturity and self-identity, a struggle that is organised around the abiding presence and jealousy of Rebecca in the girl-heroine's mind; the sinister housekeeper, Mrs Danvers; and the heroine's attempts to win Maxim from the stranglehold of the past. At the end the heroine, who remains unnamed throughout, says of herself:

confidence is a quality I prize, although it has come to me a little late in the day. . . . At any rate I have lost my diffidence, my timidity, my shyness with strangers. I am very different from that self who drove to Manderley for the first time, hopeful and eager, handicapped by a rather desperate gaucherie and filled with an intense desire to please (Du Maurier, 1938/1975, p. 13).

Throughout the novel the heroine's confidence or lack of it is measured not only, and certainly not primarily, by her social poise or a confident sexuality, neither of which she seems to fully achieve even at the end, but insistently by her ability and frequent inability to handle the servants of Manderley. The moment of her transition from a 'hopeful and eager' young woman to the confident, mature, albeit temporary mistress of Manderley is marked very specifically by her almost magical ability to deal with the domestic staff, and in particular the hitherto terrifying Mrs Danvers. She ponders, 'I had not thought it would be so easy to be severe. I wondered why it had seemed hard for me before' (ibid., p. 302).

The text articul‾tes that middle-class consciousness noted above, in which the marker ʋf a woman's psychological maturity and social identity was not only evidenced via her married status, but equally through her ability to conduct kindly but authoritative relations with her servants. In *Rebecca* the possibility of achieving a mature selfhood is constantly under threat, nowhere more than in the relationship of the heroine with the housekeeper, Mrs Danvers, which becomes as the novel progresses a struggle quite specifically over the heroine's survival and identity, both at a social and a psycho/sexual level. Indeed at the climax of this struggle Mrs Danvers urges the girl to suicide in language that overtly links the heroine's desires for love, selfhood and social power:

> She's still mistress here, even if she is dead. She's the real Mrs de Winter, not you. It's you that's the shadow and the ghost. It's you that's forgotten and not wanted and pushed aside. Well, why don't you leave Manderley to her? Why don't you go?. . . . We none of us want you. He doesn't want you, he never did. He can't forget her (Du Maurier, 1938/1975, p. 257).

As Alison Light has observed, the heroine is paralysed by her desire to be a different kind of woman, to be female in the highly sexualised and erotically powerful way that Rebecca is (Light, 1991, p. 166). The heroine also seems to me to long to be of a different class; on arriving at Manderley she imagines what it would be like to be a cottager's wife bustling 'in my kitchen, clean as a pin, laying the table for supper'. Surely, she muses, such a way of life would be 'peaceful and steady' requiring 'no set standard' (Du Maurier 1938/1975, p. 67). She recounts her meeting with the Manderley servants in language that, in its excess, precisely articulates the profound anxieties of the middle-class woman in fear of being 'ruled' by her servants: 'they were the watching crowd about the block, and I the victim with my hands behind my back' (ibid., p. 72).

Growing-up for the heroine of *Rebecca* is as much to be feared as desired for maturity allows no escape from the obligations of either femininity or middle-class status. Her yearning to escape takes the form of fantasies of domestic pastoral in which she serves rather than is served, in which the social power contingent upon being mistress of Manderley is relinquished in favour of the powerlessness of service to her cottager husband.

At the end, Maxim and the second Mrs De Winter are exiled from England and Manderley has burned, possibly at the hands of Mrs Danvers. Deprived of her position as mistress of Manderley, childless and exiled, the heroine becomes mother to her husband and 'mistress' to an ever-changing staff of hotel personnel. Certainly Du Maurier represents this as loss, but neither nostalgically nor sentimentally: the girl-heroine may have compromised her romantic (youthful) dreams of love and passion, but she has gained what she valued most. She has acquired the confident selfhood and wisdom of the English middle-class mother but without the claims of and obligations to children and servants. Like Mrs Miniver, but differently and more painfully, she has achieved a deeply internalised self-containment, a private self in which even hurt may be enjoyed because unwitnessed by children, servants or husband, '[I] keep the things that hurt to myself alone. They can be my secret indulgence' (ibid., p. 11).

We might speculate how middle-class readers of the period, acutely aware of the 'servant problem', understood *Rebecca*. Today we cannot register the sinister presence of Mrs Danvers or the girl's gaucheries in dealing with her servants in anything approaching the way these might have struck contemporary readers. For many Mrs Danvers must have appeared the embodiement of everything middle-class women feared most in their servants – overtly deferential but covertly hostile, apparently subservient but 'ruling' through her efficiency and confidence. Equally, her unqualifed admiration for and passionate devotion to Rebecca might speak to middle-class women's desires for such relationships with their female servants. Moreover, the romantic excess and gothic elements articulated in the characterisation of Mrs Danvers and Rebecca offered middle-class readers a space in which to demonise those aspects of their lives which were most anarchic and difficult to control – fears of servant hostility and contempt, and fears of 'unspeakable' sexualities. Demonisation, of course, attempts to suppress and deny the desires inherent in such fears. Rendering and reading Mrs Danvers as villain and possibly the destroyer of Manderley may have permitted middle-class women to camouflage their own fantasies of collapsing the social structures that 'forced' them into servant-keeping, desires that could only ever remain unconscious because to own such fantasies equalled the destruction of those modes of self-definition from which middle-class identity was formed. Finally, the heroine's abdication of public responsibility, her retreat into exile and her private self, offered fantasies in which the social obligations of class and gender might be circumvented via self-containment and withdrawal.

Doris Arthurs was born near Cannock in Staffordshire, North Midlands, in 1908. Her father was a miner and she was one of ten children, of whom six survived – two boys and four girls. All four girls went into service on leaving school: 'there was nothing else for the girls when they left school, no factories, not anything'. Doris left school at thirteen and worked first in the local presbytery, serving dinners and cleaning the brasses. Once she was old enough she left Staffordshire to take up a position as a nursemaid in a suburban household in Birmingham. Like many young migrants Doris gravitated to the city in search of work that could supplement the meagre income of her family as well as providing her with respectable and safe accommodation. Doris must also have dreamt of finding a husband and a home in which she did not have to sleep four in a bed or spend her leisure time whitening steps and helping with the huge washing loads produced by such a large family. Doris only stayed as a nursemaid for six weeks: she found the care of three small children plus the extra work expected of her on top of her nursemaid duties too much. She left to become a housemaid in the home of the Lord Mayor in Sutton, a wealthy suburb north of Birmingham where she worked for three and a half years.

After her marriage and the birth of her only daughter, Doris undertook a variety of jobs, one of which was cleaning and general help two days a week for a childless couple, Mr Powley, a business man, and his wife Jessie. It is difficult to discover from Doris's account how long this employment lasted, but the impression is of a long and close relationship between Doris and Jessie. Doris says of the couple, 'they were ever so good to me, they really gave me a good start in life'; Mr Powley sent a car to fetch Doris to work, they took her on holiday with them, and Jessie left Doris a small legacy. Now in her 80s Doris's memories return continually to Jessie and the relationship they shared.

In many ways Doris's account suggests an idealised version of the cultural narrative that represents domestic servants as deferential and faithful retainers. However Doris reconstructs this conventional understanding of the relations between the two women, articulating it as a familial relationship of equals: she speaks of Jessie 'as a sister to me' and tells how she would 'spend as much time as I could with her'. Moreover, whilst Jessie's husband is always referred to as 'Mr Powley', Jessie is addressed by her christian name, suggesting that Doris understood the hierarchies of the household in terms of gender rather than class and her relationship with Jessie as a personal one, whilst Mr Powley remained, despite his kindness to her, very firmly her employer. After the Second World War and Mr Powley's death Doris looked after Jessie, 'who couldn't have enough of my company. I used to hurry up and get my jobs done and race up there', and when Jessie died it was Doris who made all the funeral arrangements. One reading of Doris's story might interpret it as wish-fulfilment. Doris yearned for a family to replace the one she had left behind in rural Staffordshire and Jessie represents the 'lost' family, becoming mother, sister and child for Doris. However if Doris's story is located in history, both her personal history and the wider circumstances of a specific past, a more complex understanding of the relationship is produced.

Doris's youthful experience as a residential housemaid in the Lord Mayor's household would have taught her the hierarchical nature of domestic service. As a junior housemaid she would not have had direct access to her mistress and would have experienced her relationships with her employers through the mediations of more senior servants. As a married woman with a child, non-residential and employed as the only servant, Doris had direct access to both her employers but particularly to Jessie. Doris would have understood her position as far more egalitarian than her previous experiences of service had prepared her for and she may have experienced a hitherto unknown confidence and autonomy in her position.

Yet, despite the apparently democratic and at times intimate nature of their relations, Doris recalled it in the language of economics. Jessie gave Doris clothes for her daughter, Valerie, and cast-off household items whenever she moved house; Jessie left Doris a legacy; and Jessie and her husband paid for a holiday for Doris and Jim. Jessie, Doris says, 'gave her a good start' and 'I shall never be out of her debt'. In return Doris 'spent as much time as I could with her'. Alongside and overlapping Doris's articulation of their intimacy and close personal relationship is an equally compelling, though more obliquely coded, expression of the economic terms of the relationship. Jessie provides much needed and desired material goods, Doris 'pays' for these with her labour and her emotional commitment. Jessie is possibly lonely and

'buys' Doris's friendship as well as her domestic labour. The fundamental economic relationship between mistress and servant has not
been disturbed but the historical context in which this occurs allows
Doris to reconceive the relationship in ways that are self-dignifying and
self-empowering. Jessie needed Doris, Doris needed the autonomy such
dependence might bestow and the terms of mistress/servant relationships were in a state of flux, thus making it possible for Doris to
partially assuage and suppress the envy and resentment, endemic to her
social situation, by her satisfaction and pride in the equality she perceived herself to have achieved with Jessie.

Juxtaposing Doris's story with Du Maurier's romantic fiction may
appear to be trying to force impossible comparisons. One was written
in 1938, the other was recounted in 1987, and as forms of imagining
they are totally unalike. Yet Doris's story of Jessie and herself is as
much a narrative fiction as *Rebecca*, though not of course 'literary' in
the way Du Maurier's fiction is. Surely, it might be argued, the 'servant
problem' or relationships with domestic staff was not the point of Du
Maurier's tale of romance and mystery. Perhaps not. Nonetheless Mrs
Danvers, even today, remains the most powerful image in the novel, a
perception reinforced by the film of *Rebecca*. Perhaps more importantly
we should ask why we might be reluctant to set the two fictions alongside each other and why we resist or might wish to downgrade readings
that focus on relationships with servants? Do we fear 'the literary' will
become contaminated by the oral? Is our reluctance to confront relationships that are social and economic rather than private and sexual
rooted in a continued preference for investing such 'intimate' relationships with the power to constitute our innermost selves?

Because the search for selfhood continues to remain embedded in
belief in a root cause or essence that is most freely revealed in personal
rather than socio/economic relations, we continue to re-affirm distinctions between 'private' and 'public' spheres of activity, feeling and
thinking, and to reaffirm asymmetric social relations. Yet the stories of
Doris and Du Maurier can remind us that whilst on the one hand, as
Rebecca testifies, the asymmetric social relations of domestic service
created uncomfortable psychologies, there were historically specific
moments when the changing form of those social relations might allow
relationships that transgressed the prevailing conceptions of where intimacy should be located. However compromised by its location in a
framework of social asymmetry, Doris's account of her friendship with
Jessie articulates a belief that the barriers of class are not impregnable.

Afterword

At the end of a piece of historical writing it is usual for the writer to look back over the terrain covered, to draw together ideas and suggest conclusions, to point up significances and to identify connections. Most historical writing, like many other kinds of writing, is part of a wider metaphysical and psychological desire to seek order and coherence in the random and disparate events of not only the past, but our contemporary lives. In order to achieve such unity and coherence it always becomes necessary to reduce and suppress elements or 'voices' that threaten to disturb the ordered patterns desired by both writer and reader. As a result, as the work of Hayden White and Dominick La Capra has argued, historians inevitably find themselves using narrative structures and devices that are more commonly associated with the construction of literary fictions, and in particular the forms associated with the nineteenth century realist novel (White, 1987; La Capra, 1983). Historians frequently adopt the role of omniscient narrator, ordering the 'voices' in their narrative into a hierarchy in which the narrator's 'voice' is the most fully coherent and most explanatory, interpreting and synthesising events, practices and their representations into patterns that satisfy our desire to know 'how it really was'.

Of course historians have always recognised the partial and fragmentary nature of the evidence left by the past and the illusory nature of any 'reality' thus created. They have, as stated in the Introduction, always been aware that other versions are always waiting to be written. Yet, as Lloyd Kramer has suggested, 'historians continue to seek the account of the world as it actually existed rather than admit that their partial descriptions always exclude a great many other kinds of important information' (Kramer, 1989, p. 118). Kramer has argued, following White and La Capra, for new modes of representing the past that, whilst refusing any simple rejection of concepts of order in favour of anarchic chaos and a meaningless pluralism, allow a respect for the dialogic play of 'voices' that exceed interpretive structures aimed at containing them:

> The historian's task, then is to develop a 'dialogue' in which the autonomous past is allowed to question our recurring attempts to reduce it to order. 'It must be actively recognized that the past has

its own "voices" that must be respected', La Capra writes, 'especially when they resist or qualify the interpretations we would like to place on them. A text is a network of resistances, and a dialogue is a two-way affair; a good reader is also an attentive and patient listener'. . . . Every epoch, every important text, and every historical figure encompasses tendencies that defy and contradict the labels on which historiography depends (La Capra, cited in Kramer, 1989, p. 103).

Throughout this book I have attempted to represent a variety of 'voices', speaking from the past and in the present, one of which is, of course, my own. Neither have I simply left those 'voices' to speak for themselves, which would be one way of representing the past, but have consistently and continually throughout the writing attempted to impose certain kinds of order and claims to knowledge on the material under scrutiny. This is how I perceive my task as an academic and a writer, but it is a task that cannot remain unquestioned, raising, as it does, problems about authority, knowledge and the desire for single and teleological meaning. To return to the questions raised by Katherine Borland, which I quoted in the Introduction, how might it be possible to allow the individual woman's account of the past 'interpretive respect' without abdicating responsibility to use the power conferred by certain knowledges to rediscover and reinscribe women's experiences in the service of a feminist politics?

In this Afterword, then, I do not intend to offer primarily a summary of *my* conclusions, though undoubtedly what follows will do that to some extent, not least by its position at the end of the book, but I do want to investigate my own position in the research undertaken and I want to relate this to wider questions about the structures of oppression that function via a nexus of culturally produced representations, of which historical writing is but one, to create effects of power. In doing so I am drawing substantially on the work of Valerie Walkerdine, who has suggested ways in which the relationship between researcher and researched, surveiller and surveyed can be understood in terms that understand academic research as creating its own set of regulating effects that answer the need to control deep-seated anxieties and fears within the intellectual bourgeoise itself:

The 'social scientist' is the producer of a 'truth' which claims to 'know' those whom it describes. Together, observer and observed constitute a couple in the play of power and desire. We therefore need to examine the response of the observed to their experience of surveillance. Equally important, however, is the theorist's 'desire to know' for this contains *both a fantasy of power and also a fear of the observed* (Walkerdine, 1990, p. 195, my emphasis).

The 'social scientists' of the 1920s and 1930s who surveilled and observed the practices of working-class housewives and mothers may have been, as suggested in Chapter 3, motivated by their own desires inherent in those fantasies of omniscience so prodigiously offered in social surveys. Educated women, feminist and otherwise, found in welfare work and social surveying a space where a desire for authority, beyond the confines of house and home, could be satisfied and claims to knowledge, generated from such authority, could be articulated in the public arena. Yet, of course, despite the undoubtedly genuine but nonetheless patronising impulse to help 'the poor', the practices and representations of working-class life produced from surveys and welfare visiting remained regulative. The practice of any social observation that *only explains the observed* always functions to position those observed as pathologised or aberrant precisely because '[t]he knowledge it produces will inevitably differ from the meanings ascribed to them by the participants – meanings they produce as they live out the practices in which they are formed' (ibid.)

Hence the working-class housewives and mothers described by the Women's Hygiene Committee or the district nurses who visited them, would have ascribed different meanings to their experience than those represented in the accounts passed down to us. Equally, of course, the educated women who surveilled 'the poor' interpreted their actions and assumptions in very different ways to the ways in which I and other twentieth century academics and feminists might do so. This is not to argue for an amorphous plurality but to draw attention to the ways in which a variety of potential meanings struggle, not simply to become valid, but to achieve ascendancy.

In producing a meaning from social practices or cultural products, none of us wish that meaning to gather dust unheard and unconsidered. Various forms and methods ensure that certain meanings are transmitted from one group to another or from one generation to another, and whilst I continue to disavow any desire to produce a single definitive interpretation, nevertheless, whether I like it or not, inhabiting as I do a world whose meanings are structured around the oppressions of

gender, race, class, age, education and wealth, certain explanatory forms
have more force as 'rational' claims to knowledge than others – for
example those produced by white Eurocentric male and female academics and those produced in the present where we may consider
ourselves more 'enlightened'.

Hence the 'voices' of the past that I discuss remain embedded in
those hierarchical structures of discourse which serve to privilege the
'voice' of contemporary rational academic discourse. In consequence,
as Walkerdine asks, 'how far is it possible for the observer to 'speak
for' the observed'? In 'speaking for' those whom history has attempted
to silence I am speaking for myself, my own needs and preoccupations
in the present as much as for others (ibid.) It seems to me to become
necessary in 'speaking for others' that we recognise and make aware
the extent to which we also and equally speak for ourselves and our
deepest desires:

> You cannot open up a question without leaving yourself open to it.
> You cannot scrutinise a 'subject' without being scrutinised by it. You
> cannot do any of these things without renewing ties with the season
> of childhood, the season of the mind's possibilities (Lyotard, cited in
> Stuart, 1993, p. 80).

Walkerdine argues that claims to knowledge by the intellectual bourgeoise are predicated on the assumption that 'the best' knowledge is
that arrived at through rationality and intellectualisation and that other
knowledges, in particular those produced from the pleasures of
materiality, are precisely that – 'other'. It therefore becomes necessary
for intellectuals, concerned to produce 'the best' knowledge, to suppress or 'rationalize the pleasures of the body, to transform them into
pleasures of the mind', and insofar as this mind/body dualism is represented in terms of class, gender and occupation (mental/manual work;
male:mind/female:body) this task requires the surveillance of those (often
perceived as women or 'the poor') whose '"animal passions" . . . have
to be monitored and regulated' (Walkerdine, 1990, pp. 201, 199). Such
regulation functions to hide those fears of 'the other' which are the
motivating impulse of claims to knowledge based on rationality: to
'know' someone or something via intellect alone is to hide and deny
other knowledges that can be named 'lower' or 'perverse' knowledges
and are thus represented as requiring control and surveillance.

The task of any bourgeois intellegensia is to transform, via intellectualisation and rationalisation, 'other' knowledges that are not those of the mind, into forms that render them less dangerous. Yet, of course, such control can never be complete and the suppressed term of the dualism will find alternative forms of articulation, which in turn require further denial and/or denigration. The intellectual task of 'knowing' those whom we study is itself often rationalised as a 'crusade to save the masses from the ideology that dupes them' and as such 'can obscure the real social significance of their pleasures', which are necessarily named as 'perverse' (ibid., p. 201). Which is not to argue for a simple reversal of the opposition nor to suggest that *only* populist forms of knowledge are of cultural and social significance but rather to suggest the need to become aware of, and to acknowledge, those – equally 'perverse' – pleasures embedded in bourgeois claims to truth, authority, knowledge and certainty. This seems to me to have considerable bearing, both upon my own position vis-à-vis this research and upon the ways in which it becomes possible to consider feminism's relation to domesticity and housework.

I could say that the impulse that compelled me to undertake research into some of the practices and representations of domesticity arose from my own immersion in home and family for fifteen years. In one sense I wished to justify the desires and pleasures that immersion spoke to and satisfied (partially), and I wished to defend both the pleasures and pains of domesticity against those versions of feminist thought which sought either to glorify or denigrate 'women's sphere'. Yet, in the process of interviewing, writing and thinking about the topic I have, following Walkerdine's argument, transformed my own previous, unexamined enjoyment of, and frustration with, the practices of domesticity into 'pleasures of the mind' (ibid.) And I am left wondering how far my desire to *study* domesticity hides a fear of being returned to it: interviewing women and reading their autobiographies was in one sense a dialogue with what I both feared and desired to become. It was also a dialogue with both my mother and my grandmother, who lived during the years under scrutiny and whose own relations to domesticity and thus to me as a small child continue to frighten, anger and fascinate me. I draw attention to these possibilities not in order to attempt some psychological reading of self-motivation per se, but rather in order to demonstrate that in 'speaking for others' we must always find ourselves 'speaking for ourselves', and that to deny this aspect of research interaction is to deny the ways in which ' "our" project of analysing "them" is itself one of the regulative practices which produce *our* subjectivity as well as theirs. We are each Other's Other – but not on equal terms' (ibid., p. 200).

Thus my self-definition as middle-class academic is produced from a struggle requiring suppression of the desire to abdicate intellectual responsibility in order to return to domesticity and the pleasures of the material (see also my discussion of *Rebecca* in Chapter 4), alongside the desire for power inscribed in the position of 'intellectual' and the knowledge claims thus associated. The affluence, education and history that allow me to study 'them' (this includes both working- and middle-class women in the past), rather than the other way around, define and position me as more powerful, whether I wish it or not. In the end, at least within the framework of this research, I do have the last word. Rhetoric that insists 'academics should side with the oppressed' can represent a much-desired denial of the responsibility contingent upon power; it can be, as Walkerdine suggests, 'a way of disavowing our position instead of accounting for it' (ibid., p. 196). My somewhat attenuated attempt to insert myself into the narrative as a subject of the research, however differently positioned, is an attempt to account for that position.

Finally, I want to suggest ways in which the foregoing relates to current conceptions of domesticity and the somewhat fraught, I suggest, relationship that is sometimes seen to exist between 'ordinary' women and feminism. During the first three decades of this century middle-class and educated women were able to rely on at least a general maid or 'char' to help with certain domestic tasks such as cooking and cleaning; shopping could be ordered and delivered and washing sent to the laundry. Moreover, not only were middle-class families having fewer children but childcare itself was, as yet, not the intense, demanding and exclusive relationship it was to become in the years after the Second World War. And, for many middle-class families, children of both sexes attended boarding school from the age of about nine. Equally the conventions of Victorian family life, which had imposed stifling constraints on women's mobility and activities, loosened considerably in the wake of the First World War. As a result, as I have argued, educated women may have enjoyed a degree of privacy, directly connected to the home and its pleasures, in which to nurture forms of selfhood unknown to either their mothers or their daughters. Certainly women such as Virginia Woolf, Naomi Mitchison, Vera Brittain and Jan Struther's fictional Mrs Miniver, however different in their political affiliations, shared a common regard for certain forms of self-reflection and a conscious awareness of the 'rich inner life' that separated them, as they perceived it, from 'the masses'.

One of the ways in which this sense of 'inner life' could be expressed and 'known' was in its distinction from and opposition to the material and bodily activities of domesticity that sustained everyday life. Hence, of course, Woolf's distinction between 'Mozart and Einstein' and 'baths and ovens': the pleasures of the mind distinguished from the needs of the body; Mitchison's ignorance of 'dusters and soda' as opposed to the pleasures of Mrs Miniver's 'three library books'. As we have seen, the everyday tasks of domesticity are only acceptable to the woman with a 'rich inner life' once they have been transformed into pleasures of the mind. For example, when the heroine of *Rebecca* fantasises about being a cottager's wife her desire for the pleasures of 'ordinariness' is articulated in the form of a 'high-culture' version of idyllic pastoralism in which 'ordinariness' is idealised and loses its significance *as* the ordinary and the everyday. In similar ways, as servant help became more uncertain and middle-class women found themselves increasingly having to do their own housework, certain tasks were defined as 'creative': cooking, interior decoration and childcare required intelligence and artistry, whereas scrubbing and washing were physical tasks requiring 'brawn' rather than 'brain'. It should therefore not surprise us that the latter were, of course, the very tasks for which it remained both possible and desirable to buy help. As late as the early 1950s I remember my grandmother baking whilst Gracie, the general maid, scrubbed the outside steps, and when feminism attacked 'the housewife syndrome' in the 1960s and 1970s it was the 'mindless' routines of cleaning, washing and polishing that were seen as most entrapping and stifling.

Dorothy Holland, born in 1912, the only daughter of a Lancashire solicitor, spent her early childhood with her mother and the daily maid, Gracie. She was sent to boarding school when she was nine and thereafter, until she married in 1940, became used to the ministrations of servants and 'domestics', whether at school, home or university. When, in the 1950s, she found herself confined to the home with two small children and no domestic help she became acutely depressed and unable to cope with the demands of a domesticity she had never imagined herself having to deal with and which she could not help but see as 'below her'. Cleaning and washing clothes were, as they must have been for many middle-class women brought up in the 1930s, associated with servants and represented those 'lower' activities which required assiduous avoidance if social differentials were to be sustained.

Furthermore, many of the educated women who grew to adulthood in the 1960s saw higher education as offering an escape route not only from apparently predetermined gender roles, but also from what was perceived as the monotony and tedium of suburban life (Heron, 1985). Indeed I would speculate that for many women educated in the 1960s and 1970s it was suburbia and its limitations rather than any specific identification with gender issues – although, of course, these were part and parcel of the perceived limitations – that motivated the desire for 'escape' to the wider vistas of university and city life. It is ironic (and sad) that so many women of my generation wished to escape precisely the conditions of suburbia and respectability that were so deeply desired by the previous generation and, as I have argued, paid for in terms of emotional reserve and sexual restraint; modes of behaviour that are now seen as out of date and unnecessary. Educated women, non-feminist and feminist, have, like Woolf and Mitchison, continued to distance themselves from the 'lower' tasks of homemaking, seeing in them the dangers of those 'pleasures of the body' and the material that Walkerdine refers to, and which, along with suburbia and 'the house-wife', comprise a discourse that continues to divide women along lines of power containing traces of those earlier distinctions – 'servant' 'mistress'; 'cultivated' 'materialistic' (Walkerdine 1990, p. 201). And it is precisely this cultural dynamic that produces those 'truths' in which there is little room left for any response from women who enjoy polishing and scrubbing other than to feel 'perverse' or stupid. In failing to offer any satisfying position for those whose self-worth is or has been deeply implicated in the skills and enjoyments of housekeeping is to run the risk of alienating large numbers of women and perpetuating a continuing image of feminism as elitist and exclusive.

Thus, whilst feminism has been acutely aware of the ways in which the body/mind dualism functions to distinguish occupational categories and valorises mental over manual work in the labour market, for example masculine rationality versus feminine manual dexterity, it has failed to recognise how this same split manifests itself in the representations and practices of domestic labour and 'private' life. 'This body/mind dualism [which] valorizes mental labour as genius or creativity and denigrates the servicing and manual work which make them possible – the labour of the masses and their terrifying physicality' has structured the ways in which the home and 'private' life are experienced and understood equally as much as it has structured the ways we conceptualise paid work in the labour market (ibid.) In this context it is only necessary to recall those distinctions encountered throughout this book between domestic privacy, which created the conditions for a 'rich inner life', and domestic materialism, which allowed 'suburban neurotics' to 'fetishise' their homes. This seems to me to have far-reaching implications for the ways in which we conceptualise domesticity and 'private' life and for ways in which we might develop future approaches to the topic. For if we accept that the dualism, mental/manual, applies not only to the world of paid work but equally, though in different ways, to the privatised world of the home, then we must, it seems to me, consider domesticity not simply as a gendered formation but one that is deeply implicated in other socio-cultural divisions, including class, environment and generation. For too long feminism has focused on the gendered manifestations and oppressions of the sexual division of labour both within and outside the private sphere. In doing so we are in danger of failing to address the ways in which not only is there no homogenous or universal category 'woman', but equally there is no universally defined location, 'home', where she may be found. Whilst I would not want to deny that any history of the home and women's relationship to it has to recognise gender as one of its fundamental structures, I also believe that we need to become aware of the ways in which women's relationship to the home is not just a gendered issue but one that also encompasses issues of class, generation, education, suburbanisation and domestic service, which are themselves shaped by gender.

Notes and References

Introduction

1. The oral testimonies upon which I draw were collected in 1987 and 1988 for my doctoral thesis (Giles, 1989). Twenty-one women were interviewed, all of whom left school at 14 and spent their childhoods and/or adult lives in the urban conurbations of York and Birmingham. Further details of the criteria used in seeking women for interview and further biographical information on each woman can be found in M. J. Giles, '"Something that Bit Better": working class women, domesticity and respectability 1919–1939', unpublished D.Phil thesis, University of York, 1989.
2. Whilst I recognise that the term 'public sphere' tends to conflate 'three analytically distinct things: the state, the official-economy of paid employment, and arenas of public discourse', I am using it here in the sense primarily of public discourse and secondarily of paid employment (Fraser, 1990, p. 57).
3. See the Afterword for an extended discussion of this point.
4. Betty, who lived by herself, agreed to an interview. When I arrived she informed me that 'George' from over the road was coming in as he 'could tell me more about the past'. In the event George talked for forty-five minutes and Betty never said a word. Betty had quite obviously chosen this strategy as a way of coping with the interview.

1 'Making Do' and 'Getting By'

1. Reading the accounts of women's lives in Margery Spring Rice's *Working Class Wives* renders such a claim doubtful: ill health and disease prematurely aged working-class women throughout the 1920s and 1930s.
2. See *Home Chat*, 1895–1958, in particular issues for July, August and September 1925 and July, August and September 1935.

2 A Home of Their Own

1. See pp. 150–1 below.

3 'Keeping Yourself to Yourself': Private Lives and Public Spectacles

1. I am indebted to Sarah Lawson Welsh for the phrase 'emotional thriftiness'.
2. See p. 64 above.
3. It is not intended to suggest that visibility was the only reason for male

174

violence towards working-class women on the streets: cultural associations between the poor, animality and sexual availability all played a part.
4. See p. 52 above.
5. One of these 'boys' was to become Muriel's husband.
6. I first discussed Gertie's story in a paper given to the 'Romance Revisited' Conference at the University of Lancaster in March 1993, which was subsequently published in the edited collection of these conference papers (Giles, 1995).

4   Servant and Mistress: The Case of Domestic Service

1. Nettie Holland was the author's grandmother; Dorothy, the author's mother, was born in 1912 and died in 1980.
2. There are many accounts of working-class marriage in the early twentieth century that discuss the ways in which housewives might resist male power within the home via their control of the domestic environment. For example Ayers and Lambertz, 1986; Roberts, 1986; Tomes, 1978.

Bibliography

Alberti, J. (1989) *Beyond Suffrage: Feminists in War and Peace, 1914–28* (New York: St. Martin's Press).

Austin Motor Company (1938) *Longbridge Today*, publicity pamphlet.

Ayers P. and J. Lambertz (1986) 'Marriage Relations, Money and Domestic Violence in Working-Class Liverpool, 1919–1939', in J. Lewis (ed.), *Labour and Love: Women's Experiences of Home and Family 1850–1940* (Oxford: Blackwell).

Baldwin, S. (1926) *On England and Other Addresses* (London: Philip Allan).

Banks, J. (1954) *Prosperity and Parenthood* (London: Routledge & Kegan Paul).

Banks, O. (1986) *Becoming a Feminist: The Social Origins of 'First Wave' Feminism* (Brighton: Wheatsheaf).

Barrett, M. (1993) Introduction to V. Woolf, *A Room of One's Own and Three Guineas* (Harmondsworth: Penguin).

Barrett M., and M. McIntosh (1983) *The Anti-Social Family* (London: Verso).

Beaumann, N. (1983) *A Very Great Profession: The Woman's Novel 1919–1939* (London: Virago).

Beddoe, D. (1989) *Back to Home And Duty: Women Between the Wars, 1918–1939* (London: Pandora).

Bell, Q. (1972) *Virginia Woolf*, vol. 2 (London: Hogarth Press).

Birmingham City Council (1921–39) *Reports of the Housing and Estates Committee.*

Black, C. (1918) *A New Way of Housekeeping* (London: Collins).

Bland, L. (1986) 'Marriage Laid Bare: Middle Class Women and Marital Sex c1880–1914' in Jane Lewis (ed.) *Labour and Love: Women's Experience of Home and Family 1850–1940* (Oxford: Blackwell).

Board of Education (1933) *Handbook of Suggestions on Health Education* (London: HMSO).

Bock, G. (1989) 'Women's History and Gender History: Aspects of an International Debate', *Gender and History*, vol. 1, no. 1, pp. 7–30.

Borland, K. (1991) 'That's Not What I Said: Interpretive Conflict in Oral Narrative Research', in S. B. Gluck and D. Patai (eds), *Women's Words: The Feminist Practice of Oral History* (London: Routledge).

Bourke, J. (1994) *Working-class Cultures in Britain 1890–1960: Gender, Class and Ethnicity* (London: Routledge).

Bournville Village Trust Research Publications (1941) *When We Build Again: A Study Based on Research into Conditions of Living and Working in Birmingham* (London: Allen & Unwin).

Boys, J. (1989) in J. Attfield and P. Kirkham (eds), *A View from the Interior: Feminism, Women and Design* (London: The Women's Press).

Briggs, A. (1952) *A History of Birmingham, vol. 2, Borough and City 1865–1938* (London: Oxford University Press).

Brittain, V. (1928) *Women's Work in Modern England* (London: Noel Douglas).

176

Brittain, V. (1933) *Testament of Youth: an autobiographical study of the years 1900–1925* (London: Gollancz).

Bromley, R. (1986) 'The gentry, bourgeois hegemony and popular fiction: *Rebecca* and *Rogue Male*', in P. Humm, P. Stigant and P. Widdowson (eds), *Popular Fictions: Essays in Literature and History* (London: Methuen).

Brookes, B. (1988) *Abortion in England 1900–1967* (London: Croom Helm).

Brown, L. M. and C. Gilligan (1992) *Meeting at the Crossroads: Women's Psychology and Girls' Development* (Cambridge Mass: Harvard University Press).

Burnett, J. (1976) *Useful Toil: Autobiographies of Working People from the 1820s to the 1920s* (London: Allen Lane).

Burnett, J. (1986) *A Social History of Housing 1815–1985* (London: Methuen).

Chance, J. (1931) *The Cost of English Morals* (London: Noel Douglas).

Chanfrault-Duchet, M-F. (1991) 'Narrative Structures, Social Models, and Symbolic Representation in the Life Story', in S. B. Gluck and D. Patai (eds), *Women's Words: The Feminist Practice of Oral History* (London: Routledge).

Chinn, C. (1988) *They Worked All Their Lives: Women of the Urban Poor in England 1880–1939* (Manchester: Manchester University Press).

Chodorow, N. (1978) *The Reproduction of Mothering: Psychoanalysis and the Sociology of Gender* (Berkeley: University of California Press).

Cott, N. (1977) *The Bonds of Womanhood: Woman's Sphere in New England, 1780–1835* (New Haven: Yale University Press).

Davidoff, L. and C. Hall (1987) *Family Fortunes: Men and Women of the English Middle Class 1780–1850* (London: Hutchinson).

Davin, A. (1978) 'Imperialism and Motherhood', *History Workshop Journal*, vol. 5, pp. 9–65.

Dayus, K. (1982) *Her People* (London: Virago).

Delafield, E. M. (1927) *The Way Things Are* (London: Hutchinson).

Delafield, E. M. (1930/1984) *The Diary of a Provincial Lady* (London: Virago).

Dreyfus, H. and P. Rabinow (1982) *Michel Foucault: Beyond Structuralism and Hermeneutics* (Chicago: Chicago University Press).

Du Maurier, D. (1938/1975) *Rebecca* (London: Pan).

Dyhouse, C. (1989) *Feminism and the Family in England, 1880–1939* (Oxford: Blackwell).

Dyos, H. J. and Wolff, M. (eds) (1973) *The Victorian City: Images and Realities* (London: Routledge & Kegan Paul).

Elias, E. (1978) *On Sundays We Wore White* (London: W. H. Allen).

Elshtain, J. (1981) *Public Man, Private Woman: Women in Social and Political Thought* (Oxford: Martin Robertson).

Edynbury, R. (1938) *Real Life Problems and Their Solutions* (London: Odhams).

Ferguson, A. (1984) 'Conceiving Motherhood and Sexuality: A Feminist Materialist Approach', in J. Trebilcot (ed.), *Mothering: Essays in Feminist Theory* (Totowa NJ: Rowman & Allanheld).

Flax, J. (1987) 'Postmodernism and Gender Relations in Feminist Theory', *Signs*, vol. 12, no. 4, pp. 621–43.

Foley, W. (1974/1986) *A Child In The Forest* (London: BBC, Ariel Books).

Forrester, H. (1981) *Twopence to Cross the Mersey* (London: Fontana).

Forster, E. M. (1910) *Howard's End* (Harmondsworth: Penguin).

Foucault, M. (1978/1984) *The History of Sexuality, vol. 1* (Harmondsworth: Penguin).

Foucault, M. (1985) *The Use of Pleasure*, trans. R. Hurley (Harmondsworth: Penguin).

Foucault, M. (1986) *The Care of the Self*, trans. R. Hurley (Harmondsworth: Penguin).

Foucault, M. (1988) 'The ethic of care for the self as a practice of freedom', in J. Bernauer and D. Rasmussen (eds), *The Final Foucault* (Cambridge Mass: MIT Press).

Fowler, B. (1991) *The Alienated Reader: Women and Popular Romantic Literature in the Twentieth Century* (London: Harvester Wheatsheaf).

Fraser, N. (1990) 'Rethinking the Public Sphere: A Contribution to the Critique of Actually Existing Democracy', *Social Text*, vol. 25/26, pp. 56–80.

Fremlin, C. (1940) *The Seven Chars of Chelsea* (London: Methuen).

Friedan, B. (1965) *The Feminine Mystique* (Harmondsworth: Penguin).

Friedman, S. S. (1988) 'Women's Autobiographical Selves: Theory and Practice', in S. Benstock (ed.), *The Private Self* (London: Routledge).

Gavron, H. (1966) *The Captive Wife: Conflicts of Housebound Mothers* (Harmondsworth: Penguin).

Giddens, A. (1979) *Central Problems in Social Theory: Action, Structure and Contradiction in Social Analysis* (London: Macmillan).

Giddens, A. (1984) *The Constitution of Society* (Cambridge: Polity).

Giles, J. (1989) 'Something That Bit Better: Working Class Women, Domesticity and Respectability, 1919–1939', unpublished D.Phil thesis, University of York.

Giles, J. (1992) 'Playing Hard to Get: Working class women, sexuality and respectability in Britain, 1918–40', *Women's History Review*, vol. 1, no. 2, pp. 239–55.

Giles, J. (1993) 'A Home of One's Own: Women and Domesticity in England, 1918–1950', *Women's Studies International Forum*, vol. 16, no. 3, pp. 239–53.

Giles, J. (1995) 'You Meet 'Em and That's It', in L. Pearce and J. Stacey (eds), *Romance Revisited* (London: Lawrence & Wishart).

Gilligan, C. (1982) *In A Different Voice: Psychological Theory and Women's Development* (Cambridge Mass: Harvard University Press).

Gilman, C. P. (1935/1975) *The Living of Charlotte Perkins Gilman: An Autobiography* (New York: Harper & Row).

Gittins, D. (1982) *Fair Sex: Family Size and Structure 1900–1939* (London: Hutchinson).

Glucksmann, M. (1990) *Women Assemble: Women Workers and the New Industries in Inter-War Britain* (London: Routledge).

Gordon, L. (1986) 'What's New in Women's History', in T. de Lauretis (ed.), *Feminist Studies/Critical Studies* (London: Macmillan).

Gordon, Lyndall (1984) *Virginia Woolf: A Writer's Life* (Oxford: Oxford University Press).

Graves, R. and A. Hodge (1940/1991) *The Long Weekend: A Social History of Great Britain 1918–1939* (London: Cardinal).

Griffith, E. (1938) *Modern Marriage and Birth Control* (London: Gollancz).

Habakkuk, H. J. (1971) *Population Growth and Economic Development since 1750* (Leicester: Leicester University Press).

Hall, R. (ed.) (1978) *Dear Dr Stopes. Sex in the 1920s. Letters to Marie Stopes* (London: Andre Deutsch).

Halsey A. H. (1972) *Trends in British Society Since 1900* (London: Macmillan).

Harrison, B. (1987) *Prudent Revolutionaries: Portraits of British Feminists Between the Wars* (Oxford: Clarendon Press).

Heron, E. (ed.) (1985) *Truth, Dare or Promise* (London: Virago).

Hewins, A. (Mary) (1986) *After the Queen: Memories of a Working Girl* (Oxford: Oxford University Press).

HMSO (1923) *Report of the Consultative Committee of the Board of Education on The Differentia of Curricula for Boys and Girls in Secondary Schools* (London: HMSO).

HMSO (1926) *Report of the Consultative Committee of the Board of Education on the Education of the Adolescent* (London: HMSO).

HMSO (1931) *Census of England and Wales for 1931, General Report* (London: HMSO).

Hoggart, R. (1958) *The Uses of Literacy* (Harmondsworth: Penguin).

Hoggart, R. (1965) Introduction to G. Orwell, *The Road to Wigan Pier* (London: Heinemann).

Holtby, W. (1934) *Women and a Changing Civilisation* (London: John Lane).

Holtzman, E. (1983)'"The Pursuit of Married Love": Women's attitudes towards sexuality and marriage in Great Britain, 1918–1939', *Journal of Social History*, vol. 16, pp. 39–51.

Housewife (1890) 'Strategy with husbands', vol. 5, p. 443.

Hughes, M. V. (1940/1979) *A London Family Between the Wars* (Oxford: Oxford University Press).

Hunt, L. (ed.) (1989) *The New Cultural History* (California: University of California Press).

Hygiene Committee of the Women's Group on Public Welfare (1939–42) *Our Towns. A Close-up.*

Jamieson, L. (1986) 'Limited Resources and Limiting Conventions: Working-Class Mothers and Daughters in Urban Scotland' in *Labour and Love: Women's Experience of Home and Family 1850–1940* (Oxford: Blackwell).

Jeffreys, S. (1985) *The Spinster and Her Enemies: Feminism and Sexuality 1880–1930* (London: Pandora).

Jephcott, P. (1943) *Girls Growing Up* (London: Faber & Faber).

Johnson, R. (1979) 'Three Problematics: elements of a theory of working-class culture', in J. Clarke, C. Crichter and R. Johnson (eds), *Working Class Culture: Studies in History and Theory* (London: Hutchinson).

Keating, P. J. (1973) 'Fact and Fiction in the East End', in H. J. Dyos and M. Wolff (eds), *The Victorian City: Images and Realities, vol. 2* (London: Routledge & Kegan Paul).

Keating, P. J. (1976) *Into Unknown England 1866–1913, Selections from the Social Explorers* (London: Fontana).

Kessler-Harris, A. (1983) *Out to Work: A History of Wage-Earning Women in the United States* (New York: Oxford University Press).

Kessler-Harris, A. (1989) 'Gender Ideology in Historical Reconstruction: A Case Study from the 1930s', *Gender and History*, vol. 1, no. 1, pp. 31–49.

Kramer, L. (1989) 'Literature, Criticism and Historical Imagination: The Literary Challenge of Hayden White and Dominick La Capra', in L. Hunt (ed.), *The New Cultural History* (London: University of California Press).

LaCapra, D. (1983) *Rethinking Intellectual History: Texts, Contexts, Language* (Ithaca, NY: Cornell University Press).

Laqueur, T. (1990) *Making Sex: Body and Gender from the Greeks to Freud* (Cambridge Mass: Harvard University Press).

Levine, D. (1987) *Reproducing Families: The Political Economy of English Population History* (Cambridge: Cambridge University Press).

Lewis, J. (1980) *The Politics of Motherhood: Child and Maternal Welfare in England 1900–1939* (London: Croom Helm).

Lewis, J. (1984) *Women in England 1870–1950* (Sussex: Wheatsheaf).

Lewis, J. (1991) 'Models of equality for women: the case of state support for children in twentieth century Britain', in G. Bock and P. Thane (eds), *Maternity and Gender Policies* (London: Routledge).

Light, A. (1984) ' "Returning to Manderley": romance fiction, female sexuality and class', *Feminist Review*, vol. 16.

Light, A. (1991) *Forever England. Femininity, Literature and Conservatism Between the Wars* (London: Routledge).

Llewelyn Davies, M. (1931/1977) *Life As We Have Known It* (London: Virago).

Marwick, A. (1965) *The Deluge: British Society in the First World War* (London: Macmillan).

Mason, M. G. and Carol Hurd Greed (eds) (1979) *Journeys: Autobiographical Writings by Women* (Boston: G. K. Hall).

Mass Observation (1943) *An Enquiry into People's Homes* (London: John Murray).

Mass Observation (1945) *Britain and Her Birthrate. A report prepared by Mass Observation* (London: John Murray).

Masterman, C. (1902) *From the Abyss* (publisher unknown).

Masterman, C. (1909) *The Condition of England* (London: Methuen).

McBride, T. (1976) *The Domestic Revolution: The Modernisation of Household Service in England and France 1820–1920* (London: Croom Helm).

McNay, L. (1992) *Foucault and Feminism: Power, Gender and the Self* (Oxford: Polity).

Melman, B. (1988) *Women and the Popular Imagination in the Twenties* (London: Macmillan).

Merrett, S. (1979) *State Housing in Britain* (London: Routledge & Kegan Paul).

Merrett, S. and R. Gray (1982) *Owner-Occupation in Britain* (London: Routledge & Kegan Paul).

Miles, P. and M. Smith (1987) *Cinema, Literature and Society* (London: Croom Helm).

Mitchell, G. D. and T. Lupton (1954) *The Liverpool Estate* (Liverpool: University Press of Liverpool).

Mitchison, N. (1979) *You May Well Ask* (London: Gollancz).

Mowat, C. (1955) *Britain Between the Wars, 1918–1940* (London: Methuen).

Mulvey, L. (1975) 'Visual Pleasure and Narrative Cinema', *Screen*, vol. 16, no. 3, pp. 6–18.

Mulvey, L. (1981) 'Afterthoughts on Visual Pleasure and Narrative Cinema', *Frameworks*, vol. 15/17, pp. 12–15.

Newson, J. and E. Newson (1970) *Four Years Old in an Urban Community* (Harmondsworth: Penguin).

Nightingale, F. (1928) 'Cassandra', in R. Strachey; *The Cause* (London: Virago).

Oakley, A. (1974) *Housewife*, Harmondsworth, Penguin.

Orwell, G. (1937/1987) *The Road To Wigan Pier* (Harmondsworth: Penguin).

Peretz, E. (1989) 'The professionalization of child care: the health visitor', *Oral History Journal*, Spring, pp. 22–8.

Pollard, S. (1983) *The Development of the British Economy 1914–1980* (London: Edward Arnold).

Poovey, M. (1989) *Uneven Developments: The Ideological Work of Gender in Mid-Victorian England* (London: Virago).

Priestley, J. B. (1934/1984) *English Journey* (Harmondsworth: Penguin).

Pugh, M. (1992) *Women and the Women's Movement in Britain 1914–1959* (Basingstoke and London: Macmillan).

Rathbone, E. (1924/1986) *The Disinherited Family* (Bristol: Falling Wall Press).

Rathbone, E. (1940) *The Case for Family Allowances* (Harmondsworth: Penguin).

Ravetz, A. (1989) 'A View From the Interior', in J. Attfield and P. Kirkham (eds), *A View From the Interior: Feminism, Women and Design* (London: The Women's Press).

Read, D. (1972) *Edwardian England 1901–15: Society, Politics* (London: Harrap).

Rice, M. S. (1939/1981) *Working-Class Wives. Their Health and Conditions* (London: Virago).

Rich, A. (1977) *Of Woman Born: Motherhood as Experience and Institution* (London: Virago).

Roberts, E. (1984) *A Woman's Place. An Oral History of Working-Class Women 1890–1940* (Oxford: Blackwell).

Roberts, E. (1986) 'Women's Strategies 1890–1940', in J. Lewis (ed.), *Labour and Love: Women's Experience of Home and Family 1850–1940* (Oxford: Blackwell).

Roberts, R. (1973) *The Classic Slum: Salford Life in the First Quarter of the Century* (Harmondsworth: Penguin).

Ross, E. (1982) 'Fierce questions and taunts: married life in working-class London 1870–1914', *Feminist Studies*, vol. 8, pp. 575–605.

Ross, E. (1985) '"Not the sort that would sit on the doorstep": respectability in pre-World War I London neighbourhoods', *International Labour and Working Class History*, no. 27, pp. 39–59.

Ross, E. (1986) 'Labour and Love: Rediscovering London's Working Class Mothers, 1870–1918', in J. Lewis (ed.), *Labour and Love: Women's Experience of Home and Family 1850–1940* (Oxford: Blackwell).

Rowntree, B. S. (1902) *Poverty. A Study of Town Life* (London: Macmillan).

Rowntree, B. S. (1941) *Poverty and Progress: A Second Social Survey of York* (London: Longmans).

Ruddick, S. (1984) 'Preservative Love and Military Destruction: Some Reflections on Mothering and Peace', in J. Trebilcot (ed.), *Mothering: Essays in Feminist Theory* (Totowa, NJ: Rowman & Allanheld).

Sarsby, J. (1988) *Missuses and Mouldrunners: An Oral History of Women Pottery Workers at Work and Home* (Milton Keynes: Open University Press).

Scannell, D. (1974) *Mother Knew Best: An East End Childhood* (London: Macmillan).

Seabrook, J. (1982) *Working-Class Childhoods* (London: Gollancz).

Showalter, E. (1987) *The Female Malady* (London: Virago).

Smith-Rosenberg, C. (1975) 'The Female World of Love and Ritual: Relations between Women in Nineteenth Century America', *Signs*, vol. 1, no. 1.

Smith-Rosenberg, C. (1986) *Disorderly Conduct: Visions of Gender in Victorian America* (New York: Oxford University Press).

Spring-Rice, M. (1939/1981) *Working Class Wives, Their Health and Conditions* (London: Virago).

Steedman, C. (1992) *Past Tenses: Essays on Writing, Autobiography and History* (London: Rivers Oram).

Stevenson, J. (1984) *British Society 1914–45* (Harmondsworth: Penguin).

Stevenson, J. and C. Cook (1979) *The Slump: Society and Politics During the Depression* (London: Quartet).

Stopes, M. C. (1918/1955) *Married Love* (London: Hogarth Press).

Stopes, M. C. (1920) *Radiant Motherhood* (London: G. P. Putnam's Sons).

Strachey, R. (1928/1984) *The Cause* (London: Virago).

Struther, J. (1939/1989) *Mrs Miniver* (London: Virago).

Stuart, M. (1993) '"And How Was It For You Mary?": self, identity and meaning for oral historians', *Oral History*, Autumn, pp. 80–3.

Swanwick, H. (1935) *I Have Been Young* (London: Gollancz).

Swenarton, M. (1981) *Homes Fit for Heroes: the Politics and Architecture of Early State Housing in Britain* (London: Heinemann).

Taylor, P. (1979) 'Daughters and Mothers – Maids and Mistresses: Domestic Service Between the Wars', in J. Clarke, C. Crichter and R. Johnson (eds), *Working-Class Culture: Studies in History and Theory* (London: Hutchinson).

Taylor, S. (1938) 'Suburban Neurosis', *The Lancet*, 26 March.

Thane, P. (1991) 'Visions of Gender in the making of the British Welfare State: the case of women in the British Labour Party and social policy 1906–1945', in G. Bock and P. Thane (eds), *Maternity and Gender Policies* (London: Routledge).

The Motherhood Book (circa 1930) (London: Amalgamated Press).

Thompson, D. (1975) 'Courtship and Marriage in Preston between the Wars', *Oral History*, vol. 3, pp. 39–44.

Thorne, B. (1987) 'Re-visioning women and social change: where are the children?', *Gender and Society*, vol. 1, no. 1, pp. 85–109.

Tomes, N. (1978) '"A Torrent of Abuse": Crimes of Violence Between Working-Class Men and Women in London, 1840–1875', *Journal of Social History*, vol. 11.

Townroe, B. S. (1924) *A Handbook of Housing* (London: Methuen).

Tudor-Walters, Sir J. (1919) *Report of the Special Committee on Housing 1918* (London: HMSO).

Tupling, R. E. (1983) *The Story of Rednal* (Birmingham Public Libraries).

Vicinus, M. (1985) *Independent Women: Work and Community for Single Women 1850–1920* (London: Virago).

Walkerdine, V. (1990) *Schoolgirl Fictions* (London: Verso).

Walkowitz, J. (1980) *Prostitution and Victorian Society: Women, Class, and the State* (New York: Cambridge University Press).

Walkowitz, J. (1992) *City of Dreadful Delight. Narratives of Sexual Danger in Late Victorian London* (London: Virago).

Ward, S. (ed.) (1992) *The Garden City, Past, Present and Future* (London: E & F. N. Spon).

Webb, B. M. (1932) *The Teaching of Young Children and Girls as to Reproduction* (London: The British Social Hygiene Council).

Weeks, J. (1981/1989) *Sex, Politics and Society* (London: Longman).

Weeks, J. (1985) *Sexuality and its Discontents: Meanings, myths and modern sexualities* (London: Routledge & Kegan Paul).

White, C. (1970) *Women's Magazines 1693–1968* (London: Michael Joseph).

White, H. (1987) *The Content of the Form: Narrative Discourse and Historical Representation* (Baltimore: Johns Hopkins University Press).

Willmott, P. (1979) *Growing Up in a London Village: Family Life Between the Wars* (London: Peter Owen).

Willmott, P. and M. Young (1962) *Family and Kinship in East London* (Harmondsworth: Penguin).

Woolf, V. (1931) 'Professions for Women', in *The Death of the Moth* (1942) (London: Hogarth Press).

Woolf, V. (1931/1977) Introductory letter to M. Llewelyn Davies, *Life As We Have Known It* (London: Virago).

Woolf, V. (1977) *The Diary of Virginia Woolf*, vol. III, edited by Anne Oliver Bell (London: Hogarth Press).

Women's Housing Subcommittee to the Ministry of Reconstruction, 1918–19 (PRO. London).

Wrigley, E. A. (1969) *Population and History* (London: Weidenfeld & Nicolson).

York City Council (1921–39) *Minutes of the Housing Committee.*

Index

Walker, Betty   128–9, 130–1
Walkerdine, V.   43, 53, 57, 108,
  166–70, 172
Walkowitz, J.   17, 64, 101–3, 107,
  108, 120, 122
war   32–3
Watson, John   120–1
Webb, B. M.   21
Weeks, J.   85, 114–15, 122, 123,
  124–5, 129
welfare workers   109–10
  see also district nurse; health
  visitor
welfarism   23, 41
Westall, Lilian   156
Wheatley Act (1924)   65
White, C.   6
White, H.   165
Wilkes, Alice   91–2
Wilkinson, Alice   18
Willmott, P.   9, 59, 81, 96
Wodehouse, P. G.   138
Wolff, M.   103
Woman   6
Woman's Own   6
Woman's Weekly   6, 21
women
  access to housing   69, 71
  citizenship   70
  class divisions   11–12, 97,
    132
  history   8–10
  relationships with men   28, 51
  sense of self   99
Women's Co-operative Guild   1,
  38, 110, 143

Women's Group on Public
  Welfare   105–6
Women's Health Enquiry
  Committee   109, 110, 113
Women's Housing
  Subcommittee   68, 71, 74
Women's Hygiene Committee   29,
  167
Woodward, Kathleen   42–3
Woolf, Virginia   1–2, 3, 38, 83, 97,
  110, 116, 132, 141–3, 149,
  170–1
working-class   13
  aspirations   28
  public/private split   17–18
  'the poor'   23–4
working-class boys   48
working-class women
  'a problem'   49–50
  aspirations   37–8, 46–7, 83
  defined   97
  independence and mobility
    103–4
  self-image   27
  through middle-class women's
    eyes   38–9, 108–16
  view of present affluence   46–7
World League for Sexual Reform
  123
World War I   33, 51–2, 135, 143
World War II   135
Wrigley, E. A.   36

York   71, 73, 74–5, 76, 91–2, 112,
  119, 126, 137, 141
Young, M.   81, 96